Hard lines

This book is dedicated to John Course, who was Northern Editor of the **Guardian**

Hard lines

Voices from deep within a recession

Geoffrey Beattie

with photographs by Bill Stephenson

MANDOLIN

Published by
Mandolin, an imprint of Manchester University Press
Oxford Road, Manchester M13 9NR, UK
and Room 400, 175 Fifth Avenue, New York, NY 10010, USA

Distributed exclusively in the USA by
St. Martin's Press, Inc., 175 Fifth Avenue, New York,
NY 10010, USA

Distributed exclusively in Canada by
UBC Press, University of British Columbia, 6344 Memorial Road,
Vancouver, BC, Canada V6T 1Z2

British Library Cataloguing-in-Publication Data
A catalogue record for this book is available from the British Library

Library of Congress Cataloging-in-Publication Data applied for

ISBN 1 901341 08 9 *paperback*

First published 1998

05 04 03 02 01 00 99 98   10 9 8 7 6 5 4 3 2 1

Typeset in Hong Kong
by Graphicraft Typesetters Limited

Printed in Great Britain
by Redwood Books, Trowbridge

A boxing trainer's most difficult task is said to be to persuade a young boxer to get up and continue fighting after he has been knocked down. And if the boxer has been knocked down by a blow he hadn't seen coming – which is usually the case – how can he hope to protect himself from being knocked down again? and again? The invisible blow is after all invisible.

Joyce Carol Oates (1995) On Boxing

Contents

Acknowledgements

I am grateful to Chatto & Windus for granting permission to use extracts from *Survivors of Steel City* published in 1986, to Weidenfeld and Nicolson for granting permission to use extracts from *Making It*, *All Talk* and *England After Dark*, which were published in 1987, 1988 and 1990 respectively, and to Victor Gollancz for granting permission to use extracts from *On the Ropes: Boxing as a Way of Life* published in 1996.

Introduction

This is a book about Britain during a time of change. Britain in the 1980s and the early to mid-1990s. Britain under the Tories, Conservative but with a radical political and economic agenda. A series of Conservative governments, who did not wish to keep existing conditions unchanged. Conservatives who were anything but cautious or moderate. Conservatives who had a mandate and a mission to halt Britain's sharp economic decline which had, most analysts seem to agree, been going on since the end of the Second World War. It needed strong measures, they said, to halt this decline. Immoderate measures. This is a book about the human consequences of all of these immoderate measures.

This was a period of what political economists call 'negative de-industrialisation'. The statistics tell us something about the period. Coates (1994) points out that the total number of workers in the paid labour force in 1993 may have been at the same level as in 1979 when Mrs Thatcher came to power, but the number of people employed in manufacturing declined from 7 million to 4.5 million. A fall of about 36 per cent. There had been, it must be admitted, a steady loss of jobs in manufacturing in Britain since the mid-1960s, but the trend accelerated under the Conservatives. In 1960, 36 per cent of the total civilian population of the UK was employed in manufacturing, by 1986 the figure was 22.5 per cent (see Cairncross, 1992, p. 29).

The North, forged during the first industrial revolution, was based on and around its manufacturing industry. This is where the negative de-industrialisation hit hardest.

These changes altered the fundamental industrial structure of the country, which changed from a predominantly manufacturing economy towards a more service-orientated economy. Economic change was happening in other developed economies as well, but as Cook and Healey (1995) point out 'Unlike other developed nations, however, which possessed relatively high levels of agricultural employment the UK compensated for the growth in service sector employment by a reduction in manufacturing employment' (p. 18).

With this negative de-industrialisation, unemployment rose, although because of changing definitions of who was or was not unemployed it was sometimes difficult to keep track of the real extent of the problem. Coates (1994) tries to see through the official government figures:

Conservative ministers are prone to claim that more jobs were created in the UK in the 1980s than in any other European country (an extra 1.59 million in the first decade of Tory rule), as unemployment levels here settled to below the EC average. But this

Neepsend, the old industrial heart of Sheffield, November 1997

achievement is as much a product of their massaging of the figures (changing the definitions of who is unemployed more than nineteen times in that period) and downplaying the kinds of jobs now on offer as of widening employment opportunities per se. In fact, the officially defined numbers of the unemployed rose until 1985 (to reach 3.3 million), fell back until 1989, and have now risen inexorably towards 3 million again.

However, there was hope. That, at least was the political message. And it was in our hands, or in some of our hands. Our salvation was to be the free market and enterprise. Thatcher proselytised about the enterprise culture. It was to be the new age of the entrepreneur. It is perhaps worth reflecting on what this term actually means. The word 'entrepreneur' was used originally in France in the early sixteenth century to refer to men engaged in military expeditions. Two centuries later it was expanded to cover those engaged in adventures of a rather different sort, including bridge building, road contracting and architecture (see Silver, 1985, p. 14). Finally, an Irish economist living in France, Richard Cantillon, identified the entrepreneur as an important component of the economy when he described entrepreneurship as the process of bearing uncertainty. According to Cantillon, the 'entrepreneur' buys services at 'certain' prices with a view to selling their product at 'uncertain' prices in the future. 'Thus the entrepreneur was defined by a unique constitutive function: the bearing of non insurable risk' (Kilby, 1971, p. 2). As Kilby points out, a few decades later Jean Baptiste Say (1817) was to describe the entrepreneurial function in more general terms by emphasising the bringing together of the factors of production and the provision of continuing management, as well as the risk bearing function.

Entrepreneurs took risks for profit. Thatcher saw them as Britain's saviours, the instigators of good new jobs not bad old jobs. In 1984 in a *Panorama* interview she said,

If many of the people who criticise us for unemployment, and I'm the first to want to get unemployment down, went out or were capable of going out and starting up wealth-creating businesses of their own, we'd be a great deal better off. There are not a lot of people who can; fortunately there are more and more who are doing it, but employment, good employment, profitable employment, good jobs are created by those who can start a business, expand it, build it up, please the customers, make a profit, plough it back, expand.

Many responded to her admonishments. But sometimes the risk was too great. In 1992 for example, there was a record number of bankruptcies in this country. Sixty three thousand in that one year alone. Individuals were going bust, whole cultures, mining villages and steel towns were being closed down.

This decline seemed to come in a series of stops and starts with the steel works and the mines and the various engineering firms going to the wall, or being thrown against the wall, in quick successive bursts, and in certain parts of the country you could see it happening before your very eyes – the human side of all this negative de-industrialisation, the cost in people. The cost was often just too high. Colin Thunhurst wrote about just one such case in the *Sheffield Star* in 1985:

On Monday June 24th a 19 year old Derbyshire youth threw himself from the top of High Tor. He had on him a note simply saying 'Put it down to unemployment'. The reasons why people kill themselves are never simple. Everybody, at some time or other, asks him or herself what life is about and whether it's worth continuing. For most of us this comes at an occasional time of crisis. For the unemployed, particularly the increasing number of long term unemployed, crises are no longer occasional.

Then there was the shame and the embarrassment of losing a job. The narrowing of horizons, the closing in, the long days of shame.

Sheffield was full of ex-steelmen with shopping bags. You could see them in the supermarkets in the afternoon. They didn't talk a lot, even to each other. It was embarrassing. Straight in and straight out; back to the house; back to Wimbledon, cricket, old films and the housework. Many of them quite liked the housework – they didn't like to be seen doing it, mind, but it was still alright; it was still something. One former steelworker I knew had just got a job on a building site, so his brother, another unemployed steelworker, slipped in to do the housework one day a week. He slipped out again as cautiously as he went in. Burglars would have envied his stealth. (Geoffrey Beattie, *Guardian*, October 1984)

Some political change of direction may, of course, have been necessary to halt Britain's decline. But what change? There were a lot of theories to explain our economic decline. What was to be done depended upon your theoretical understanding of what had gone wrong in the first place. Coates (1994) reviews some of these conflicting theoretical accounts which pointed this way and that. Some economists blamed the unions and argued that our decline was largely attributable to the entrenched industrial power of organised work groups and their representatives. Others went further and proposed that the basic problem was that trade unions were not interested in management and efficiency. Others suggested that the unions had too much political power. But there were alternative points of view, other people to blame, other sections, other interests. Some blamed the poor quality of UK management. Others pointed towards the anti-entrepreneurial culture which, it was argued, exists in this country. Others suggested that the basic problem was that the more dynamic elements of UK industry were going elsewhere. Some even pointed to the adversarial nature of our political system, with each party vying for short-term electoral advantage. Some said that there was too much state intervention, some said too little state intervention.

There were a lot of theories. You could pick and choose depending upon your political leaning and your own particular set of values. You could explain our economic decline in a variety of ways and many did so. But you still had to face the consequences. You still had to live through it.

Of course, some tried to persuade us that their analysis was the only right one, and that their particular attribution of why Britain had fallen so far was the only one worth considering. Every time Mrs Thatcher spoke she told us about her explanation, and she also warned us that she was going to do something about it. She had been elected by us to fight our economic battles for us. She was there to win the war of the economy. She told us that we had to 'be fit to compete with the Germans and the Japs and French when we get an expansion in world trade.' (See Beattie (1988), Chapters 5 and 6 for selected quotations from Margaret Thatcher's political interviews.) We had to go forward with vigour and with determination.

I do want more jobs, obviously, so does everyone who is suffering from unemployment. What we have to consider is how best are those jobs of the future going to be created. They're not going to be created if we shy away from taking on new technology. They're not going to be created if we shy away from getting rid of old labour practices. They're not going to be created if we have two men doing the work of one and taking two men's wages . . . We're going through a period of new technology. We're going through a period when many countries overseas are producing the sorts of goods which we used to produce and sell from here. All of that requires great adaptation.

She told us that she was there to lead us at this critical time. We had to look to the future – an entrepreneurial future. 'So we have to embrace new technology. We have to try to give help, and we are, to small businesses, to start up and to expand.' Not to the past. 'Now the public sector, you're quite right, where it has a monopoly, has muscle. And the tragedy today is that the trade unions have more capacity to harm their fellow trade unionists and fellow citizens than they have to defend those trade unionists and citizens from the harm they cause.'

These were her buzz words and therefore ours – adaptation, competition, flexibility, change, entrepreneurial vision, risk. These were the images we had to contend with – well-muscled public sector monopolies, bullying unions picking on their own kind, an individual prepared to stand up to unions, ready and willing to cut the unions down to size – to scythe the weeds, the green shoots of recovery nourished by a caring Conservative government, the swash-buckling entrepreneur, with traces of its original meaning as men engaged in military expeditions somehow woven into it. Then there were the polarities constructed for us – new entrepreneurs/old labour practice, new technology/old obsolete equipment, new information superhighway/old industrial plant, new flexible workforce/old jobs for life, new good jobs/old bad jobs, new job seekers/old unemployed.

And as Thatcher's commitment to the task at hand grew and grew, the language became more powerful, the images more elaborate. She knew who to blame alright. So she painted pictures in words to tell the rest of us. She told us all about her economic fight to get Britain back on its feet and she warned us that 'We have to fight our economic battles every day – they're never won.' And sometimes she strode out in her white coat of the imagination, telling us about how she was going to 'cure unemployment' and that she could see signs of 'healthy trends in aspects of economic policy'. Then she would warn us about 'bouts of inflation', and about 'palliatives not working in the short run'.

George Orwell (1946) wrote that the function of the metaphor is to produce visual images. 'When these images clash – as in "The Fascist octopus has sung its swan song, the jackboot is thrown into the melting pot" – it can be taken as certain that the writer is not seeing a mental image of the objects he is naming; in other words he is not really thinking.' Thatcher never mixed metaphors quite like this, never quite as blatantly as this, but they still came thick and fast with her sometimes painting herself as the general in battle dress, sometimes as the doctor in the white coat, sometimes as the nation's favourite gardener having 'to get rid of dead wood and cultivate new growth'. Sometimes she was the nation's footballing coach: 'We can put the ball at people's feet – some of them will kick it.' And sometimes she was the nation's shopkeeper telling us that 'You have to run your finances in a sound, honest way', and reminding us that she was looking for 'a fair deal for the weaker members of our society' and that she was interested in finding 'a good value-for-money-deterrent'. Justifying the nine billion pounds to be spent on Trident she said in a *Panorama* interview in 1984 with Sir Robin Day: 'We could not possibly get such good deterrent value for that money as we get in Trident.' Good deterrent value. She sounded as if she was talking about washing-up liquid.

And at times you would just sit there and listen and wonder, and watch what was happening around you and wonder again. There were a lot of theories to explain Britain's economic decline and a lot of rhetoric. A lot of powerful images were created for us in our living rooms, but sometimes in the end you were none the wiser. Were the unemployed 'dead wood' or 'casualties of the economic battle', 'sick men' or 'poor footballers'. Sometimes you needed your own metaphors to understand what was happening. You could see men and women in that ring getting a pounding. You could see them sinking down onto the canvas. I lived in Sheffield, I had a ringside seat. And as Joyce Carol Oates (1995) wrote, 'a boxing trainer's most difficult task is said to be to persuade a young boxer to get up and continue fighting after he has been knocked down. And if the boxer has been knocked down by a blow he hadn't seen coming – which is usually the case – how can he hope to

Drop-forge workers, Turton & Platts, Sheffield, 1988

protect himself from being knocked down again? and again? The invisible blow is after all invisible.' Some of them never got to their feet again.

This is a book about people living through this period. A book which takes Britain's economic decline and more specifically the de-industrialisation of the North of England as its backdrop, but it is not a book about economics or statistics, but about people and the lives they lead in the midst of all this change and uncertainty. It is about men and women getting up off the canvas, or staying down. It is about individual adaptation to being unemployed. It is about individuals trying to get a business off the ground, and living with the risk, and trying to get through the consequences of the failure, or the success. But mostly the failure. It is about crime and vice and all the other distractions in life. It is about threat and survival and trying to be somebody at a time when the green shoots of recovery were still not visible through the stony ground of Northern industrial Britain, during those critical years of such negative de-industrialisation.

It is a view from Sheffield, which was, of course, at the centre of the first industrial revolution and at the very centre of the devastation caused by all this de-industrialisation. A town synonymous with steel. Metal goods and textiles were the two most important products of British industry in the first industrial revolution. They called Sheffield 'Steel City' then. They still call it Steel City today, as they try to market it as a new city of leisure with modern sports facilities and the largest, most up-to-date shopping complex in Europe.

Foundry workers, Turton & Platts, Sheffield, 1988

But the lower Don Valley seems eerily quiet as the shoppers go in search of Meadowhall. It all looks two-dimensional sometimes, and not just because there doesn't seem to be anything behind the façades of some of the preserved outer walls of the redundant factories. In the book, I work my way out from Sheffield, in an attempt to build up some kind of picture of adaptation to change, of psychological survival in hard times.

The first industrial revolution turned Sheffield into a polluted, dirty town. Edwin Chadwick in his report on the sanitary condition of the labouring population of Great Britain wrote, 'Sheffield is one of the dirtiest and most smokey towns I ever saw . . . one cannot be long in the town without experiencing the necessary inhalation of soot, which accumulates in the lungs, and its harmful effects are experienced by all who are not accustomed to it. There are however numbers of persons in Sheffield who think the smoke healthy' (1842).

It is cleaner today, and quieter, like the rest of the North. On the surface it can all look quite pleasant, but sometimes you have to dig a little to see what's underneath, to view the lives, to discover what's going on, sometimes to see the desperation.

Of course, all of this change in the manufacturing base of this country may have been necessary in the end. I'm no economist, so who am I to say? But I think that it's worth sometimes just reminding ourselves of what it was like to live through this period, to be there at the sharp end when the foundries and the furnaces and the mines all stopped, to see the human cost of negative de-industrialisation, to see how some survived.

It was after all their hard lines. It's perhaps worth remembering that.

References

Beattie, G. (1988) *All Talk: Why It's Important to Watch Your Words and Everything Else You Say*. Weidenfeld and Nicolson: London.

Cairncross, A. (1992) *The British Economy since 1945*. Blackwell: Oxford.

Chadwick, E. (1842) *Report from the Poor Law Commissioners on an Inquiry into the Sanitary Condition of the Labouring Population of Great Britain*.

Coates, D. (1994) *The Question of UK Decline. The Economy, State and Society*. Harvester Wheatsheaf: New York.

Cook, M. and Healey, N. M. (1995) *Growth and Structural Change*. Macmillan: London.

Kilby, P. (1971) 'Hunting the Heffalump', in P. Kilby (ed.) *Entrepreneurship and Economic Development*. Collier Macmillan: London.

Oates, J. C. (1995) *On Boxing*. Ecco Press: New Jersey.

Orwell, G. (1946) 'Politics and the English Language', in G. Orwell (1969) *Inside the Whale and Other Essays*. Penguin: Harmondsworth.

Say, J. B. (1817) *Catechism of Political Economy*. M. Carey & Son: Philadelphia.

Silver, A. D. (1985) *Entrepreneurial Megabucks: The 100 Greatest Entrepreneurs of the Last 25 Years*. Wiley: New York.

No work

A similar disturbance in family relationships takes place when children do not pay lodging money as such, but are the sole breadwinners in a family when the parents are unemployed . . . a father rebuked his two daughters for frequenting a public house, and they turned on him, saying that they no longer recognised his authority: 'Damn you, we have you to keep.' They said that they were entitled to spend at least a part of their earnings as they pleased. The girls left home and abandoned their father and mother to their fate. (Friedrich Engels, *The Condition of the Working Class in England*, 1845)

A funny old-fashioned street

Summer had to come to Netherfield Road some time and the mist eventually did lift from the Rivelin Valley so that you could see the grey slab flats of Stannington (they turned out to be brown and white, but they had looked grey all year). Swallows appeared overhead, dipping for flies. Boys with fishing nets set forth. Funny, I thought that sticklebacks had gone for ever, but they obviously knew different. Old familiar smells – hot tarmac, rain on warm pavements – returned to haunt the memory and tease the imagination. Steel City was heating up after a year of wind and rain. Cold Steel City to chill the bone and dampen the spirit, but now the chill had gone.

But Netherfield Road was different this summer. The noises were different. The feeling was different. People were getting up later. There was no bustle. It was now a street of people who didn't work. Some were retired, some hadn't got a job yet; but most had been made redundant. Work was never really discussed. People were bitter. Casual enquiries about work or job prospects could hurl you into an endless spiral of accusation and complaint. 'Thatcher.' 'Foreign steel.' 'Bloody recession.' Most people only fall down this well once. Some things are better left unsaid; everybody knows that everybody else knows who's to blame and that's all that matters. And anyway, there were more important things to talk about – the decorating, the price of houses, the weather. This summer, especially the weather.

The women seemed to rise first. Two old retired dears brought their milk in first. They lived side by side and hated each other. Both were in their seventies, both were widows and both natives of Sheffield. One had a son, one hadn't got anyone. Mrs Hill's son came to visit her once a week in his old Polo. He would sit for an hour in her house on a Sunday, then leave. If it was a good day they would drive for an hour. But one Sunday he had his two corgis with him. He was supposed to be taking his mother to Chatsworth for the day but, Mrs Hill said, 'There was no room with the dogs in the back. I don't mind. It would have been too cramped. It's a good day for just sitting out anyway,' and then she went off to the bingo. Her luck was in – she won a tenner. 'It pays me to go,' she said.

Mrs Hill's neighbour, whom she always referred to as Mrs What's-her-name (despite the fact that she had an excellent memory), was new to the street. She had bought the terraced house after her husband died – it was a step down for her from lower-middle to upper-working. She had lived in Sheffield all her life, but not in this street. Mrs Hill didn't like her – she didn't like strangers. Mrs Hill left her living-room curtains undrawn well into the night and watched the comings and goings. Mrs Hill patrolled up and down her living room pretending to tidy it but really she was just watching the street. Her black and white television was always on. (Errol Flynn in the afternoon, Magnum at night.) Mrs What's-her-name also watched the street, but from behind drawn living-room curtains and after she had gone to bed she liked to watch from behind the bedroom curtains (Mrs What's-her-name was from a higher social class). You didn't have to page the oracle in our street; you just asked Mrs Hill. She knew who was moving and why; she was good on the

Unemployed steelworker and pregnant wife, Kelvin Flats, Sheffield, 1988

price of houses, she was tops on adultery and divorce. She told Mrs What's-her-name the spicier bits, but they were both a bit deaf, so they shouted. It was strange to hear yourself talked about in this way, but of course they thought they were whispering – it would have been too embarrassing to tell them. Mrs Hill went to the shops at 10 am and 3 pm. Mrs What's-her-name went at 11 am and 4.30 pm. Mrs What's-her-name also went somewhere at 7 pm, although no one knew where. Mrs Hill had tried to wheedle it out of her but Mrs What's-her-name's lips were sealed. Mrs Hill suspected that she took a drink.

Mr Smith and Mr Forrest were another unlikely pair. Both were steelworkers, both redundant for two years. Both bitter. Mr Smith was in his forties. His wife was a clerk, his daughter had just left school but hadn't got a job yet. Fred Smith had been decorating his home all year. Now he had reached the outside, he was replacing the window frames and varnishing the door. He started at about 9 am and took breaks every few hours out in the sun. He didn't sit out in the sun before he started, but only after he had worked for a couple of hours and at the end of the day. At the end of the day, he didn't wash immediately, he liked to leave the dirt on for a bit, he liked to feel he had been grafting. He could then sit and enjoy the sun for a while – he'd earned it. He liked this stage of the decorating, it was hard work, plenty of graft; all the poncey bits done. He didn't know what he'd do when the decorating was finished, though.

Mr Forrest, the other former steelworker, was fifty-seven, and lived at the bottom of the street. In a street overlooking the Bole Hills and the Rivelin Valley – a street which was really exposed – Mr Forrest had the most exposed house of all. The wind tore at his house, he was constantly replacing his tiles and his guttering. He had been made redundant just over two years earlier. He didn't mind much at the time – his wife was very ill with kidney failure. This summer she wasted and died. He always referred to her as Mrs Forrest. 'Mrs Forrest is in a better place now,' he said. But he didn't let her death get him down. He was constantly on the move, constantly busy. He ran everywhere with his dog Suki. 'I could be out dancing every night,' he said, 'if I'd got the brass.' He was always up ladders replacing people's guttering, unblocking their drains, digging their gardens – he needed any money people could afford to give him. He'd work for a day for a couple of quid. He got business by worrying people. 'The next time we have a good storm that drainpipe is going to come right off.' 'Oh,' said Mrs What's-her-name. 'I could do it for you tomorrow.' 'Oh, all right then.' And off he went, whistling his happy tune. He talked in the same kind of shout as the old people because he was deaf from the years in the noisy steel mill. The whole street shouted their private messages at each other. There was little privacy here.

It was a funny, old-fashioned street. There was no graffiti, little vandalism. There were too many people watching what was going on for these to occur. Everybody knew everybody else's business. And yet the houses themselves with their neat little gardens were very private. No posh houses, mind. They were just stone terraced houses or fifty-year-old unfashionable red-brick terraced houses. Privately owned houses for the working class with the discipline and the thrift, once a way station for the economically mobile

Shelley, age 13, Hyde Park Flats, Sheffield, 1986

steelworkers reared in council houses. And houses for the retired folk when they found themselves with a bit of money.

But now things were different. Instead of standing on the parapets and planning their advance into new unconquered territories, these people were in a state of siege. Constantly reworking their decorations, their fortifications, constantly mending their guttering, varnishing their doors, constantly polishing their J-registration cars. These people wouldn't be leaving their castles and they knew it. They also wouldn't have to retreat, thanks to redundancy payments.

So this summer, the sun was shining and the temperature rose but they were not tempted out. These were the working class, reared on discipline and hard work; sitting in the sun was redolent of idleness and waste. Sitting in the sun was skiving. And these were the people who didn't skive, who had timetables fixed and immutably etched on their brains, the people who thrived on overtime. But now the overtime had gone, as had the work. So they were poorer and a bit disillusioned. Some of them had lost all their aspirations and yet the little foremen in their heads still made them feel guilty for enjoying the hot summer sun.

And the sun was shining and the grey slab flats of Stannington across the valley seemed even closer. And the three-bedroom semis of middle-class Shef-field seemed a million miles away.

August 1983

'We came out a week before everybody else'

Bobby was a 25-year-old South Yorkshire miner. He had been on strike for the full thirty-four weeks – 'Thirty-five actually, we came out a week before everybody else.' His allegiances were clear. 'Arthur Scargill's the best leader the miners ever had. Joe Gormley sold us down the bloody river, when he retired they sent him forty pieces of silver. As for Margaret Thatcher, it's simple – I hate her.' What about the Nottinghamshire miners? 'They make me bloody sick. If it had been the other way round, Yorkshire would have supported them. They're just out for themselves. I'm one hundred per cent behind the strike. I didn't think it would go on this long, mind. I thought it would last a few weeks at the most and I really thought the government would back down, but after this length of time it's like fighting a battle. We've lost so much there's no point in turning back. It's us or them now.'

Bobby had been attracted to mining for the money, pure and simple. There was no romanticism attached to mining in his mind. He started when he was seventeen after a brief spell in an engineering firm. 'I doubled my wages right away. I started with two mates – one stuck it for a day, the other for six months – he's selling Ferraris for a living now.' Bobby trained as a fitter in the pit and spent eighteen months working on the surface before going underground. 'It's no bloody joke down there, gobbling coal dust all the time. Down the mine it's always either too hot or too cold, but there is unity among the men. You get the odd back-stabbers, mind, but most of the men are great. You've got to stick together.' Bobby was earning a flat rate of £130 plus up to £75 a week in bonuses. He drove a Triumph Stag. 'I always liked flash cars,' he said. 'I had to be ready to go down the pit at 6.30 and I lived ten miles away from the pit. Mind you, we'd finish at a quarter to two and I'd go home and have a good kip. Before I started courting I used to go out every night until about 3 am. I was always knackered at work, but it was good money.'

Before the strike began, Bobby had been managing to put a little money away. 'Well, my girlfriend's always talking about marriage,' he said, almost

Solid fuel industry worker, Grimethorpe, 1984

apologetically. 'Then the government dropped a bollock,' said Bobby. 'They forced us into it – bringing in MacGregor and forcing a confrontation in the spring, when coal stocks were high. They wanted a fight – they wanted to get even for what we did to Heath in '74. Scargill may be a bit pig-headed, but he's a good leader.'

So how did Bobby survive? He was luckier than most – he didn't have a family to support and he lived with his parents, although his father was unemployed. 'The best I can,' he said. 'I got £12 for the first week on strike because we were picketed out and £65 in food tokens from the Sheffield Labour Council – I gave those to my mum. But that's not enough to survive on. Oh yes, and I had two food parcels from the local Miners' Club. The lady who dished them out said the food was from Russia and Poland but – 'he laughed – 'they were all local brands – two tins of Heinz beans, a tin of skimmed milk, a packet of tea bags and a tin of stewed meat. You can get food parcels every fortnight if you like, but it's a long way to go for a few tins of beans.

'The first things to go when the strike began were my savings and then my car. I knew from the start I couldn't afford to run the Stag. I sold it and bought a Mini but my savings clearly weren't going to last too long, so I had to have a look round for other jobs. The first job I got was store-detective work – this was two weeks after the strike began. I just worked Saturdays – six hours a day in one of the big stores in Sheffield. £1.50 an hour, cash in hand.'

'But what would have happened if you'd seen one of the hard-up striking miners nicking something?' I enquired.

Bobby just smiled at the irony of the situation. 'On the first day I did see somebody nicking something. I don't know whether he was a miner or not, but he got away anyway,' Bobby said with relief.

After that Bobby got a job on the door of a nightclub for a few months – £12 a night. Here he heard some strong views expressed about the miners. 'I couldn't believe it – these women who worked in the club were worse off than me and yet they supported Thatcher and suggested Scargill should be shot.' During the day he was doing a spot of window-fitting and installing double glazing. 'I also do up cars for people I know, I'm quite good with engines.' Over the summer months he did some labouring on building sites. 'A friend got me the job,' he said. On Saturdays he now worked in a trendy shop selling expensive and fashionable clothes. 'It's a friend of mine who runs the shop.' His full week, however, with all these little jobs lined up end to end and all yielding cash in hand, didn't get him more than £25 a week. 'Enough to get by on though,' he said. He was not alone in working during the strike. One of his mates from the pit was steel-erecting in London. Another was working for the family garage business. Another was doing property repairs. Yet another was a bouncer.

But what did the miners who do picket duty every day think of Bobby's commercial ventures? 'They just laugh,' he said, 'and ask how I'm fixed for a drink. They thought it was hilarious, me acting as a bouncer. Some of them are right big blokes, and I'm not that big. In fact when I was working at the nightclub, the other bouncers had to keep an eye on me to make sure I didn't get into any trouble. I've seen some miners in the shop and they don't mind me working. When I went down to Orgreave to do some picketing I told all my mates about my jobs.

'Orgreave,' he said, 'was an experience.' He told me that most miners phoned their union representative to find out where to go picketing, but he said he just heard about the 7000 pickets at Orgreave on the radio, so off he went. He didn't go dressed for trouble. 'I was dressed as if I was going up town with some nice clothes on and these fashionable slip-on shoes on. When I got there all the miners were laid in these fields. It was a beautiful sunny day. There were these riot police with shields but they all went for a break. Then these guys started going round telling everyone to get up. They wanted the riot police to sweat, out in the heat. So some of the pickets rolled a tyre at the police line and some started throwing stones. The police backed off. The next minute the riot police were back all banging their shields and chanting, like something out of bloody *Zulu*. Then came the horses. It was a pitched battle. We all ran off chased by these bloody horses. One of my shoes came off and I had to pick it up and run back to my Mini. It was an eye-opener to see those police with their shields and batons, all chanting. You hear all this bollocks about pickets getting £15 a day, but anyone I've talked to only gets £1 a day plus their petrol.'

Bobby was extremely pragmatic in his approach. 'My view is that if the miners win this one we'll have a good run before anything else happens. I just want to earn a little bit of money like everybody else. I want a bit of security. I don't want to end up on the bloody scrap heap. People say the strike's political, sure it is, because we're opposing the government. I support

Scargill because he's our leader. I know he's supposed to be a communist, but to be honest I don't know a hell of a lot about it. I only know about the political parties in this country.

'But sometimes,' he added, 'I think anything has to be better than Thatcher.'

November 1984

Hell, but with a career structure

Fred Smith was a Sheffield man, born and bred. Sheffield is famous for its steel and for twenty-two years Fred had worked for Hadfield's, the private steel firm in Sheffield. But not any longer. He had been made redundant in 1981 when the Leeds Road plant closed. For two years, Fred had had time to sit and think about what might have been, to sit and brood. Two years is a long time. Not surprisingly, Fred was bitter about the industry which had paid him off and about the country which had allowed it to happen. 'I couldn't go back now if you paid me,' said Fred, not noticing the irony of what he has just said.

Fred started in the firm of Brown–Bayley in Sheffield in 1959. (It was taken over by Hadfield's in 1974.) He was twenty-one and had just completed his national service in the RAF. He was born and brought up in Darnall in the east end of Sheffield. This is where the big steel mills and factories were situated. Once they operated twenty-four hours a day, the furnaces in constant use, manned by three eight-hour shifts. The air thick with smoke. Now the mills were silent and the furnaces had been extinguished. Cold, dead hulks. When Fred started in 1959, Hadfield's employed about 10,000 workers – now there were fewer than 800. The Leeds Road plant was closed completely, leaving just the Vulcan Road plant in operation. In a town which owes its worldwide reputation to steel, these figures clank ominously.

The steel industry was, and is, a tough manly business. Fred didn't have any misty-eyed view of his former work. 'Hell' was the way he described it. 'Up to your ankles in dust from the insulation tiles. Swept out once a week by a special gang on overtime but a few days later you were up to your ankles in it again.' There were three eight-hour shifts; one from 6 am to 2 pm, one from 2 pm to 10 pm and one from 10 pm to 6 am. Fred laughed as he remembered the shifts. 'In them days, the pubs closed at 10 pm. The afternoon shift used to start really at 1 pm and finish at 9 pm so you could have a pint on the way home. By mutual consent with the other shifts, of course. In the melting shop they had to send out for their beer. It wasn't just a practice, it was a custom. It was the only way of stopping the men going outside for a pint. They brought the beer in, in half-gallon cans, and allowed a ten-minute break. The heat in the melting shop was fierce. You needed a pint.' It may have been hell but there was companionship – what Fred missed most about his work. 'When the afternoon shift finished, the gang would go to the Greyhound pub or the Attercliffe Liberal Club for an hour's drinking,' said Fred.

Coalite plant apprentice, Grimethorpe, 1984

Working in a steel mill was a hot, dusty and dangerous job. Three of Fred's friends had been killed during his time at Hadfield's, the last one not long before Fred was made redundant. 'A load fell off a fork-lift truck on top of him,' said Fred, 'and I was sitting playing dominoes with him in the canteen ten minutes before it happened.' Despite the obvious changes, safety equipment seems to have been minimal before about 1967. Before then, Fred said that they would make their own protective clothing out of any sacking they could find lying about to cover their trousers in a giant apron. Clogs they bought themselves. 'Shoes didn't last a day,' he said. 'Steel helmets only arrived in '67 and even then, many people did without. It wouldn't have done a lot for my friend anyway, would it?' There were also no showers. 'You travelled back to Attercliffe or Darnall dirty.'

It may indeed have been a hell but it was a hell with a career structure. Fred started as a pit labourer at just over £8 per week in 1959 – 'the lowest of the low – the general dogsbody'. He was part of a four-man gang consisting of a header man who made the feeder heads for the moulds, a second pit man who raked the dirt out of the mould before casting with a vacuum, and the first pit man – the gaffer in charge of the gang. His promotion was rapid – 'it was in them days – there was a big turnover as men headed for cleaner jobs in the cutlery industry and elsewhere.' Fred became 'header man' within a year, then he did charge-wheeling in the blast furnace, then became trainee foreman, then shift supervisor, all within another year. As shift supervisor he had to accept a drop in salary at first but it was a cleaner job. 'Anything was better than working on pit side,' he said, 'it was really dirty, really scruffy.' In

1962 he earned £14 per week as shift supervisor. By 1981 it was £8500 per annum – good money by anybody's standards. But then came the crash. He heard in May 1981 that the Leeds Road plant was to close. It came as a shock. 'We always thought it would be the Vulcan Road plant – its equipment was older – nearly thirty years old. The equipment in the Leeds Road plant was only five or six years old. It didn't make sense. Me and all my mates were sick. We thought we were all there for life. All my mates, who I'd been to primary school with, were all made redundant at the same time. We went to London to lobby our MP but it did no good.' Fred still quibbles about the productivity indices which suggested that British steelmaking was comparatively poor in performance compared with other EEC countries. He could argue his case well – 'but,' he said, 'no one listened'.

When the news of the closing sank in, the local technical colleges were invited to send guest lecturers to the firm to tell the men about what retraining courses were available. Fred opted for a course in electronic servicing – and while he was on the course he got full pay for fifty-two weeks but he failed to get a job afterwards. 'All the firms want experienced men and here am I at forty-five with paper qualifications but no experience. What use is that? I wish I'd done something else like getting an HGV licence, it would have been more useful.'

Money had recently started to get tight for the first time. With his £5000 redundancy payment he had paid off his mortgage on his terraced house in Crookes – another working-class district of Sheffield, but upmarket from Darnall. He had bought a neat little house which now had red tulips overflowing in a small, well cared-for garden with a plaque outside which read 'Mr and Mrs Smith live here'. Since being made redundant, Fred had worked his way through the house, decorating every room in turn. It was in good taste – no flying ducks or swarthy beauties on the wall. But since his retraining course finished, he was down to his dole money and his wife's salary (his wife was a clerk). 'It's down to essentials now,' he said.

But money wasn't the only problem. His wife was now the breadwinner. She went out to work every day. She brought back the bacon. He stayed at home and got their sixteen-year-old daughter ready for school. 'She's doing O levels at the moment. She's applied for forty jobs but only had one interview.' He made the dinner and did the cleaning and the shopping. 'I don't mind cooking,' he said. 'I did a bit when I was at work because of the shifts. I don't like cleaning, though. My wife says I don't do it right. She's always telling me off about cleaning. I only do the surface stuff really. She does the deep-down cleaning at weekends. I do like shopping, though – I like to see what the prices are and to make sure that I'm not being fiddled. I'd never done any cleaning or shopping before but I do nearly it all now. I've no timetable. I just do what I feel like, except of course for the tea which I have to get ready for half five. Most of my old mates don't do anything about the house. Especially the older ones in their fifties and sixties. They're just not used to it. They just sit about the house. In the old days the man of the family would be served first in Sheffield. But luckily in our family it wasn't like this. Just as well. I'm just one of the family now, not head of the family.'

But wasn't he glad to be out of that hot, dusty and dangerous place – to be sitting in the spring sunshine in his garden full of tulips? 'Not really,' he said. 'I miss the lads at work. I've no male company any longer. I still see my mates from work. The problem is they live all over Sheffield. We meet for a drink about once a month and I meet another friend who was made redundant at the same time who's now a bus conductor, once a week, but it's not the same. Up in Crookes when I go into Shoppers Paradise supermarket, it's full of young mums or grannies. There's only about three other redundant steel workers in all of Crookes and I didn't really know them before. Darnall's not the same. Most of it's been knocked down and the last time I went to the Greyhound pub it was in new hands – it wasn't doing any business since the steel mill closed down. There's not much happening in Sheffield any more. It's a dead town. But I've just got an allotment. I like to see things growing.'

June 1983

'How would you get them to leave?'

It was midday, and I was standing in the blinding spring sunshine looking for the security agency offices. This was where the interviews were to be held. 'Opposite the skating rink, and upstairs from the car hire business,' the voice on the phone had told me. Just next door to Cee Bee (busy, busy, busy) variety agency. I spotted the sign on the window and went into the hallway. It took my eyes a few minutes to adapt to the dark, after the bright sunshine. All other senses, however, were working overtime. The damp, dank smell hit my nose first, the sun had never had a chance to dry out this carpet. I made my way up the stairs, they creaked below my weight. There was one other candidate outside the door, sitting on the stairs and gripping a pink form. He was wearing a denim jacket and jeans. He looked strangely proportioned, but I assumed that it was just the way that he was sitting. He eyed me up as I approached, as if to say 'no chance mate'. I asked him if he was waiting to be interviewed. He said that he was, but that you just had to wait.

There was a notice on the door. It said, 'Please knock and wait. Thank you.' So I knocked, and waited, and nothing happened. So I knocked again, and still nothing happened. So I stuck my nose around the door. Two women stared at me through a cloud of smoke. 'Would you mind waiting *outside* please?' said the woman from behind the desk. 'You've come for the interview . . . Fill this in and wait *outside*.' 'Yes, but . . .' I tried to reply before I was pushed back on to the stairs. I was gripping my pink form, as if it were a comforter.

'That's just what happened to me,' said the other occupant of the stairs. 'I don't think we've made a very good start so far. You'd better start filling your form in. Look I've started mine already.' And sure enough he'd already got to question 4: 'Marital Status . . .' and 'Husband's Occupation . . .' I didn't know how long it had taken him, but he seemed to have been there quite a while already. 'Hey, I think this form's just for birds,' he said suddenly. '"Maiden Name, Husband's Occupation," do you think this is part of the test.' I said that you couldn't be sure, indeed anything was likely in a place like this. Just then someone from the Cee Bee Variety agency opened their door, knocking me down a few of the stairs. I thought that this was more likely to be part of the test, as I hauled myself back up, staring at the offending door. It too had a notice on it – 'Sorry but due to increased work load visits by prior arrangement only (THIS MEANS YOU).' It wasn't a very welcoming place.

Suddenly we heard the stairs creaking. 'This must be the bloke coming to do the interviews,' said my companion hopefully. Or another candidate for the job, I thought to myself – the top stairs were cramped enough as it was. It turned out to be a woman in her thirties wearing a bright yellow sweater and sunglasses. She greeted us, and my new companion sprang up to say hello. If we had been standing outside at the time, it would have been quite likely that he would have blocked out the sun. I couldn't see round him. The woman in the sweater looked impressed. When he eventually stepped aside, she looked me up and down. I could see her disappointment even through her shades. She told us to hurry up with the pink forms. I hadn't started mine yet. The man who could eclipse the sun was writing very slowly indeed. The other two women left the office, they said nothing as they passed.

My new companion was called first to be interviewed. I was pleased, I wanted to hear the type of questions which were to be asked. I listened through the door which wasn't properly closed. I discovered that he was nineteen years old, and had been unemployed for six months since the fitness studio he worked for had gone bust. He had no criminal convictions and could start straight away. And then the really tricky question – 'Do you have a dark suit? 'No, I can't get one to fit me,' he said – 'I've got a 54-inch chest, you see.' The woman in the yellow sweater sounded most impressed, and she was just in the process of recommending a shop which produced suits for men 'with a good build', when another candidate made his way wearily up the creaky stairs.

This one was in his mid-forties, with receding hair. He was wearing a green Parka jacket and grey flared trousers, the trousers had a patch on the inside of the thighs. He eyed me up and down as well, and this at least seemed to give him a little confidence. I nodded towards the door, on which he then knocked. A pink form was thrust his way. He glimpsed the young man being interviewed, through the crack in the door, and his confidence seemed to ebb again. 'Jesus, look at the size of that thing in there. I hope they're not just looking for blokes like that.' There was a bit of a gap in the conversation, which he proceeded to fill, he clearly needed to talk – 'Oh well. I've got a job already, you know, I'm not unemployed, I work in an engineering firm not far away. I'm just looking for a bit of extra cash. I saw the advert in the paper. I've always fancied a bit of security work on the doors of clubs or pubs or whatever. I really wouldn't mind a job with a uniform, even a dickie bow. But I thought that bouncers were changing their image lately. I thought that they wouldn't be looking for heavies anymore. But I wouldn't fancy having to throw five of somebody like that animal in there out of a pub.'

Just then the young man with the 54-inch chest made his way out. He threw me a confident smile. The man in the Parka jacket looked even more

Rock night, Rebels nightclub, Sheffield, 1995

crestfallen. I told him that he could go first, that I was in no hurry. 'Better to get it over with, eh?' he said as he walked manfully through the door.

This time the rate of pay was explained at the beginning – £10 a night on the door of pubs, working from 8.00 to 11.30 pm, £16 a night for clubs – working from 9.00 to 2.30 am. 'How do these rates of pay strike you?' enquired the lady in the yellow sweater, who I couldn't help noticing was chain-smoking. 'Magic,' said the man in the Parka. 'Right, now some questions to assess your suitability for the position,' said the interviewer. 'Say there were five lads in the club, and it was after 2.00 am, and you wanted them to leave. How would you go about it?' The man in the Parka jacket looked pensive, this was his opportunity to show that brains were better than brawn, and that a little initiative can go a very long way. 'Well, I'd not go in heavy, that's for sure.' 'Fine,' said the lady interviewer. 'What would you do instead?'

'Well, I'd ask them to drink up please, and say something like, "Would you mind making your way out of the club, thank you very much indeed." The man in the Parka looked satisfied with his answer, the interviewer didn't. 'What if they still didn't move?' she enquired. There was a very long pause, during which the man in the Parka moved forward in his seat, and started twisting his ear. 'I'd say to them – "come on lads, haven't you got any beds to go to? Move along." '

'But what if they still didn't move?' asked the interviewer again. The man in the Parka slumped back in his chair.

'Look,' said the man in the Parka, 'I'm not desperate. I was just looking for a nice cushy job on the side. I don't want a load of bloody hassle. I thought

that it might be simple security work. Would you mind if I had my application form back?'

'I would,' said the interviewer.

'Why?'

'We just want to keep it, in case you apply for any other security jobs.'

'I don't want any other security jobs, I just want my form back.'

'Why?'

'I just want it.'

Things were now turning nasty.

'Okay,' said the interviewer, and she started to tear the pink form up right
in front of him. 'Is that better?' she asked sarcastically. The man in the Parka
grunted and pushed his way out. He didn't say 'cheerio'.

It was my turn now. The interviewer was reading some notes, it gave me a
few seconds to look around the office and get my bearings. I was trying to
compose myself. I could just make out the little notice on the wall – 'This job
is so secret that I don't know what I'm doing.' It sat above a tyre in one
corner. There were press cuttings about the woman in the yellow sweater –
'A normal day for the danger girls,' ran one headline. Below it was another
headline – 'Why a shy guy stole sexy gift for bride.' Was she the bride? Did
she catch the shy guy? What was the sexy gift? What was I doing here? My
eyes flitted to a pile of application forms. I could make out the form of the
man with the 54-inch chest – '54 inch chest' had been written in red ink at
the top. The one just below it, and visibly jutting out of the side of the pile,
was covered in a childish scrawl. 'Why would you like a job as a Store Detective?' asked the pink form, even though the interviews were for positions as
bouncers. 'I WUDE LIK A JOB AS A STORE DETECTIVE BICOS I LICE IT' was the
reply. All printed in thick capitals. The 22-year-old respondent, who had last
worked on a Community Programme, had lived at his current address for '4
MUMFS', the form said. Unfortunately, it wasn't a joke, but I started laughing anyway.

I thought that I'd take the initiative. 'I've got a thirty-eight-inch chest,' I
began, 'and if I was in a club and the five lads refused to leave, I'd leave
instead. Okay? With any luck they'd follow me out.'

On that cue, I got up and skipped down the creaky stairs and ran back into
the bright, fresh spring sunshine, passing one more hopeful on the way in.

April 1988

Ken's obsession

Kenneth Clark is the little man. The man who goes to work on time
every day, without complaining. The man who goes to war whenever he's
called, whistling. He believes in bettering yourself in this life, through books,
through friends, but mostly through work. Work for him isn't wages or self-
actualisation – it's the very stuff of life. 'In the sweat of thy face shalt thou
eat bread, till thou return unto the ground, for out of it wast thou taken,' as
Genesis says. Ken Clark is the kind of man who believes that you work until

Ken and Vic Whittles, Dial House Working Men's Club trip to Blackpool, 1983

you're not able – anything else is immoral. He's the kind of man who suffers most from unemployment. He's always had a heart condition, and research in psychology now tells us that people with chronic health problems tend to undergo severe physical deterioration with unemployment. Ken Clark could tell you that from experience. He was made redundant in 1980; today he's a broken man, his health has gone, and so have his dreams of a bungalow for him and his wife in retirement. He misses his friends at work, he misses the responsibility of the job, he misses getting out of the house. He's angry and resentful – more so than most – because he believes that he was victimised by the bosses of the steel firm where he worked, who, he says, he caught fiddling; and by a system which refused to take his accusations seriously. The little man is often ignored – Ken Clark always knew that.

The funny thing is, Ken might just have been right.

Ken Clark was born in Sheffield in 1919. He started work in the city at fourteen with Laver's Timber Merchants. He subsequently tried for a job with the railways, but was rejected because of heart trouble – he was sixteen years old. He joined Effingham Steel in 1936 – a friend offered him the job. Effingham Steel had a good football team and the friend thought that Ken would make a useful centre forward. Ken started as a steel-cutter's assistant – it was his job to run the steel through the cutter and slit it into three strips. At the time they had a regular monthly order for Yokohama, Japan. 'All the lads used to say, "What the bloody hell do they want all this steel for?" One of the bosses said it was for toys. It was only after the war that we found out what it was really for – cartridge clips.'

Ken joined up in 1939 and served for six and a half years. He finished up as a sergeant in ordnance. 'I've always been meticulous,' he says. He was badly injured in a fall in Iceland when he was in the infantry. His army records describe his conduct as 'exemplary'. They identified him as a man 'to be trusted with responsibility'. He met his wife, Ann, who was in the WRAF during the war, at a concert on Spital Hill. 'It was money for a tank that night, I think.' They married in 1943 when he was home on leave. They couldn't get a house of their own and were on the council list for five years. They lived with in-laws and got their first council house on Manor Park estate in Sheffield in 1951. 'It was a very nice little house, very well-built – all except one thing: there was no dividing wall in the loft. God knows how many bricks were saved by the company that built it with this little fiddle. Somebody obviously pocketed a fair bit.'

After the war, Ken started with Sheffield Forge as a general inspector – checking the quality of the steel. 'They were the good days of the steel industry – there was plenty of work – we were supplying steel for nuts and bolts for the motor trade – most of the workers were ex-servicemen and we all got on very well. The funny thing is, there were few charge hands in them days – you didn't seem to need them.' Everything was working well, 'except for one little incident where I had an appointment with my union man who was also a councillor. I missed watching the Blades to go and see him on a Saturday afternoon. His secretary said he was in conference. I found him in the pub. I said to him, "I didn't know this was where you did your business," and gave him a good piece of my mind. Sixpence a week to the union – it seemed a lot to subsidise his boozing.'

Ken then got a job at Dunford's – 'another good firm – I was centre forward for their football team as well'. He then applied for a job at Denton's in 1959 as a steel inspector. It was there that he first met William Kelsey, then Managing Director of Inca Steel. Mr Denton set up a finishing shop at Inca Steel and Ken became manager under Bill Kelsey. 'Bill was just the type of bloke I wanted to work for at the time. The machines were running twenty-four hours a day – Bill gave me a completely free hand, he just said, "Run it as you see fit – anything you can't handle just come to me." Bill was a good boss. He knew I was a keen football supporter so he used to give me tickets to go to Bramall Lane to watch the Blades. He also gave me tickets to watch Yorkshire play – all Yorkshiremen are cricket lovers. Bill used to entertain the visiting Australian team at his home – Kelsey's Folly. Everybody knew he had a lot of money. In 1969, Inca Steel was taken over by Osborn's. As soon as this happened Bill left to join Napier Steel at Oughtibridge in Sheffield as Managing Director. It's been pointed out since that he joined Napier Steel on April Fool's Day 1969.'

Ken was transferred to Osborn's main plant as shift foreman and assistant safety officer – reliable, meticulous, trustworthy. Good old Ken. Ken was in charge of the night shift at Osborn's. 'It was while I was there that I first came across scrap men in operation. Some of the bigger scrap men in Sheffield are millionaires. There was a pub – the Woodbourne Hotel – near Osborn's where all the scrap men and the police would meet and drink after hours. I was always shocked by the camaraderie and the fact that there was so much obvious backscratching going on. The scrap men would shop small thieves to the police and in return they'd get away with lorryloads of dodgy scrap. It all seemed wrong somehow.'

Ken moved again – to Sheffield Twist Drill in 1973 as a result of a personal invitation from Bill Kelsey. 'There was a lot of movement between steel firms in those days,' says Ken. 'Bill wanted me with him at Oughtibridge.'

Ken's job was to reorganise billet preparation and despatch to mills. At the time they were running up to six months behind schedule. By May 1975 schedules were back on target. In early 1976 Ken was appointed Works and Transport Manager of a new site at Darnall. 'Meanwhile at Oughtibridge the alloy store had metal doors fitted, security padlocks installed and an alarm fitted. It was called "Fort Knox" by everybody who worked there. It was meant to be the safest store in Sheffield. Bill Kelsey had the key.'

Ken's problems started in 1977. Eighteen tons of steel came in from West Valley Steels to the Darnall site. Ken took one look at it and rejected it. 'I rang West Valley Steels immediately and told them it wasn't on – "It's no good to us, it's cogging" – a much rougher steel than we used. They said, "Oh yes – it's what you've ordered." I rang Bill immediately and said, "Bill, some-body's playing silly buggers with us – West Valley Steels have sent us cogging. It's no bloody use to us at all." But Bill surprised me – he just said, "Get in touch with the buying department." I rang down to buying and I said, "I've got a load here that's no good to us at all." So this chap from buying said, "Who says?" and I said, "I say." He said, "Well, it's urgent." I said, "It's no good." Anyway, he went to a higher authority, a person called Hopwood who was head of buying, and he said, "Get it inspected." So I inspected it and rejected sixteen out of the eighteen tons. I could tell by the appearance that it wasn't right. I sent some to our research department and they rejected it as well.

'The next thing I knew, I was summoned by Mr Huddy, Managing Director of Sheffield Twist Drill, and I went down to see him – all innocence. Bill Kelsey was with him. Huddy said to me, "This steel you've been throwing out, can't we get anything out of it? You know how desperate we are." I said to him, "Look, it's no good at all, it needs finishing."

'Huddy said to Bill, "What's he trying to tell us?" I interrupted. I said, "What I'm trying to tell you is that you're paying for sirloin steak and you're getting stewing meat. I can't put it any plainer than that." So Kelsey says, "Thanks for bringing it to our notice." Huddy was going to sack Hopwood, but Kelsey apparently suggested (as I found out later) that they should put it down to Hopwood's inexperience – just a little error – despite the fact that Hopwood had paid five times more than the steel was worth! Somebody should have smelt a rat. Kelsey obviously didn't want Hopwood fired – at the time, I didn't know why.

'Kelsey asked to see me and told me that Hopwood would be after me. Kelsey was jubilant – he didn't want Hopwood fired but he did want him brought down to size. Kelsey told me if I couldn't handle Hopwood to go to him and he'd straighten him out for me. Hopwood was severely reprimanded for this and West Valley Steels were struck off the Suppliers List.

'Things then quietened down a bit. It was common knowledge I'd upset the apple cart. Huddy, the Managing Director, then moved elsewhere. Things were now running smoothly. In 1979 I got to hear that they were going to start having future deliveries of steel from West Valley Steels. The funny thing was that after Huddy had gone, Hopwood got the buying job back. I got straight on the phone to Bill and said, "What's this, you're dealing with West Valley Steels again?" Bill assured me that they could meet all our specifications now. The first load from them was three loads of shank – they'd been "bright-drawn" – the steel was perfect but it was bowed – you couldn't feed it through the machines. It was useless. I got straight on the phone to Kelsey and said, "They're up to their old tricks again, Bill." Bill said, "Look, send it back and get it straightened and then get it back to us." It's very rare to have to reject 100 per cent of a load like this but I just never suspected Bill Kelsey at the time. In the next few years West Valley Steel became our firm's main supplier despite numerous competitors.

'In 1980 the time ran out at the Darnall site and I was told to run the place down. We bought a place at Bramall Lane. I wanted to find out where the move left me personally. I talked to Bill and he said I'd be all right. But when I went to Bramall Lane, a Mr Wainwright, who had been just a junior buyer at Darnall, was appointed as overall manager. I was responsible to him – I had no role in setting it up. As soon as I got there, I did me nut – "Bloody organised chaos, this place," I said. Bill just told me to keep my head down and have a free ride. In August of that year Wainwright and Hopwood were abroad on holiday. This steel came in from West Valley Steels. The driver, who was going to unload it, said to me, "Have you seen this lot, Ken?" There was 50 per cent too much and it was being delivered five months early and I had a memo about destocking! We were down from 800,000 drills to 400,000. I said to the driver, "You're not offloading that, mate," and he just said, "You're desperate." It was a nonsense – we had forty weeks' supply and we were losing orders right, left and centre. He said, "There's three loads as well." I got on to West Valley Steels and said, "You're playing silly buggers again." They said, "What do you mean? We've got strict instructions from your buying department – it's got to be rushed in – you're desperate for it." I said, "Well, I'm not accepting it," and I gave strict instructions that no one was to sign for anything.

'I rang Bill and he said, "Just put it on the floor and Hopwood and Wainwright will sort it out when they get back from holiday." I knew something was going on, so I started photocopying everything in sight, and sent a memo to Kelsey, Hopwood and Wainwright. We had this steel everywhere, you know, and we were having to walk over these greasy bars. When Mr Wainwright came back from holiday, he had a meeting with Bill and Hopwood and said the top brass told him that it had to be accepted and pushed through for immediate payment. It was passed by research in a ridiculously short time – the tests just couldn't have been done. The steel was invoiced on 8 September and payment went out immediately on the 9th. This just wasn't Bill Kelsey's way of doing things – he never paid anything until the final demand came.

'On that same day, I was sent for by Wainwright. He said, "I've got news for you, Ken – you're redundant." I couldn't believe it. I rang Bill and asked him to intervene on my behalf. He didn't want to know. I was devastated. When I tried to ring him, he was never in. I got £1,520 redundancy.'

Ken Clark is a meticulous and honest man – he had smelt a rat and the rat had bitten his hand off. 'I appealed against my dismissal. Hopwood said that irrespective of cost they would contest any industrial tribunal. At a pre-hearing assessment in November 1980, I was given permission to go to tribunal in February 1981. At the tribunal, I challenged the code of conduct of Sheffield Twist Drill. They denied the existence of certain documents and ignored a tribunal directive to produce them.' He produces a photocopy of the decision of the industrial tribunal. The tribunal unanimously rejected his complaint. It's worth quoting from the original document:

Mr Clark made a complaint that the job he did is still there. He cannot get over the fact that the work which he did is now shared between those who were above him in management and those who were beneath him on the shop floor . . . there clearly is no possible grounds for his complaint that he was not redundant because his functions must still be performed . . . he has a further complaint that the reorganisation itself and everything that was done by the company in its redundancy situation so far as he was concerned was done with the idea of getting rid of him . . . He is not prepared to accept that the person above him who decided that the deliveries should be accepted might be aware of *other factors in management of which he was not aware* and he is not prepared to accept that his good advice should not be readily welcomed by his employers. He has therefore assumed that as they did not accept his advice, they regarded him as a nuisance and wanted to get rid of him. We find that there is no substance whatever in that complaint . . . The real problem here is that Mr Clark is quite unable to understand that having expressed their appreciation of his qualities, they still made him redundant . . . This application must be dismissed.

Ken Clark was out of work – depressed and very angry. He believed that he had been victimised. Nobody wanted to listen. He had stopped whistling. The little man started complaining for once. In fact he just wouldn't shut up. He became a real nuisance.

And then a very funny thing happened. In November 1981 – thirteen months after Ken's redundancy and eight months after his industrial tribunal – Stephen Elkington, Sheffield Twist Drill's financial controller, was shot in the leg by a gunman outside his home in Derbyshire. The gunman escaped leaving both Elkington and the police baffled about the possible motive for the attack. One theory apparently entertained by Derbyshire police at the time was that the shooting was a case of mistaken identity – the intended target, it was thought by some, was Mr Hopwood. As part of the police enquiry, a number of employees recently made redundant by Sheffield Twist Drill were interviewed to see if anyone bore Elkington (or Hopwood) a grudge. Ken Clark was one of those the police spoke to. He told police that 'Elkington was probably shot because he caught Hopwood with his fingers in the till'. 'But they never followed this up,' says Ken. Overlooked by many people at the time was the fact that Stephen Elkington was due to supervise an audit of the alloy store at Napier's. A year later, on 2 December 1982, South Yorkshire Police were called to Napier Steels where there had been a report of a burglary at the alloy store. Not a small burglary either – one million pounds' worth of steel was said to have been stolen. Ken Clark rubbed his hands. 'I knew what they'd really find,' he said.

What they found at Napier Steel triggered the largest enquiry South York-shire Police ever had to mount – the investigation lasted eighteen months and the resulting court case four months: £1.7 million had gone missing. In September 1984, Bill Kelsey was jailed for seven and a half years for twenty-five offences of fraud and corruption. Patrick Hopwood was jailed for three and a half years on four corruption charges. Between 1976 and 1982, alloys that should have been delivered to and stored at Napier Steel were in fact rerouted to a Sheffield scrap firm where an accomplice of Kelsey's sold the alloys to unsuspecting dealers. Audit stock checks would obviously have exposed the theft. In 1980, the audit simply involved the counting of alloy drums in the store. Nobody disputed Bill Kelsey's authority, and drums of scrap filings and 'swarf', in disguised alloy drums, were put on display. In 1981 Twist Drill's auditors requested a more thorough stock check – the drums were to be actually opened and alloys inspected. Kelsey meanwhile had obtained more drums with rubbish topped up with a layer of ferro-chrome. A thorough audit would have revealed the deception, however. Stephen Elkington insisted that this more thorough audit had to proceed. A few days later he was mysteriously shot; his deputy carried out the check, but Kelsey had the pipe leading to the cutting equipment shortened. Only the three nearest drums could be reached. These were open and passed. The deception continued.

However, in 1981, SKF, the Swedish firm that now owned Sheffield Twist Drill, announced the impending closure of Napier Steels. Hopwood was in-structed to sell off the alloys which should have amounted to £1 million at 'Fort Knox'. On 2 December, Kelsey finally agreed to meet the auditors and open up the store. The keys could not be found and the store was cut open. There was not an ounce of alloy to be seen. 'Oh my God!' Kelsey is reported to have said. The 'burglary' was reported, but suspicion fell on Kelsey imme-diately – he, after all, had held the key. Ken rubs his hands again. 'All sorts were implicated. Bob Green, a notorious Sheffield criminal, got four and a half years for conspiring with Kelsey to commit arson, and a Detective Ser-geant Graham Storr from Sheffield got five years for conspiring with Kelsey to commit arson and conspiring to corrupt. Kelsey had all kinds of connec-tions, you know. Also Hopwood admitted in court that between 1975 and 1977 he accepted a £700 bribe from West Valley Steels in return for his firm choosing West Valley Steels as a supplier. Kelsey admitted knowing Hopwood received bribes from West Valley Steels, but Kelsey himself was bribing Hop-wood in a separate swindle. Everybody was bribing everybody else, but they knew there was no point in trying to bribe me,' says Ken. 'No point at all.'

Ken appealed against the decision of the original industrial tribunal armed with this new information. This tribunal had to provide an answer to the question 'whether the evidence that we have heard establishes that Mr Clark was dismissed as part of a desire on the part of senior management to pursue criminal activities within the respondent company'. Mr Wainwright appeared as a witness and his evidence was crucial. He testified that he was not told by senior management, i.e. Hopwood and Kelsey, whom to make redundant, and that he had personally selected Mr Clark – on purely eco-nomic grounds. The review tribunal confirmed the original decision and finished with the admonishment:

it is time to close the book on this episode finally and to consider that it might be that however suspicious it seemed and disturbing the truth might be that this was a simple dismissal for redundancy, upsetting and disturbing though that in itself no doubt was.

'Of course, I can't prove anything different,' says Ken, 'but no one listened originally and look what skeletons they found in the cupboard. I'll keep on till somebody proves it. I know in my heart why I was sacked. I know exactly why. And the funny thing is, the worst part of the whole affair is, that when I moved into my little terraced house in Robinson Road I nearly borrowed a thousand pounds off Bill Kelsey to build an extension. I would have been in his debt along with everybody else. That's how Bill Kelsey worked. I have more sleepless nights about that than anything else. When Bill Kelsey gets out of prison he'll go back to his big grand house – his future secured. My future has gone down the Swanee along with the Sheffield steel industry which people like Bill Kelsey managed to ruin.'

'Managed to ruin, geddit?' I said, laughing.

Ken nearly cried.

January 1987

Dust everywhere

Brian had always looked forward to going to town. When he was a boy he loved going to the stamp counter of Woolies with his father – just once a week. It was the highlight of his fairly routine schedule. And then on to Lipton's with the smell of cheddar cheese which hung over the whole shop and the sausages on sticks out to taste. And when he was working, he had the whole weekend to look forward to. The pub on Friday and Saturday – not that exciting in itself, but wonderful when you didn't have to get up the next day. And Saturday afternoon shopping sandwiched in between. Time to get the overalls off, get really clean and go round the shops with the wife. If he ever had to go to town during the week, it was always a quick dash in his overalls, but on Saturdays, he had the whole morning to sit about, dress and get ready. And here he was in town, midweek, nice and clean, no overalls, no dirt down his fingernails, plenty of time, and it wasn't even raining. Yet it was all so depressing.

The problem was time, he thought. The days were so long and a trip to town wasn't a break from anything, now he was redundant. He went to town to pass time and when you're trying to pass time you see things differently, you notice things that the rich and famous, the busy, even the employed never see. It's as if you pick out all the bad bits and then that's all you end up able to see. He could remember his father used to say that you could tell when a storm was coming by the way the wind whipped the litter along the pavement. He really noticed the wind today – and the litter. The wind was so low and it led the chip papers and the Wimpy boxes and the Coke cartons all in a merry little dance. The red and white cartons flashed along the grey pavement like so many grubby tropical fish. And yet there was no storm in the making – nothing to break the monotony or the mood. Shows

Supervisor in the solid fuel industry, Bolsover, 1984

what my bloody father knew, he thought. And he was sure there hadn't been that much litter in the good old days. He felt like picking some of it up and putting it in the litter bins but he was afraid people might think he was some nutter out on day release from Middlewood.

He went into the Wimpy bar and ordered a Coke. It came in a carton. He kept thinking about what his wife's cousin had told them. She worked in a building society, the one that gives a little Xtra help and the cashiers tilt their heads while they're smiling. She had been telling them about customers these days making deposits of 25p or even 15p. It never happened before, and it wasn't for a joke. They were quite serious, and they all could justify it by saying they were just evening up their accounts. It meant they came in four or five times a week for a bit of a chat, even a formal and ritualised one, centering on the exchange of a few coppers. Perhaps it'll be like that in a couple of months for me, he thought. Perhaps I'll start ringing Directory Enquiries for an intimate conversation. He wanted to down his Coke in one, but he knew he had to make it last.

So this was life on the dole, he thought to himself. Making a trip down Fargate – all 200 yards of it – last an hour. Funny, in the good old days of Saturday shopping, it did last an hour – but then he used to be weaving in and out of shops, instead of weaving between the chip wrappers. And there were mates to chat to. Now he didn't like meeting old friends – it was too embarrassing. Most of them were still working, and those that weren't all felt sorry for themselves. So now he did the Fargate run every day except Saturdays. Better to be out when your mates were locked away behind the factory doors, he thought.

Brian was forty-six and had been unemployed for only two months but it felt like years; before that he worked for a big engineering firm in Sheffield for twenty-five years. He was an electrician. He always knew the firm would run into problems. It was large, too large; he used to boast that because of its size it could carry a lot of dead weight, including himself. And he had always been amazed how little anyone had to do. He worked on a test bed on the production line. Things were always slack at the start of the week and he and his mates would sit around reading, and then go in at weekends on time and a half and double time to get the work done. On nights it was even worse. The night shift was from 9 pm to 7 am, but they'd be able to get the work done in three hours by stretching some of the safety rules a bit. ('Well, rules were made to be broken,' they would all say.) After that it was time for a kip. Brian chose the dark room. The only disadvantage was that it was a bit cold in there so he'd lay some corrugated cardboard down on the floor. The night foreman just didn't bother. But every so often there would be a bit of commotion at the top and all the foremen would be given strict instructions to stop people getting their heads down. This purge would last for a couple of weeks – then it was back to normality. The management, Brian thought, was a joke. They ruled without any authority. Brian had always feared the worst. He knew that the survival of such a factory in a recession was going to be difficult anyway, and with a workforce accustomed to sleeping on the job, and a management without the power to stop it, it was going to be impossible. And the worst came to pass. In November 1983, they were told that the factory would close in six months. Three-quarters of the workforce were paid off in March 1984. Brian was one of the 'lucky' ones – he got to stay until the end.

Those were the days of hope and prayer, and considerable recrimination. Hope and prayer that the factory could somehow survive, and recrimination as to why it had to happen in the first place. Management blamed workers and vice versa. Local MPs took an interest in the cause and hopes rose. Sheffield Corporation considered the reintroduction of trolley buses to provide some work for the factory, and hopes rose still further. But the economics just didn't make sense in the end. The trolley-bus order would have guaranteed jobs for about ten. Hopes shot through the roof and plummeted to earth. It was like pissing in the wind, thought Brian.

Brian stayed on till August 1984 in a deserted factory, trying to finish off an order for the Ministry of Defence. Production lasted until June 1984. During the last eight months, representatives from the Department of Employment and a team of redundancy 'counsellors' came in to give a series of lectures in an effort to ease this particular rite of passage. Brian found the lady from the Department of Employment somewhat disconcerting when she suggested that the rules and regulations about unemployment benefit were so complicated that nobody really knew what anybody was entitled to. The redundancy counsellors gave a lecture on finding a job. All that Brian remembered of it was that they suggested dog-walking, pet-sitting and fish-feeding for neighbours on holiday as real possibilities. They also gave lectures on interview technique, but it all seemed so obvious. Dress reasonably and don't squirm or fidget. Brian didn't squirm or fidget anyway. So, equipped with his knowledge (and £6500 redundancy money) Brian joined the army of the unemployed, with strict orders to sign on and search for jobs and trudge the streets for the long, long, empty hours.

So he sat in a Wimpy bar with no one really to blame. He would have liked somebody to blame – anybody would have done, the Japanese, Thatcher, the multinationals – but he couldn't stop thinking about the dark room and the corrugated cardboard. It made it all that much worse. And he thought about his mates from the night shift who worked in the machine shop and who weren't able to slip off for a kip, and he thought how depressed they must feel. They grafted while others slept and here they were all in the same boat – all up the creek without a paddle, and just a lifeline dangled by the Department of Employment for minimal assurance. He tried cheering himself up – he wasn't as badly off as some. At least he had some interest outside work. He was a keen marathon runner. When he was still employed he would sometimes do 20 miles during the day (and sleep off the running fatigue during work hours). So when the axe was threatened, he thought that it wouldn't be that bad. It would leave him time for extra training. He might even be able to break the three-hour marathon barrier.

But things didn't turn out like that. On his very first day on the dole he went out for a run with his wife. She had just taken up running and he was going to be her mentor. He says he was quite relaxed and quite happy about redundancy, but that day, that critical day when it finally materialised, he found that he just couldn't keep up with her. He tried going out with his old running club and the same thing happened – they left him behind. He had never had asthma in his life but suddenly here he was puffing and panting and gasping for breath. The other runners couldn't understand it. It got so bad that he couldn't even walk home from the Jobcentre without continually stopping. He read somewhere that nerves could bring on asthmatic symptoms but he refused to believe that was what was happening with him. He thought perhaps it was his house-cleaning, which he did while his wife went to work, or the fact that there was a lot of dust in the factory for the last few weeks before the closure. He was looking for some physical cause, something that he could put his finger on and say, 'That's it', something tangible. He didn't want to believe that it was something psychological, that it was all in the mind.

He had never liked work, he had often told people. He had a lot of outside interests and unemployment would just mean he could spend more time doing them, he kept saying. Between gasps, that is.

He could see the bitter irony in the whole thing. If it goes on like this, he thought, it'll soon take me an hour just to walk down Fargate. I'll not even have to drag my feet. And he left the Wimpy bar and positioned the Coke carton with meticulous precision right in the middle of the litter bin. The whole careful movement took nearly a minute and a half. Just as well nobody's watching, he thought.

November 1985

Work

The most unhealthy type of work is the grinding of knife-blades and forks which, especially where a dry stone is used, always leads to the death of the operative at an early age. The unhealthy nature of this work is caused partly by the fact that the grinder works in a bent position. His breast and stomach suffer from the pressure put upon them. But the main danger of this trade comes from breathing in particles of sharp metallic dust thrown up into the air during the grinding process. The average expectation of life of a dry grinder is barely 35 years, while that of a wet grinder is rarely more than 45. (Friedrich Engels, *The Conditions of the Working Class in England*, 1845)

'Wake me when I get to London'

It was the middle of the night. A quarter past three to be exact, in a village called Holton le Clay, just outside Grimsby. The snow was falling heavily and the wind from the North Sea whipped it right across the road. It was a very good night for snow drifts, but very little else. Dave Cowley opened the front door of his little semi, the wind blasted him in the face. 'Bloody hell,' he said. He'd left his wife wrapped up in bed, in the middle of her eight-hour sleep cycle. He was in the middle of his sleep cycle as well, and that was why it felt distinctly odd to be up and about. He pushed out through the blizzard, and into his mini-van. The temperature was way below freezing. Luckily the van started first time. But the snow was starting to lie. 'That's all I bloody need,' he said, as he roared off, 'I'll have to push it a bit now with this bad weather, or I'll get caught up in the traffic, as I get near London.'

His housing estate was asleep, Holton le Clay was asleep, all of Grimsby was asleep. Nothing at all stirred. 'That's the bloody problem basically, it's dead up here now. The fishing industry's been killed off, and Grimsby was the fishing industry. Don't ask me why it died, that's political, and I'm not into politics, especially at this time of the bloody morning. But I've always been one of those that got on their bike basically. Just as well really.'

Dave made his way through the town, and into a cul-de-sac with more warm semis. There was one light on in the whole street. 'That'll be George,' he said. Dave pulled up. There was a slight delay as George made his way slowly through the blizzard and loaded his gear into the back of the van, between the portable bed and the empty buckets. 'The bed's in the back in case I can't find anywhere to kip tonight,' said Dave. 'I'm moving on to a new site today in Mansell Street near Tower Bridge. I haven't got any digs lined up yet.' George got into the van beside him, he was bleary-eyed and shivering. He wrapped himself in his donkey jacket. 'Wake me when I get to London,' he said. George was fifty-five years old, 'and I feel it, I'm getting too old for this bloody game.' This game being commuting from Grimsby to London for work on a building site. Dave and George were both crane operators for the 'Expanded Piling Company' of Grimsby. George had been commuting like this on and off since 1957, Dave since 1971. 'But there's been one big change in the past five years,' said Dave. 'There's more blokes having to do it now. You'll see when we get on to the A1. You used to be able to do the 180 miles in two hours, but now the traffic is terrible near London. It takes nearer four hours now. You have to leave earlier and earlier to get there on time. It's dead in the North, that's the basic reason.'

'When I started out,' explained George 'you used to go down for a month or six weeks at a time. I never saw my kids grow up. I prefer coming home for weekends, but all this travelling is very hard on you. It's worse when you're travelling on your own though. This morning we're going in convoy with a couple of lads from Hull – they had to leave home at half two this morning.'

And sure enough, through the blizzard you could just about make out the other little 'Expanded Piling Company' van, with the snow settling in layers on its roof. Dave screwed his eyes up even tighter to try to see the van

Mr 'Shifter' and mate, coalmen, Doncaster, 1984

through the snow on the windscreen. 'And the worst thing is that with this weather we're gong to have to push it all the way there,' he said.

Dave was thirty-eight, but he looked, in fact, much older. He had been getting on his bike for the past seventeen years. He did it, he said, for the job security. It cost him his first marriage. 'She found somebody else while I was away. But she wasn't a patch on Sheila, my second wife anyway. Sheila is more independent, she needs to be. She understands why I have to work away. Most building sites, you see, operate on a hire and fire basis. One week you've got a job, the next you're out. With this company, you've got a bit of security.'

For a basic week of 50 hours, Dave took home around £200. 'But the hours can stretch a bit. I've had to work a 20-hour day before now, and once I had to work 27 hours on the trot. It can be risky work mind. One time my crane nearly tipped over on the Cenotaph, it's risky enough even without these long hours. But I've made as much as £400 in one week, absolutely fantastic wages by Grimsby standards, so I can't really complain. But you don't get money like that every week.'

With wages like that, he had been able to buy a three-bedroom semi in Holton le Clay for around £32,000. 'You'd get nothing in London for that kind of money,' he said, 'and don't forget within a few miles of my house I've got both countryside and seaside – Cleethorpes is only six miles away. I wouldn't swap it for the world. But,' he added after a moment's contemplation, 'the sea is a bit shitty around here, and to be honest if it wasn't for the people from Sheffield and Rotherham, no-one would come to Cleethorpes for their holiday. I only go there for some decent fish and chips. But I'd never move to London. It's a horrible place, it's too fast and too expensive. I'm a big bloke, but when I go down the street, everybody's flying past me.' George stirred for a second and said 'the people are all like ants, the way they pour out of the tube stations and that. Just like ants.' He curled up again, and his eyes closed – 'five days a week in London is plenty, believe me.' Dave took over again, 'but that's where the money is basically. If I'd bought a house in London when I first started working there, I'd be one of them now, I suppose – the rich. But I've left it a bit late. For me it's up and down this bloody road, week-in, week-out.' Dave squinted even harder at the windscreen, trying to follow the white line in the centre as it wound its way through the sleeping Lincolnshire countryside.

'The main problem with this job,' said Dave, 'is the travelling. I've had a few scrapes already. In 1976 I was off work for a year when I broke my spine in an accident on black ice. I was in hospital for four months. The bloke who found me just said, "I thought you were dead mate." I said, "Well, I'm bloody well not." I've never been so happy in my life to see the inside of a hospital. In '84 on the way back from London I went straight into a woman doing a three-point turn right in the middle of the road. There was a three-tier wedding cake in the back of her car, after the smash it was just a trifle.' He guffawed with laughter, but George didn't stir. 'But luckily she wasn't hurt. Six weeks after that I rolled my car right over a hedge and into the grounds of a detention centre. My son Jason was beside me and he fell out of the car, luckily he wasn't hurt. There wasn't a straight panel on the side of the car though. I'd just bought it as well, but I hadn't got round to insuring it yet. It's just the law of averages though. You're bound to have a smash going up and down this road all the time. I think I've been pretty lucky so far. One of my best pals was killed a few months ago, I guess his luck just ran out. I've worked out a few ways of keeping myself awake on the drive – I'll sing at the top of my voice, or talk to myself. Who cares if people think I'm a nutter. Sometimes I have a shave when I'm driving, with an electric razor. I don't shave all week when I'm down in London. So when you start pulling your beard off with this thing, it keeps you awake alright. At times I'll drive really daft to keep myself awake. There's nothing more boring than driving slowly.'

The blizzard stopped rather abruptly, as we headed toward the A1. The road was dry now as Dave started to accelerate. I couldn't stop thinking about his sojourn in hospital, as we started to drive faster and faster.

'It's not a bad life,' said Dave. 'In addition to your wages, you get £12.36 a day subsistence allowance. That's not bad – it's a quid over what most firms pay. You can usually get a bed-and-breakfast for around £14 a day in London in the Kings Cross area. The only problem is that we're out in the morning before breakfast and back in the evening after tea. We get fish and chips most nights, or a kebab. We live on that kind of food. Nearly everyone prefers working out of London, up in Morecambe you can get bed and breakfast and an evening meal for £8, which is very reasonable.' 'And a cup of tea for 15 pence,' added George. 'In London it sets you back about 25 pence.' George shut his eyes again. 'The only problem is,' continued Dave, 'all the work is down in London. They're always pulling office blocks down and putting up new ones. I've built all sorts – the Lloyds bank building – that's a real space oddity, the extension to the Covent Garden Opera House. I've even drilled a hole in the House of Commons car park. I don't talk about my work much at home, and Sheila has only been to London a couple of times, so she's never really seen anything I've built. There's too much to be crammed into a week-end to have time to talk about it. We have to do the shopping at weekends, and visit all our relatives. My dad has farmer's lung disease, and if I don't take him out, then he doesn't get out. It's as simple as that. And Sheila often says that some things that you're dying to tell each other about during the week just seem trivial by the time the weekend comes around. Sheila would like me to work at home but she knows the score about the job situation up in Grimsby. Once you couldn't move down at the docks early in the morning, now you can drive straight through any time of the day or night. That says it all. You either go in search of work, or you stay on the dole and commit Hari Kari, and I don't fancy that somehow.'

We passed Lincoln Cathedral at around 4.30 am. Lincoln slept.

'I'm going to a new site today and I don't know what it's going to be like. If I can't get digs, I'll have to just kip down where I can – in the site office or whatever. I always say that after a few pints it doesn't really matter anyway. The truth is I don't even go out drinking much in London these days. After a day at work I'm too knackered. We used to go up Soho and that sort of thing – into the sex shops. When I was looking at this magazine once, this bloke came up behind me and said, "this ain't a library mate." I'm big, but he was huge, so I legged it. But I'm getting too old for that sort of thing now. I usually go to bed before 10.00. I bring a little portable telly with me and that's about it. Sometimes I'll go round some model shops in the evening – that's my hobby, you see. Now and again the blokes will bring a blue video to watch in the site office, but I'm more content with a good fishing book to tell you the truth.'

The A1 got noticeably busier near Leicester. It was, however, still pitch black. 'The other problem with this journey is that there are so few transport cafes open all night. But luckily there's one around here – time for a cup of tea,' he said and we pulled into Truckers restaurant. The other 'Expanded Piling Company' van was already sitting outside. Inside sat another Dave, who was a foreman, with Mark and Jim. Nobody talked, and somewhat incongruously the TV in the corner was broadcasting an American news pro-gramme about the Republican Primaries. 'You know, I'd prefer to work any-where in the country except London,' said Dave the foreman – 'anywhere.' This was followed by a long silence.

We left the cafe at 5.45, and got back on to the A1. The road was starting to fill up. Dave still pushed the pace along. Dawn started to creep up as we entered Hertfordshire at around 6.20. Ten minutes later the A1 was solid traffic. London was still twenty-nine miles off. 'Five years ago this road would have been empty at this time,' said Dave, overtaking another mini-van full of workers. 'To miss the traffic jams now, we'd have to leave at 2.00 in the morning.' George started to wake up. 'Do you know what you're building at the moment George?' asked Dave. 'No, but it's probably an office block, they're all office blocks – going up or coming down. It's always the bloody same.'

Cathy, carpet maker, Leeds, 1985

We started to drive through Mill Hill, it was now 6.45. A green Mercedes, with a personalised number plate, raced the van at some lights, and finding itself unable to leave the van behind, simply cut right in front of it. Dave muttered something, you could see that he hadn't really got the energy to shout anything stronger. 'It's like this,' said Dave, surveying the posh houses of Mill Hill. 'There's so much money floating about down here. I was on a job where they offered the residents £30,000 each not to complain about the noise. Thirty grand a piece. Straight up. There are some Cockneys on the site, and they're all the same – they've all got their heads screwed on alright. And look at all those wanted criminals on the Costa del Sol, they're all bloody Cockneys. They don't just go for the odd grand, they go for the whole bloody lot. They think big down here, that's why all the bloody money in the country has ended up down here. It's nothing to do with effort. Nobody worked harder than the Grimsby fishermen, and look what they got for their trouble.' George just squinted out at the roads paved with gold and litter, before getting out of the van at his site at Tower Bridge. 'See you on Friday,' he said.

It was now 7.25 am as we pulled into Mansell Street. It was still freezing, but thankfully there was no snow. I made my excuses and retired to bed. Dave started a day's work.

May 1988

The nightshift

It was 10.30 pm, and the room was very noisy, even though there were only two machines working in the decorating room through the long, long night. John, the foreman, was on his dinner break – he had come on at 6.00 pm, and he was not due off until 6.00 in the morning, so he had an hour for dinner – unpaid, which he could have taken at any time. John settled the night men down – they came on at 10.00 pm – then he took his hour. He read the *Sun* from cover to cover twice, there was no-one to talk to, no music, no laughter, no crack, just the super, soaraway *Sun* for company. 'Come into the office,' he said and he led me to a group of dirty plastic chairs covered in pages from the *Sun* clustered in one corner, of the factory. I had to sit on a Page 3 girl.

He was going to explain about the work that is done in Grindley's in Stoke-on-Trent at night, but we couldn't make each other out over the noise of the machines. 'You get used to it,' he said, 'even if you can't ever hear what people are trying to say to you.' We made our way past Kevin and the other machine operator on the way to the other office. Neither of them looked up, as we passed by. 'They're interested in a professional performance,' said John. 'In this business if the goods don't come up to the mark, you don't get paid, it's as simple as that. You have to concentrate on what you're doing, or you can come out at the end of the week with bugger all.'

John works a 59-hour week with five 12-hour nights for a gross pay packet of around £210. 'That's very good money by pottery standards, labourers here who work days earn only £91.28 gross for a 39-hour week. The wages in the pottery industry tend to be a bit behind the times. I don't mind nights, I've no family, I live with my step-father. I get in around 6.30 am, and read the morning papers and watch a few films that my brother has recorded for me the night before. He's got cable TV – I've thought about it myself, but I hear that they're going to phase it out around here. I go to bed at 9.00 am with a couple of good books, mainly science fiction. I used to have my own bookshop, you see, before I started working here four years ago. This job is a bit different to running a bookshop. I get up about one o'clock in the afternoon. There's this little dog that starts yapping about this time every day without fail. I can't sleep through it. The whole thing can get you down sometimes to be honest.

'You only get paid for the best ware you send out, you understand, and we're paid on a piece-work basis. So you're always trying to do the best work as quickly as possible. It's great if you're on a good shift, but on some shifts you get some right dozy buggers that are always stopping and starting the machines, or dropping the plates. We have one Pakistani that's always dropping plates, he pretends that he doesn't know what I'm saying to him. They just act daft. When you give them their pay packet, they can tell you where every penny has gone. It's always "me no understand" until you start talking about money. They take advantage of being foreign, if you ask me. By the weekend I'm usually that keyed up that I just can't relax. By Saturday night I'm just unbearable. I'm not myself until Sunday night, then it's time to start the week all over again. For me it's one week of days, followed by a week of nights. I've no social life.

'I started work here four years ago as a labourer, and I've made very good progress. Believe it or not, I've also been made redundant four times during that time as well – but I've always been taken on again. The pottery industry has been going through some very hard times, you see, but Grindley's has got some new owners now, and I think that things have really improved over the past few months. Things are definitely on the up-and-up.' John then returned to his *Sun*. 'I've got ten minutes yet,' he said, so he stayed on the plastic chair in the corner – 'the office' – for a further ten minutes, and got up exactly at the end of the one-hour break.

I wandered off in search of the other workers – bowls were being revolved around and around on one of the machines in the decorating room. Two silicon pads with stamps on them, or the 'bombs' as they are known, plunged down on the plain bowls. The first bomb deposited the fruit part of the decoration in brown, the second bomb deposited the corn and the leaves in a blue/grey colouring. Kevin stood beside the machine lifting the finished bowl off and putting the next plain bowl on. He has to check whether the decoration has been put on properly, and stack the perfect plates with a series of refractory pins between them, because the plates are still wet. A pile of rejects also built up beside him. Kevin works nights from 10.00 pm until 6.00 am, with one break of twenty-two minutes. He gets paid for ten minutes of the break, but not for the other compulsory twelve minutes. Everything is worked out to the last minute and the last penny. It is the foreman's job, John's, to change the silicon pads, and it is his job to add the colour to the machine and to wheel away the trolleys stacked with the 120 dozen plates. Kevin just lifts one plate off, and puts another one on, constantly scrutinising the fruits of the forest – a million miles away from this place – hour after hour after hour. As the personnel manager later explained, 'It may be boring to you, it may be boring to me, but the incentive is there. They are trained people, specialists in their own field. They know how many plates they have to get through in a night, they know that we don't pay for mistakes. We know how to motivate these people.

'Kevin will get thirty pounds and twenty four pence for tonight's shift, assuming that he manages to do the same number as last night,' said John, as we watched Kevin and the machine in perfect harmony, or almost, as another bowl came off with a band that didn't go all the way round.

'It's the fairest system when there's a bit of night-work thrown in, provided that everybody's prepared to play the game,' said John. 'Everybody should have a crack at night work because the pay is so good – in comparison to the day I mean. They're trying to bring in a system of continental shifts with two day shifts followed by two noon shifts, from 2.00 pm to 10.00 pm, followed by two night shifts. Most people are prepared to go along with this – except one that is. There's always one, isn't there. Here it's Mr Saddique.'

Everywhere I had gone in the factory, I had heard the whispers about Mr Saddique. He refused to change his habits, or conform. He worked permanent nights, every night – five eight-hour shifts, and two twelve-hour shifts at weekends – sixty-eight hours a week – week in, week out, year in, year out. You might think that he would be commended for his hard work and industry, but not here. Saddique was earning at time and a half, double time on Sundays. In a factory where everything is calculated to the last minute and the last penny this creates all sorts of petty and not so petty jealousies. 'His wages must be fantastic,' said John. 'It's the other poor buggers that can't have a crack at night work that are suffering because of him.'

Mr Saddique works with the earthenware going into the kilns. He and his helper, who is also Asian, push the trolleys loaded with the earthenware into the kilns and remove them from the other side. The stacked trolleys are heavy and not easy to push. Mr Saddique and his helper dug their shoes into the dusty floor to get the trolley moving. This went on all night long without any real breaks. The kilns are extremely hot and radiate a good deal of heat into the surrounding area. When the doors of the kilns are open, the heat is quite unbearable. Mr Saddique allowed himself a wry smile as I backed off from the open door of the kiln. If, for whatever reason, the trolleys break down inside the kilns, Mr Saddique and his helper have to enter the kilns to drag the trolleys out. Their only protection is the wet towels they use to cover their heads. You can only bear the heat inside the kiln for a few seconds at a time.

The night I was at the factory, Mr Saddique had come on 55 minutes early to get everything ready for his shift. Some trolleys had been overloaded, and he wanted to unload some of the earthenware so that everything would run smoothly. He did this for no extra pay. You might say that he's a dedicated worker.

Mohammed Saddique came to Britain from Kashmir in 1963. His wife and children still live there. 'If they came here who would look after my elderly parents?' he said. He lives with his brothers in Stoke-on-Trent. His life doesn't so much revolve around the work at the factory in Stoke, his life *is* the work at the factory. He goes to bed each day about 9.00 am, gets up in the afternoon, watches some TV, and gets ready to go back to work again – seven days a week. His 'fantastic' wages come to £246 a week gross. I watched him working in the formidable heat, bending forward until he was nearly parallel with the ground in order to get the trolley moving. He didn't complain – except about his shoes. 'They only last about two months here with all the wear-and-tear they get.' And you couldn't help noticing that although they were covered in a fine dust from the earthenware, they had evidently been recently polished – probably that evening, probably every evening. Virtually all his wages, except the little he needs to live on, and replace his shoes with, goes back to his family in Pakistan.

'I came to England for the work, basically,' he said, 'and I found it. I've never once signed on the dole. England is still a fine country, it gives you such opportunities to better yourself and earn a decent living.'

And on that note he was off into the mouth of the gaping hot kiln once again – for another load of plates and bowls for light, airy kitchens – somewhere far, far away.

September 1988

Big Paddy

Sheffield was full of ex-steelmen with shopping bags. You could see them in the supermarkets in the afternoon. They didn't talk a lot, even to each other. It was embarrassing. Straight in and straight out; back to the house; back to Wimbledon, cricket, old films and the housework. Many of them quite liked the housework – they didn't like to be seen doing it, mind, but it was still all right; it was still something. One former steelworker I knew had just got a job on a building site, so his brother, another unemployed steelworker, slipped in to do the housework one day a week. He slipped out again as cautiously as he went in. Burglars would have envied his stealth. A new brand of domestic help, bred of frustration and resentment. There were no jobs for them to go to. They were in limbo.

Patrick had been in limbo many times – or perhaps purgatory is a better word for a good Catholic lad. He'd had a number of periods of unemployment between joining Brown-Bayley's, the Sheffield steel firm, at sixteen as an apprentice electrician, and his current unemployed state at thirty-four. But he was confident something would turn up – it always had. 'Well, it's not so much a matter of something turning up,' he said, 'it's what you can get, it's what you can grab for yourself. I made a list of all the jobs I've had – it's thirty-two different ones so far, and I've got a few ideas at the moment. I've been everything from store detective to chauffeur, plumber to debt collector. My size helps of course – I'm six foot two and fifteen stone. It comes in handy.' He sat back to expose his great bulk. He was accompanied by a formidable French bulldog. 'Don't worry about the dog,' he said, 'it won't bite you – it may suck you to death, but it won't bite.'

Solid fuel worker, Bolsover, 1984

Patrick was from Irish stock. His father crossed to Liverpool with his brothers in 1949. They made their way to Sheffield for the industry and there they worked on the roads, the ubiquitous trade of his class from Belfast to Barnsley. Patrick was born a year after the family exodus. He always wanted to be a policeman, 'but my father distrusted the police; well, they do, don't they – my father liked a drink. He couldn't stand coppers.' His father meanwhile had progressed to steel erecting in Brown-Bayley's and got his son an apprentice-ship there. 'He wanted me to have some security; he was laid off not long before I started.'

Like most steelworkers Patrick had a love/hate relation with the mills. 'The noise and the dirt was bloody awful – I used to sit with my hands in neat bleach for half an hour when I got home, to get rid of the grime – but the men were great. When I started I was six foot two but really skinny. I worked with a guy called Arthur Smith – he asked what they called me at home. I said "Paddy". He said, "We're not going to call you Paddy, you look like a big daft lass; we'll call you Pat," so Pat it was. They used to take the piss because I was Irish, of course, but I never took offence. Any time I made a mistake it was always "What do you expect from an Irish bollocks?" or "We'll never educate you as long as your arse points downwards", but it was just part of the crack. It wasn't so funny, though, when someone painted WOGS and IRISH BASTARDS GO HOME on our wall. Before they got into black men, we were the wogs, weren't we? But the men at work weren't like that. When they called you an Irish bastard you knew it was just a joke.'

The Irish bastard finished his apprenticeship in Brown-Bayley's but not without a struggle. 'I'd discovered nightclubs and was going out until 3 am and getting up at 6 am. Pete Stringfellow was a DJ in Sheffield in those days and used to run all-nighters at the Mojo Club. When I finished my apprenticeship I packed it in. Well, you could in those days – there was a lot of work about.'

He got a job house-wiring before being unemployed for a bit. During this period of unemployment, he got a job as a bouncer. 'It was cash in hand three quid a night, but it was rough –' he laughed – 'because I was basically rough, I created a lot of trouble. In those days I'd just say, "Would you mind leaving?" If they said no, I'd just clip them.' Pat had metamorphosed into Paddy. 'Yeah, I'd put on a bit of weight in the meantime. And I was young and fit and keen; really keen. Well, it's part of growing up, isn't it, of proving you're a man.' His father had meanwhile died of cirrhosis of the liver.

'I got the odd hiding, of course. One night a girl came up to me to say she'd just tried to get some cigarettes but some guy wouldn't let her near the machine. So I went with her and there was this bloke with long hair leaning up against it. I said "Excuse me, please" but he just thumped me. He didn't say a word. His friends grabbed me and he gave me a good going-over. I shook free and ran off. I found the other bouncer and we worked out a plan of attack. I sent him round the back to corner this guy. The owner of the club then came out and saw what was going on. I'd lost my tie, my shirt was torn, my clothes were all over the place. He tried to stop me. I just knocked him aside. He thought I'd gone mental. Me and the other bouncer got hold of this guy and gave him a taste of what he'd been giving me. This guy was wriggling all over the place and eventually he got free. He tried to run off and my friend tried to get hold of him by the hair – it came off in his hands. My friend and him both shrieked. It was a bloody wig. He ran out clutching it, blood everywhere.'

Patrick then went self-employed as an electrician for a couple who were opening a nightclub and they offered him a job on the door in the evenings. 'It was outside Sheffield and people would go to the club just to have a crack at the bouncer. I was getting four pounds a night plus a meal. But the wages went up from the first fight. I seemed to be on bonus. In the end I was getting seven pounds a night. But one fight finished it. They were all little blokes as well. The chef had to help me out. I went wild, though. It ended with the nightclub owner's wife jumping on my back because she thought I'd gone mental. I was hitting everything in sight. I thumped one guy and he ended up against a grandfather clock. It chimed and everyone stopped, just for a second. The owner wasn't too pleased because he'd just been offered 150 quid for the clock. I was really keen in those days, though. One Paki pulled a knife and I just kicked it out of his hand. Now I'd just walk off. It's not worth it for that money.'

Patrick eventually went back to Brown-Bayley's, only to be made redundant when it closed. When he was made redundant he signed on for a diploma course in construction and land use at Shirecliff College, but at nights and during the holidays, he tried his hand at different jobs.

'I was a cocktail barman first, but the owner tried to diddle me out of my wages so I threatened to stick him to the wall. He paid up. Then I was a waiter. Then through my work on the door I was offered a job by a rich Arab to chauffeur him about. Then I got a job as a chauffeur–handyman at a garage – delivering cars and cleaning the toilets. People used to see me sweeping up and think I'd got what I deserved. Then I got a job as a debt-collector – licensed of course. It's usually debts for small businesses. If cheques bounce, I get 20 per cent commission if I get the debt. The secret is not to go in as a heavy. I often send a female friend who's also a debt collector. It's embarrassing if a girl asks you to cough up. The last debt I collected was for a cheque for a car. The last instalment – £300 – my commission would be £60. It was a guy in the haulage business. I called on him and he said, "Have you come as a heavy, then?" I said, "No, it's just a job." I'd a smart suit on – no sleeves rolled up or any of that bollocks. He said he hadn't paid because there was a fault on the car and he'd been threatened three times by a heavy. You have to be subtle,' Patrick says. 'I couldn't hit anybody in cold blood anyway, could you?' (I grimace – probably not even in hot blood, but that's beside the point.) 'Most pay up. It's embarrassing for them.

'I've also tried my hand at painting and decorating, plumbing, carpet fitting, car breaking, window cleaning and I've done a bit more chauffeur work. I met this businessman in the club where I worked and he said he was looking for someone to drive him around a couple of nights a week in his Roller. So I said I'd do it. I put on a grey pinstriped suit and drove him up to Leeds. I was sitting in the front seat with him and he was telling me about how many birds he'd pulled. Two in one bed, the whole works. I thought this was going to be a right boring job, hearing him rabbiting on all the time, but he was right chatty, calling me Paddy, telling me all his tales. So we get to Leeds and he gets me to park in this back street and he says he'll be back in a minute.

'He comes back with this bird. All the way there he called me Paddy, now he suddenly starts calling me "driver". His voice had completely changed – he'd gone real posh. He's saying "Driver, take a left" and all this bollocks. I get a bit annoyed so I turn the mirror round to give the bird the eye. She's a bit tasty and he's got a face like my dog.' He points to his obedient French bulldog sitting morosely at his feet, its slobbering jaws a grim reminder of the perils of the business lunch. 'So he directs me to the hotel and he tells me to park right in front of the reception. I'm doing the business, opening doors, saying "sir" and "madam". They leave me for three hours. A couple of coppers came by and I'd noticed that the car wasn't taxed, so I had to lean up against the window as they walked by. After they came out, we set off through Leeds, we drove through this council estate and then on to this private estate. He said "Driver – pull up" and they got out. He told me to wait there but I followed them in the car. He escorted her back to the council estate. He went mad when he saw me, but I loved it – he was pretending that she was higher class. He offered me six pounds for the night – I asked for a tenner and got it.

'I bumped into the girl a few weeks later in the nightclub where I worked. She'd met him through the lonely-hearts column of the local paper. The funny thing is he's broke – he can only afford to go out two nights a week. I saw his house – the curtains are in tatters. I've only ever seen him in one white jacket and red shirt. It's pathetic really – just bullshit, but she was impressed. She asked me for his number because he hadn't contacted her again.'

Patrick's most recent job was store detective work. He'd formed an agency with a female friend. They'd found work in some of the big shops in Grimsby and now they're looking further afield. 'Scunthorpe is a likely place,' he said. 'It's all psychology really, looking for those little signs is a bit like being a bouncer. You have to notice things. It's not without its dangers, though. At Christmas I got glassed by this skinhead with tattoos all over his face. He and two girls nicked a nine-pound dress. I followed them outside with another store detective. He threw a punch, so I nipped the nerves on the back of his neck and he passed out. I learned this trick from a guy in the steel mill who'd been in the army.' He offered to demonstrate it, but I declined. The dog, whom he called Fat Man, declined as well. 'I drag him inside and he comes round in the lift and he goes for these two women shop assistants. So I nip him again and he passes out again. In the manager's office he's really groggy but he had a go at the manager, so I pulled him back and he picks up this ashtray and hits me in the face with it. There was blood everywhere. He got four months for it though, and he was only seventeen. The kids today have got it hard, though. If I'd had no work when I was their age I'd have been a real tearaway.'

October 1984

The tunnellers

The circular shield, the pipe in which he works, is damp and cold. The jigger in his hand bites into the moist red earth. Large clumps are pulled loose. He squats in the shield, which is barely four foot tall. His left leg is bent, his right leg stretched out far behind. It looks like a very uncomfortable position, but he manages to hold it. The jigger makes a hell of a racket. He doesn't use ear protectors. He has large dark eyes and almost translucent white skin, as if the sun has never touched it. The jigger stops for a moment, and he starts to shovel the clumps of wet red earth into the skip. All by hand. He swivels his broad, muscular torso in a fluent and practised movement. He wears a weight lifter's belt to protect his back. His tee shirt is damp with sweat. The skip is pulled out. The jigger starts again. There are no breaks. The shield starts to shudder with a train going overhead. He points upwards – towards the heavens if they'd been there, towards the roof of the shield, towards the layers of clay in which we sit buried. We are six feet under – almost literally. 'The railway track is exactly six feet six inches above our heads.' The accent is soft. Northern, but not Protestant, more Northern than that. Donegal. 'Ardsbeg to be exact – a wee place in Donegal, you'll not have heard of it. It's just a wee place with no work. That's why I'm here.'

This is a familiar story. Since the Great Famine of the late 1840s, the Irish have been leaving their homeland *en masse* in search of work.

We are sitting in the damp earth just outside a picturesque village. The by-pass is being extended by Alfred McAlpine Civil Engineering. They sing about McAlpine's in Ireland. 'And down the glen came McAlpine's men/With their shovels slung behind them.' They call the song 'McAlpine's Fusiliers'. The extension of the by-pass is classed as a small job by this famous company – in the region of five million pounds for two kilometres of road, with four major structures (three bridges and a subway) plus three roundabouts. There are about sixty men working there, a number of them living in caravans on the site. The tunnelling is sub-contracted out. I was told that they had Donegal miners on the job for the tunnelling – the very best. 'Go to any big tunnelling job and you'll find the boys from Donegal', they told me. 'They're the boys who did the Channel tunnel.' But today Tommy Meehan and his team are putting in four pipes under a railway line to act as a relief water flow system for the by-pass. It's hard, demanding work but on the site, the miners make the big money. 'But you don't get the big money by sitting on your arse. You have to work for it. We are paid by the metre.' The whole team is from Donegal. 'The Irish make very good workers', says Tommy. 'Don't ask me why. We've got the right attitude to work. But I recently worked with two miners who were English and I have to admit that they were pretty good. We never have any problems from the English boys over here. On the site we get a lot of respect from the other men for the job that we do. It's back-breaking work and it's also a highly skilled job. If the pipe is more than 75 mm out at the other side, you can end up not getting paid for the work. But the three pipes that we've got in so far have been right on target. Bang on. We use a candle and a spirit level to get the pipe in straight. We earn our money.'

He shows me his pay packet. Last week he picked up nearly one thousand pounds. His brother-in-law who is twenty three picked up six hundred pounds last week. These pay packets are dramatically higher than the average wage on the site. His brother-in-law throws another dry tee shirt into the shield. Tommy has had to change his tee shirt four times in the first two hours. 'You could wring them out after a few minutes of this shovelling'.

He goes back to work. 'I never kneel on this job. Kneeling is bad for your knees. You have to look after your body in this game. I train three days a week even after all this shovelling and I'm a black belt in karate. I don't smoke or drink. Some people find that very surprising. Last Christmas I was stopped by the police and asked if I'd mind taking a breathalyser test. I told them that I didn't mind at all, because I don't drink. So this policeman tells me to pull the other one. "All you Paddies drink." I know that the Irish in England have got a terrible reputation for their fondness for a drink, but I've got my own idea about that. If you've worked hard all day and you've nothing to go home to, what else can you do. There's nothing else except the drink. That's why I choose to live at home and commute in every day. A lot of the Irish fellas live on the site in their caravans but that can be awful lonely even if you're from Donegal.'

The very mention of Donegal mists his eyes. Even down in that damp hole. Especially down in that damp hole in the English soil. 'Sometimes I'd love to go home, but there's no work back there. I miss my family. I miss the pace of life there. It's so easy going. People wave at you as you pass them in your car. They salute you. That's how I describe it. Jesus, it's a beautiful country. But to make something of yourself, you have to come here. With the money that I've been making, I've been able to buy a house in England and a house back in Donegal. I rent that one out to a young family there. I've heard it said that there's one little village in Mayo that has seven millionaires, with all the money made in the building game. There's another famous Irish builder who died recently and left ten thousand pounds to each of his long term workers. It's stories like that that got me over to England in the first place. People ask me how I put up with the English always saying that the Irish are thick, but we have a wee saying. "The only thick people are those that think the Irish are mugs." There's no shrewder people on God's earth. We're here to make something of ourselves. The average Englishman might be happy earning one hundred and twenty pounds a week and living in a council house. That's no good for your average Irishman. No good at all.'

Far up above in the bright sunlight, the site is buzzing. The works manager has a great wide grin on his face. 'I'm Packie, by the way, that's Packie as in Packie Bonner, the Irish goalie, not Paki as in Pakistani. This is the way I like it. Everybody at it. Everybody's busy – they're topsoiling the roundabout, they're topsoiling the verges, they're doing the drainage, they're kerb laying, the tarmacking is on target. We've put in fifteen concrete beams this morning, each one weighing forty tons. Everything is ticking over nicely.' I had heard about Packie from one of the other senior administrators on the site, Jonathan Jones – 'Packie has got the knack of being able to organise dozens of things simultaneously and get things done. You couldn't programme a computer to organise some of the things that Packie does.' Packie is another small man from Donegal. That accent again. Jonathan who has worked with Packie for fifteen years off and on couldn't place the accent. 'I've no idea where he's from. I don't even know whether he's from Northern Ireland or the Republic. An Irishman's an Irishman to me.' Packie, on the other hand, knew exactly where Jonathan Jones was from (Birmingham, as it turned out).

Packie hails from Lettermacaward in Donegal. 'A little place with a big name. It wasn't the money that brought me away from home, it was wander-lust. I decided to have a ramble around the world. When I was eighteen me and four others rambled as far as Birmingham. One of the lads had worked there before. We arrived on the Friday night straight off the Heysham boat from Belfast, and we started work on the Saturday. We were earning up to a hundred pounds a week then. That was in 1966 when the average wage was something like twenty pounds. A couple of the lads who came out with me have done very well. Funnily enough, none of them did badly. One of them had now got his own timber business in Tyrone.' Packie started as a joiner on building sites, but soon got bored with that. 'I wanted something more adventurous. I learned the ropes from Tommy Harrington from County Mayo. That man was a legend in McAlpine's. I've been responsible for some of the really big jobs in this country – the M42, the A40 at Gloucester, the A604 at Godmanchester, the M40 at Oxford.'

Packie lives with his wife, who is also Irish – from Tipperary, and his four children from Friday night to Monday morning. He leaves his home at 4.15 on a Monday morning to get to the site. He shows me the chicken curry that his wife has sent up with him. The next four nights he spends in this caravan at one side of the site. In the corner of the room sit his organ, guitar, and penny whistle. I ask him for a song. It's a strange request. I can't imagine asking some man that I've only just met for a song. But then the Irish are different. He doesn't look surprised. 'We have this wee joke when we're in the bar and we're all having a sing song. Some of these English lads will ask why we sing so much. So I ask them for a song and you get these blank faces. I then ask them to recite a poem or even part of a poem, and you get a blank face again. I tell them that they need the Irish to fill the silences left by the English.'

He sets the penny whistle back down. 'I'm not in the mood for singing. I'll give you the lines instead. "You're the pride of them all/Your people are so kind and so true/And no matter where you roam/I am always going home/Donegal I'm coming home to you."' Here was the man who controls the site, sitting with misty eyes. 'I was home at Easter, I'm going back in August and I'll sneak back at Christmas. Jesus, I miss that place. But after three weeks back home I want out again. You end up not being able to settle anywhere. But I can still visualise every stone and tree where I played as a young boy. Sometimes I go back and walk those same paths again in my spare moments.' Those great sad eyes drift off again. Back to rural Ireland of the fifties, and all those sanguine dreams of foreign lands to visit. Like this one, with the silence and solitude of wild Donegal replaced with the silence and solitude of manner and custom, where men that you've worked with for fifteen years still don't know where you're from.

The caravan is remarkably tidy for a man living alone. The gas cooker is spotless. There is a colour TV in one corner, and a shower in another corner. The caravan has a separate bedroom with a duvet and clean sheets. 'After work tonight I'll play nine holes of golf. Later I might have two glasses of wine. I don't drink porter. The only big night for drinking is a Thursday. That night we lose the head and drink until 3 o'clock in the morning in the local, but the rest of the week I drink very little. But even when we're drinking all night, I'm never late for work the next morning. My saying is that if you're ever late for work through drink, then it's time to give up the work. I've drunk two bottles of whisky in a night and still been out of the caravan in time the next day. But I'm here to make money and I never forget that. I've got a good-sized house in Bristol, and two houses back in Donegal with fifty acres of land. I rent the houses out. It's not most people's image of how the Paddies live, but there's an old saying that when the Englishman understands the Irishman then it will be the time for the Paddy to leave England.'

Packie's full name is Patrick McGettigan. But for the first ten years with the company he was known as McGilligan. 'The foreman wrote my name down wrongly when I got started. It was too embarrassing to correct him. I met all these directors of the company in the next few years who knew me as McGilligan, Jesus it was embarrassing having to correct it. The only reason that I did in the end was that I was put in to do some building work at the Royal Ordinance Factory. They ran a security check on all the men. Mine took a lot longer because I'm from the Republic of Ireland. But I needed to give them the right name, or they'd still be checking the files now.'

We're back out in the bright sunshine again. 'Och, it lifts your heart when you see the black top going down.' Every few yards Packie is approached by some worker or other wanting instructions. 'I get on with the English alright, and because I'm the boss of the site I get a lot of respect from them. But they all call me "Packie", never "Paddy". This one driver says to me once "Excuse me, Paddy. Where's this loaded stone to be tipped?" So I say to him "Why don't you have a guess". So he says "Don't be so bloody stupid. Why should I do that?" "Well", I say. "You were prepared to guess that my name was Paddy." I'm proud of my background. All of my children think of themselves as Irish. The eldest girl asked for an Irish passport for her latest birthday. And that was all without any prompting. Most of the lads on the site, if they're not straight from Ireland, then they're second generation Irish. We've a load of second generation lads from the Midlands. There are very few genuine Englishmen about the place, but then that's the problem with England. At the end of the day, when it's all trawled out, there are very few real English-men in the country.'

Packie laughs loudly. 'On the sites the English are surrounded. They have to find our jokes funny.'

Packie worked his way up. Others are still trying. 'It's difficult for the young lads now with this recession. Everything in the building game is so tight at the moment', says Packie. One nineteen-year-old called Michael was rolling the top soil. Packie has taken him under his wing. Michael left Donegal six months ago. This was his longest time away from his family. Michael dreads the weekend. Unlike the married men on the site Michael has nowhere to go at the weekend. Usually he gets a lift from a friend to the local shop on the Friday night but this week his friend is on holiday. So the trip to the shop is out. 'It would drive you mad just sitting in you caravan looking at those four walls all weekend', he said. 'There's a pub down the road but I don't really like it. I don't feel that comfortable yet mixing with the English fellas. I think that it sometimes pays when you're out to keep your mouth shut, so that they don't know that you're Irish. I miss the people back home. I think that they're a lot easier going than the English. The English seem to get very excited about nothing. At the weekends I feel terrible homesick. Even the grass smells different over here. In fact, it doesn't seem to have any smell at all.'

Unlike Packie and Tommy, Michael still has that thick brogue, which imme-diately signals the outsider, the boy from Donegal who does not know the ropes. The boy from Donegal who doesn't yet realise that English accents often disguise a background in Birmingham with a little house with a picture of the Pope on one wall and an Irish cottage surrounded by sweet-smelling grass on the other. But the accent also signals the boy who is prepared to try. 'There are men here who are on the really big money. When I tell my family what some of these men are making they can hardly believe it.' It is Michael's ambition to pass his driving test and drive a dump truck on the site – to make his way gradually up the building hierarchy. 'My family will be expecting me to come home a millionaire next year.'

'If I can take it that is', he adds after just a moment's pause.

October 1992

They call me 'Masher'

Gentle sounds filtered through the suburbs – birds singing, children laughing in the distance, and Keith, the painter, whistling as he painted the outside of the semi. You could envy him his job on a day like this – up there in the warm air, whistling away with not a care in the world, or so it seemed. Spring, the season for nature's steady regrowth and man's hasty repainting, had arrived (if a trifle late) and here he was, as natural as a daffodil, as happy as a lark. The workers on their way to the afternoon shift in the factories, or what remained of them, cast envious glances his way. Theirs was a world of heat and dust and noise, and here he was soaking up the first sun of the year. His daffodil-yellow Datsun had a sign fixed to the side proclaiming his status – 'Keith Metham, Interior Decorator, Estimates free'. He was his own boss and they were envious all right.

And Keith came down off his ladder. 'Mind you, I know what life in the steel mills is like, I worked in them for nineteen years. I left school at fifteen back in the early sixties and served my time as a fitter – in Doncaster's. My dad got me a job there. He said, "Get on down there, son, they've all got cars, them that work there." He didn't tell me, though, that they were working seven days a week for them. Doncaster's weren't bad, mind, it was an easy-going firm. The money weren't right fantastic but there was plenty of over-time. It's gone downhill a bit since then – when I started there were thirty-odd fitters and thirty-odd fitters' mates, now there are about five fitters left. They got rid of the fitters' mates years ago. It weren't bad being a fitter in Doncaster's – if you wanted to be at it eight hours a day you could, but you didn't have to. It was up to you. You got a lot of freedom, most of the work was maintenance but you weren't tied to any particular machine. You could have a walk around the factory and nobody would say, "What are you doing here?" You could really go where you pleased. You could have as many tea breaks as you wanted. My nickname used to be "Masher Metham" because I'd have a brew-up every couple of hours. But I left Doncaster's in 1976 be-cause overtime was getting a bit scarce. There had been quite a few strikes. So I moved to a small strip mill in Sheffield, Effingham Steel, but I just stayed there for about twelve months. I left because there were one or two rumours about them closing. Accurate, as it turned out. I moved on to an iron foundry – William Cook's – my father-in-law got me the job there, but after a few months I moved on again to a better-paid job at Niagara Forge. I got that job through one of the gaffers I'd known from Doncaster's. So you see I've been through quite a few steel mills and most of the jobs I've had were through friends or relatives. That seems to be how you get on in life, you know.

'Niagara Forge were great, very steady, if you know what I mean, very cushy actually. If the machines weren't breaking down, there wasn't a lot to do. As a fitter you could always find something to do, but most didn't bother. There was no supervision. At Doncaster's there had been a foreman on every shift but at Niagara all the gaffers just worked nine while five. After five there was no one in charge. I used to work on the afternoon shift from two while ten. The production workers had a quota to meet, and when they reached their target, they'd go home, usually about nine o'clock. That would just leave me and the lads in the saw shop in the factory. I lived locally and sometimes I'd nip home at night and get some supper and then go back to work to clock out. Well, there weren't a lot to do, and no gaffers about. If anyone spotted me I'd just say I'd nipped out for a packet of cigarettes. There was no real harm in it, but sometimes we used to take it in turns to clock each other out. This was very common in the steel mills. This one night one of the lads from the saw shop was clocking four cards, one of which was mine, but a couple of gaffers nipped back and caught him. We all got the sack. We were really surprised because everybody did it and none of us had been in any trouble before. I just reckoned they were looking to make a few redundancies and they saw the opportunity to get rid of another four. It was bloody sickening actually, especially when I found I couldn't get another job. I'd get the interviews all right but then they'd ask why I left my last employment. When I told them I was sacked for a clocking offence, that were it.

'I got desperate. I was unemployed for a few years in all – quite a long time to think about things. I'd got two young lads and I felt bloody stupid. I should have used my loaf and not been caught like that. But there were no gaffers on at Niagara and perhaps the firm should have kept a closer eye on things. We'd all got into a rut there; when you had to do a hard day's work you really felt put out. We'd all got into this rut and just couldn't get back out of it. It were too easy to skive. So here I was – sacked and without any chance of a job. Who was going to employ me?

'During the time I was unemployed I did a hell of a lot of redecorating of my own house. It was the flashiest house in the neighbourhood. I had to keep active. I could see others, who were just happy to plod along, deteriorating badly. I was getting desperate for a job – at one point I thought about buying an ice-cream van. What I was really interested in, though, was painting and decorating. I've always done quite a bit myself and people always said I had a flair for it. My brother's a decorator and even he reckoned I were all right. So when I heard about this particular scheme from the Manpower Services I thought I'd give it a go. It's a scheme to finance new businesses – they pay you forty quid a week for the first year to see you over the worst period. The only qualification is that you should have been out of work for three months, and I qualified for that easily. One problem was that you need a thousand quid of your own money. After four years on the dole I hadn't got that kind of money. So what I did was put an advert in the local Sheffield free paper and got 600 quid's worth of business lined up. I then took the orders to my bank manager who agreed on a loan. I was away.

'I'm my own boss now. I have to make it work. I've nothing else to turn to. I got my name put on the side of my car for forty quid. It makes you feel a little bit above the other blokes going to work for somebody else. And I've got a chequebook with a business account number. It makes you feel as if you've gone up a little bit in the world. My rates are very reasonable – thirty quid a day in summer, twenty-five in winter. Mind you, they have to be – there's all these blokes on the fiddle in Sheffield who can charge less. It's a cut-throat business. I've got work fixed up for the next four weeks. There's no guaranteed work in this business. If anyone cancels at the last minute and I have to stay at home, I get right irritable – I'm in a right mood. I know it's all up to me. If I sit on my ass I don't get paid. There's no long tea breaks now, it's just a quick wet and half a cig, then back to the job. I've always really been conscientious, it's just that in the steel mills you didn't have to do the work. If you made work for yourself, people would say, "Who's this clown trying to impress?"

'The only thing that really bothers me is that I've always believed in every man to his own trade. I served my time as a fitter, not as a painter. I bumped into an old friend recently and he said, "What do you know about decorating?" And I said I must know something about it, because I'm being paid good money for doing it. But he had a point, I suppose. I don't know all the technical jargon for the job, but I know I do good work. Ask any of my customers.' (I did, and he does.) 'I'd always done a fair bit of decorating and I picked up a bit at a course at college.

'As far as the future's concerned, I believe the steel industry in Sheffield has gone down the Swanee. The Japs can do everything more cheaply than we can, and we just can't be like them. It's not that the British are work-shy or anything, it's just the incentives aren't there. I've two lads, one thirteen and one eleven, and I hope that one day they'll come in with me. Not as painters or decorators, mind, I'd really like one to go into the building side of things and one into the joinery side. Then I could finish up with a little building firm, we could do house extensions and owt like that. But that's all a long time in the future.'

Keith glanced nervously at his watch. Time was clearly money, now, and he mounted his ladder again. 'Well, it's back to the grind, I suppose, but I love it really. No matter how hard I've got to work, I still enjoy it. I'd work through the night if I had to, to finish a job. I know my future depends on what I do today. I suppose I didn't so much take the plunge into self-employment, more a case of being pushed. But the gaffers who gave me the sack did me a favour really. I've discovered some joy and some real satisfaction in work at long last. And not before bleedin' time.'

November 1985

The secret mental life of used-car salesmen

'That big one's sticking. I just know it is.' He started to leaf through a thick wad of invoices sitting neatly on one corner of his desk. The invoice was there. The date jumped out at him. 'Oh, I just knew it was sticking.' The car was approaching its sixtieth day. Nearly sixty days old and still in the showroom. He glanced up at the clock. It was just after 7.30 am. He had the time. 'I just have to be systematic. You must never panic in this job. There's always somebody out there for any car. Somebody, somewhere. The secret is finding them.' The office started to shake with the rumbling from the steel foundry below. It had a slightly threatening feel to it. Like distant thunder. Like low deep shock waves from some far earthquake. Like impending doom. Roy never noticed the thunder anymore, but he felt the waves of doom rolling in.

He gestured across to his fellow salesman stranded like him in a neat office in the far corner of the building. He needed to share his anxiety with someone. From the outside the neat white office looked like a cell. The paint inside was peeling, the second hand BMW Z1 sitting just outside was marked

Sales representatives, solid fuel industry, Doncaster, 1984

up at thirty two thousand pounds. He pointed at the large green motor vehicle to his right. The large shining shell stretched right back to the far wall. There wasn't room to manoeuvre yourself past the car. It reminded him of how big the car was. A big prestige car with a big powerful engine. Too big, too powerful for this day and age. 'Bloody Conservatives with their company car tax. Big cars like this fall outside the permitted range. Companies want something smaller. That car is sticking, and it's going to stick a lot worse. I just know it is.' He started to pace up and down inside his little cell.

He needed to cheer himself up. He had his wage slips neatly folded in the inside pocket of his suit. All in order. Nice and methodical. 'I won't touch computers', he said. 'I'm very old-fashioned. Very stuck in my ways.' He started to leaf through the wage slips. 'There are many men who are jealous of me. They see me driving my BMW. They know that it's the ultimate car, the ultimate driving machine. They know where I work. They assume that I must be earning a packet.' He laid the wage slips neatly on the table. 'They don't realise that I have to work for my money. I get £340 basic. Who could live on that? You'd be better off on the dole. The rest is commission, the rest is graft.' He smiled gently. The graft sometimes slipped the figures up to four thousand pounds a month. 'Just good old-fashioned salesmanship based on trust. That's what it's all about in this business. You can't rip people off now like you could in the old days. I've been in this business for forty years. In the old days there was a shortage of cars. You could sell anything. We used to file starter rings, braise new cogs on them to get a car going. It would work for a fortnight. But today, it's all different. Now even the back street lads have to keep up to standard. Now the boot's on the other foot. It's the customers who get up to all sorts of tricks. You offer them a price for their car in a trade-in, and they bring it back the next day with a set of bald tyres on it, and a cheap stereo instead of the decent model they had in when you valued it. They have this image of the used-car salesman, and they try to get one over on you first. The customers don't seem to realise today what good value they're getting.'

Roy sells second hand BMWs. He also handles all corporate sales for the Hallamshire Motor Company in Sheffield. Last month seventy eight cars were ordered. He likes to study the invoices. Whenever the gloom starts to descend, he likes to flick through the invoices. 'Not a bad month. That's a hell of a lot of money.' He keeps records of all sales in old school exercise books. The exercise books date back to 1956. Everything is methodically recorded. A Hillman Super Minx went for £550 in 1956. He sold an Austin Westminster to a customer in 1959. That same customer has bought a new car from him every year since then. In 1991 he sold 167 cars, eight more than 1990, and fifty six more than 1989. 'There's been no sign of a recession as far as the kinds of cars that I sell are concerned. The only bad year that I ever had was 1988, and that was because I was off sick for a lot of that year. Nobody else could do my job as well. I'm the most successful salesman that they've got here. Old-fashioned but successful.'

A dark-haired man in his early thirties entered the showroom. He was wearing jeans and a black leather jacket. Roy watched him carefully. 'I'm very traditional. I don't like jeans. I call them overalls. But I daren't let this interfere with business. I know salesmen who have made classic mistakes by trying to judge people by their appearance. A few years ago, I had this man come to see me with his son. They were both very scruffy, their boots were filthy. I was tied up with a customer at the time, and this other salesman went to them. They said that they would only deal with me. He told them that I'd got a customer and he said that he didn't want them to waste my time. The man in question was a scrap-dealer and a multimillionaire. He just left but he gave me a ring the following day to order a brand new BMW 735 for himself and a 635 for his son. You mustn't go on appearances. I've had other customers who have looked very smart, but have had nothing. I had this one tall man come in who was very dapper, and he told me that he was a pilot in the RAF. He could hardly drive the car on the test drive. When I rang him at home, his wife told me that he was an inmate at the local psychiatric hospital. They must keep the patients very smart up at that hospital. Very smart, indeed. You just can't go on appearance.'

He went back to scrutinising the man in the black leather jacket. 'On the other hand, I don't know this man. Many of my customers are regulars. They come back year after year. A lot of my customers come on personal recommendation. I like to float about this town and get known. The most important thing for a salesman is to be known. People will come to this establishment and ask for me by name, but I've never seen this particular gentleman before.' Roy approached the customer. 'Are you looking for anything in particular, sir, or are you just browsing?' The man with the overalls said that he did have one particular car in mind. I thought that I detected small involuntary shakes of the head from Roy. Almost imperceptible. I felt that Roy had already made up his mind. 'There's no such a thing as a time waster in this business. Even if they haven't got any money themselves, they might know somebody who has. They might mention one of the cars to a friend. This gentleman has just come for a look around. I ask customers straight out what they're looking for, and then I watch their eyes. You can always tell if someone is sincere or not. This customer isn't. He just wants to look around. I've had forty years experience of this. A lot of salesman go on courses on body language and high pressure sales techniques these days. I had none of this. I was just trained to say "please" and "thank you", and that if anyone offers you a deposit then you should take it. There is no substitute for experience.'

The man in the leather jacket was now asking pointed questions about a black BMW. He looked under the bonnet, and in the boot, he even tried to peer up the exhaust. Roy asked if he would like a test drive. 'Not today. I'm in a bit of a rush at the moment. I'll try to get in tomorrow lunch time, if that's alright.' Roy's slight head shakes started again.

'He might know someone', said Roy. 'He might, you never know, he just might.' As he settled back down to peruse his invoices to the sound of that distant rumble in the background.

'Hey! These are the cheapest cars in Sheffield! Rock bottom prices! Silly prices!' I stood in a big, bright aircraft hangar of a place – the Motor Vehicle Supermarket. The thunder had gone. Nigel sat with his feet up on the desk. Nigel had just the one BMW on offer. Large, less than pristine. 'A bit lumpy, actually', he said. He had described it in the advert in the local trade paper as suiting an up-and-coming pimp. 'Well, you've got to be truthful.' He flicked some paper at his jet ski suit in the corner. 'I've got expensive hobbies. I need to move cars to pay for them.' It was a Sunday afternoon. Three young lads were looking at a bright red F reg. Alfa. Nigel was free associating. 'I see three young lads wandering around, looking at anything. They look gorm- less. If they didn't look so gormless I might go out and stand about with my chamois in my hand. If you want to sell cars, you don't sit about in your office and then jump out on them. You stand about with your chamois in your hand looking busy. You don't intimidate them that way. But they look too gormless to be bothered with.'

Nigel went up to the office window to take some cash off a man paying his car off. The exchange took place in total silence. 'It's a fatal error to ask how the car is going. It's better just to take their money and be done with it.'

A young couple entered the aircraft hangar. Nigel told me what he saw. 'They're in their late twenties. He's probably a plumber, possibly a builder. Serious punters. They've lived together for four or maybe five years. They probably live in Woodseats or Mosborough. They're buying their house, but they're still interested in the finer things of life. They've got some readies. They're not time wasters, because if a man is really interested in a car he'll bring his wife or girlfriend with him, and there she is. Most men are under the thumb.' Nigel started reaching for the chamois.

'You have to be a bit of a psychologist in this game. I have learned that people are very strange. They'll try to tell you all kinds of stories. We had this one posh family who bought a Volvo saloon from us, and they brought it back a week later, and said that the exhaust had backfired and broken one of the rear windows. I just stared back at them in disbelief. This same family had a 1976 Jaguar XJS with a private plate, but they were so concerned with appearances that they kept ordering parts for the 1979 model from their local Jaguar dealer. They couldn't bear to say that it was a 1976 car. They kept complaining that the parts didn't fit. Our customers want to get one over on us. They'll try to trade in cars that have been written off, cars which they have finance on, cars full of faults. Our punters will even clock their own cars. If dealers do that we're in serious trouble. Some reps will even clock their cars forward to get their new car sooner and to fiddle their petrol receipts. So if some dealers clock the cars backwards the cars can end up showing the true mileage! That's poetic justice for you.'

Nigel paced up and down his office staring at the three gormless lads. They got the message and left. 'Our customers are basically trying to rip us off. I don't have any sentiments about the general public. I just find them very strange. The second-hand car trade lives off the fact that the general public have this insatiable desire to change their car periodically. A car will last a lot longer than people realise it – if it is looked after properly. People change their cars for the most trivial of reasons. But mine is not to question why, mine is just to take their readies.'

The plumber was ready for a test drive in the red Alfa. Nigel had put his chamois away. 'We take them out to the far end of Totley for a test drive. We drive them up the hill and we let them drive back down themselves. That way, we can hide any lack of performance. It's quite straightforward really. A lot of customers wouldn't notice whether the car was performing well or not. Punters tend to go for the gadgetry in the car. They like plenty of knobs to twiddle about with. On the test run, they'll play with all the buttons. When they get back they'll be able to tell you if the sun roof works or not, or if it's easy to tune the radio in, but ask them about the performance of the car and you'll draw a blank.'

Nigel and the plumber set off up the hill, I couldn't help noticing that Nigel was driving. Nigel has been in the used-car game for eight years. The company was started by his father. 'I love this business. People think that we're all rip-off merchants, but the mark up on used cars is lower than fruit and vegetables, lower than clothes, lower than . . .'

'Sandwiches', added Peter his long-term friend and now his employee. 'People don't go on about sandwich shops ripping people off all the time', added Peter. Peter is the gofer. 'We're a team here. I don't get commission. I think that's fair because I give everybody the same attention.'

'This game is all about attention to detail', said Nigel. 'There are a few simple rules. For example, when you're offering a punter money for his car, you should never say fourteen hundred pounds, you should say "one thousand four hundred pounds". It sounds more.'

'It really does', added Peter.

'And when you approach a customer, you should never say "Can I help you?" you should say "What can I do for you?" or "How can I help you?" And as for body language, they say that you can read a punter like a book. I

have to say that I've never really found this to be true. Body language is important in this game, but all it ever tells you is that the punter in front of you is a very nervous person who thinks that he's going to have his leg lifted. The biggest hassle in this game is that you must be prepared to haggle endlessly over price. I have this one associate who likes to demonstrate this from time to time. He will say to punters "You're not a wanker, are you?" The punter will go "Sorry? What was that?" "You're not a wanker? If you're not then you'll make me an offer on this car." Say the car is marked up at £2495 then the punter will say "I'll offer you £1600." So my mate will go "Done! You've just bought yourself a car, sir." But the punter will try to back out of it, no matter how low they've gone. "Oh, I don't know. I'm not very sure now." So my mate will go "I said that you were a wanker." '

'You've got to bargain, you see. The punter expects it. If you just agree with the price he offers, no matter how low it is, he'll think that there's something wrong with the car. You have to go through the motions. It's all a bit of a waste of time in my opinion. But you have to do it. The world is full of mugs trying to be clever. We have to entertain them. That's our business.'

April 1992

Selling jewellery on the never-never

You could hear the laughter out the back. Behind the jewellery, behind the glass cases, behind the gold and silver. Somebody was telling a funny story. The laughter was dampened down. Then it erupted again. Great guffaws of laughter. Bodies curled up in spasms of mirth, behind those four walls. Behind the thick, blue velvet curtain. I edged closer. The voice had a Black Country accent. 'I've sold vacuum cleaners to people without a carpet in the house.' The laughter started again, slower this time, but quickening. The pitch rose with the volume. 'I sold a woman two ironing boards – one for upstairs. She only had a hundred pound credit limit, so she couldn't have the iron.' This time the laughter sounded harsher, it came out like 'tak, tak, tak.'

'I've sold a woman velvet windows for every window in the house including the toilet.'

This time there was no response. 'Velvet windows?' 'Velvet curtains, I mean.' He had fluffed his lines, and the laughter never came. I could see in now. The man with the Black Country accent had a ruddy complexion. Too much time out in the biting wind, knocking on doors, canvassing – as they put it. His partner sat in a leather chair. Balding with a paunch, but with a brightly coloured shirt. A large, chunky Rolex glinted on his arm, thick gold rings on two fingers of each hand. Two women were doing the accounts in an adjoining room. Brian, the owner of the shop watched as the fifty pound notes changed hands. He listened intently to the tales from the field. His employees had been out there and survived.

Keith Laycock, pawnbroker, Sheffield, 1991

It was his turn in the round of stories. 'I remember Ron telling us about having to go back to this customer who had complained about his carpet, which had a hole worn in it. He went into the house and said "What have you been doing here then? It's not for walking on this, you know." The punter said "Oh, I'm sorry." So Ron said "You've worn it out because you're supposed to pick your feet up when you walk. You're not supposed to shuffle along on it." The laughter crackled, as Brian shuffled along in his imitation of the gait of the hapless punter.

In the background, you could hear the quiet but confident tapping of the calculators, as the figures were being totalled. 'A very good week', said Brian. 'A very, very good week', said the bald man with the Rolex in a parody of the AA advertisement. 'A very, very good week', echoed the man with the ruddy complexion.

I was at the very centre of the whole operation. The control room, the nerve centre – the little backroom of a jeweller's shop in Sheffield. His car, all fifty grand of it, sat outside the shop, looking just slightly incongruous in front of a shop that size. The shop, despite its tasteful jewellery, didn't look capable of sustaining a car of that sort. And it didn't. It was the backroom that paid for the car, the backroom with the little charts on the wall, and the rows of noughts after each figure.

This little backroom was the centre of a highly successful company selling jewellery in what it called a 'direct sales operation'. In the past they had sold other items in a similar fashion – duvets, ironing boards, sheets, hi-fi, carpets, vacuum cleaners, even frying pans. But now they were concentrating on jewellery. Brian explained to Mark how it all worked. The company worked hand in glove with a credit collection company. The basic idea was very simple and very neat. Agents from the credit company would go out on a weekly basis to collect outstanding debts from clients. They obviously got to know their clients very well. A representative of the jewellery company would then accompany the agents to certain targeted customers – customers who were paying off their outstanding credit. 'But only to the very good payers, or to the "crème-de-la-menthe" of the good payers as we put it', explained Brian. The jewellery would then be offered to the customer on the never-never. They showed Mark and myself the attaché case with all the gleaming, glittering merchandise inside it. Rows and rows of gold horse shoes and gold coats of arms, and rings inlaid with semi-precious stones ('*semi-precious* covers a lot of bloody things', explained one of Brian's salesmen helpfully – 'it's better than saying the stones aren't real'). All this temptation to clients already in debt.

'We're doing a social service to the public', continued Brian. 'We sell directly to some disabled customers, who can't get out to the shops. We bring a jeweller's shop right to their own doorstep in some of these high-rise flats they live in.'

I noticed that Brian was drinking out of a Pudsey Bear mug. Mark noticed it too.

'And don't forget that ninety nine per cent of our customers couldn't go out and borrow a tanner from anybody else. And if a customer decides not to pay, there's not a lot you can do about it. If a guy's unemployed and you take him to court, the court won't have lot of sympathy for the guys who have got him into debt. The court will end up telling him that he'll have to pay you off at 50 pence per week. We're in a business where we have to take a lot of risks. You can't go in with a hard edge, because they're your customers.'

Brian blew on his coffee. 'And believe me there are some right evil bastards out there, who just want to screw you for what they can get. They'll borrow money, they'll take your jewellery, they'll take anything that's going with no intention of paying any of it back. Then when the credit company says that they have to pay up, they'll try to return the goods. We had one of our agents ring up and say that his customer wasn't going to pay because she was dissatisfied with the ring we'd sold her – the stone must have been loose or something because the bloody thing had fallen out. So we got the agent to send the ring back in. The stone was still there, but the ring was so dirty that you couldn't see the stone. It was all misshapen as well. We've had rings returned where the punters have obviously punched somebody with the ring on their fingers. These are the kinds of people that we have to deal with.'

Two more salesmen arrived back. A case of jewellery lay open on the table. One of the salesman stood well away from the attaché case, as if it might contain a hidden, unexploded bomb. 'I hope that's not the case that the dog tiddled on last week', he said. 'Perhaps, you should sniff it, and see. How did you let a thing like that happen? The worst thing that ever happened to me with a dog was when this little Jack Russell ate one of my rings. I put the dog's name down on the voucher. My boss, at the time, went mad. But what else could you do? Anyway, we got the ring back after a week, although the label had disintegrated.'

They all laughed. These were people on a high. You could see that everyone here was a winner. The jewellery company had a group of customers targeted for it, plus the introduction from someone who was almost a friend of the family, and the credit company got its customers to continue to borrow. The jeweller got his money directly from the credit company, which in turn took a hefty commission. The credit company had, however, to collect the debt, but this was their business. Sweet. Very sweet. Everyone was a winner.

Except perhaps the customer.

A customer buying a £300 ring over 120 weeks would pay £204 on top of that for credit, and this is an individual with a low income already in debt. 'But the customers themselves care little about the interest rate being charged. All they're interested in is how much per week the ring or the gold chain or whatever will cost them', explained Brian. 'This one hundred pound ring will cost them £1.60 a week over two years, this gold horse shoe ring, on the other hand, will cost them £2.80 a week over two years. We always say in this game that we leave all the multiplication up to the customer. It's not our problem, after all. But you couldn't walk into a High Street shop anywhere in the world and get a ring like this for a fiver a week.'

I looked at the ring with the horse's head on it. 'It's Red Rum, I think', said Brian. 'You see, many of our customers are unemployed. But we always say that the unemployed are often better managers of money than those in work. They know exactly how much is coming in. They might be paying between ten and thirty quid a week to the credit company – for all sorts of things – household goods, car repairs, plus, of course, to clear previous debts, but they know that they have to meet the repayments, because they have nowhere else to go for credit.'

'We're basically salesmen, we're not their financial consultants', explained one of his salesmen. 'Our customers often tend to be at the very bottom of the heap. You should see some of the houses that our men have to go into. I've been in a house in Winsford in Cheshire where the mother was selecting a £300 diamond ring, and the six kids were sitting around having dinner out of a jumbo tin of processed peas. I've been to houses where you can see piles of disposable nappies chucked out the back and left to dissolve in the rain.'

'I've been to houses where I wouldn't crap in the bog', said Brian not wishing to be left out of all of this. This notion that the customers are somehow different from themselves, somehow alien, is very important to maintaining the spirit of the team. 'It's a different planet out there', added Brian unselfconsciously.

Mark and I left that cosy little office for a look. It was a bitterly cold night on the dark side of the town. Brian parked his jeep at the end of the street. Some teenagers on the street corner eyed us suspiciously. This was a regular call. Brian was on his own tonight. He poked his head in through the broken window between the kitchen and the living room. The house may have been poor, but still it had a colour TV, a video recorder and a library of videotapes, including, incongruously, Jane Fonda's *Workout*. Brian was welcomed into the house like an old friend of the family, which he undoubtedly was. Angela's husband was not about. 'He's off again', said Angela. Brian told her not to worry. 'You've got some new curtains since I was last here . . . I've got some goodies here for you to look at.' Angela's father sat beside her. Things, you could say, were not going too well for the family. 'I was married forty nine years, eleven and a half months. If she'd just lived another two weeks we would have made our golden weeding anniversary', said the father. Brian was settling in – 'It's like coming home, you know, coming here. When I sit down on this settee, I don't want to get up again.' 'I always have a right good laugh when Brian comes round', said Angela. 'It's one of the few good laughs that I ever have.'

Angela's son was waking up. He was eating some ice cream out of a plastic bowl. A pile of coins had fallen into the bowl. The coins remained there, as he ate the ice cream. Angela said that she wasn't interested in any jewellery, until the case was opened. The rings sparkled brilliantly in those surroundings. 'Ooooooh, come here, let's have a look then.' 'Try it on', said Brian. 'Now let me tell you how much that would be a week if you were to buy it. That would be four pounds eight pence a week. Very reasonable, eh?' Brian turned to Angela's father. 'We've got some nice men's tackle here, if you're interested.' He unfurled the gold chains in their velvet case with a practised flourish. The old man sat up straight for the first time. 'Try it on', said Brian. The old man fingered the chains, as Angela started pouring her heart out to Brian mainly about her financial worries.

'I'm more like a social worker sometimes', said Brian as he climbed back into his jeep. 'Some of our customers are really decent people in hard times, and it's all very sad, but what can you do?'

If Brian was the social worker, Billy was the clinician. 'You can't afford to get involved', he said. His technique was quite different. 'I'm a master at this game. It's all done as a series of moves. Watch me.' The frost was worse the following night. The punter looked as if he had just been roused from a deep sleep. He looked like the sort of man you wouldn't like to upset. Probably early forties, but could in real time be younger. 'What are you trying to sell me this time? Not more bloody rubbish, I hope.' This was Billy's cue. Mention 'rubbish' and Billy is right in there. 'Not rubbish, sir. Certainly not rubbish.' Billy had explained to me previously that selling works on objections. 'I've got some smashing jewellery for you today, sir, and a little bit special it is.' Billy was now ushering the punter, the agent and myself all into the front room of the little house. This house was a good deal more orderly than the previous one. Billy was in charge, and we could all feel it already. The wife emerged from the kitchen. Billy had told me that the first thing that you must do when selling is to assess the situation – see what priorities the customer has got. The wife had obviously just finished washing up, so there were no problems there. The telly was blaring in the background, but they'd obviously only been half watching it. The situation was 'ripe', as Billy liked to say.

As the agent sorted out the financial transaction, which was ostensibly the real purpose of the visit, Billy started to open his attaché case. All that glittering gold. He had their attention, their undivided attention – well, almost. 'Is anyone watching that?', said Billy, pointing at the television, and then without waiting for an answer, he nipped across and switched it off. There was a stunned silence for a moment. That television probably acted as a backdrop to every conversation that had ever taken place in that front room, at least since the time when someone like Billy had last visited.

'Now, madam', said Billy – 'if I said to you that you could have whatever you wanted from this box free of charge, what would you have?' There was another slightly stunned silence, as everyone in that room tried to work out whether this was a genuine offer or some elaborate ploy. 'I'd have one of those rings. I love rings and so does Frank there.' Frank nodded enthusiastically. If there were any rings going free, he wanted to be in there as a potential recipient of any largess. So Billy now knew that it was a ring that they were both after, and he knew exactly what they could afford. 'Ripe', I thought I heard him muttering, but he may just have said 'right'. Billy guided them through the rings. Rings were no longer now £180 or £220, they were just a couple of pounds a week over two years.

It was now just a case of selecting the items. 'What job do you do, Frank? Lorry driver? Right then. You don't want anything with a stone in it, that's for sure. It will make your finger go black.' Frank nodded, and his gaze shifted to the solid gold Horse shoe rings. Billy started to chuckle. 'You know, I once said the very same thing to a blackie. It took me a few seconds before I realised what I'd just said. I apologised and told him that it was just a figure of speech. 'No offence taken, mate', he said. You can't be too careful though, can you Frank? You have to watch what you say to them. Now what about this smashing ring here with the horse's head on it. Are you a gambling man yourself, Frank? I like a bit of a flutter. I'm sure that's Arkle. Just think – you could be wearing a racing legend on your finger for years. It could be a family heirloom. Leave it to your kids, Frank, there's a little bit of history on that ring. And don't forget the price can only go up, especially with inflation. That ring's only £1.80.'

You could see that Frank was far from prepared to carry out the necessary mental arithmetic, which would tell him exactly how much this nag's head ring at £1.80 a week over two years would eventually cost him. He didn't care. One look around the house told you that here was a family very short of heirlooms. Ripe.

It was now Alison's turn. 'I would have thought something with one of these ruby or emerald stones would be right up your street, madam', said Billy. 'They are real, aren't they? asked Alison nervously. 'A friend of mine bought a ring with fake stones in it a while ago. She'd been taken in, but I'd never fall for that.' Billy adopted a tone of some seriousness. He wanted to sound sincere, scholarly – 'They're what you call semi-precious, love. They keep their value very well do semi-precious stones. They're a really good investment.' But it was time to get off that track double quick. 'Here, let me try to guess your ring size, love. 'P', I reckon. Is that pretty close? Now try this one. Didn't I tell you – a perfect fit. That one's only £1.20. What do you think of it, Frank?'

Billy had drawn Mark and myself a graph of the whole procedure from going through the door in the first place to finding the egress double quick at the end, before we had gone anywhere near the house. Even I recognised where we now were on the graph. We were, at that very moment, sliding down the hill, on the other side from the sale. Billy had now only to do the paperwork and then we were out. His rule was to talk about anything other than the sale at this stage. A little bit difficult with two customers still mulling over the concept of *semi-precious* on the very same settee as him. 'Aren't you going to put the kettle on then, love? We're all parched in here, and I'm sure that Frank could do with a cuppa. Isn't that right, Frank?.'

Friday was the day when all the salesmen came back from the field with their tales of survival out there with the punters. They swapped stories, and had a chance to compare sales. 'Now, Bob, are you going to explain to us all how you managed to lose an eighty six pounds gold chain? I wouldn't have thought that a salesman with thirty three years in the business would have fallen for something like that?' The rest of the salesmen all laughed.

'Well, it was like this', said Bob. I went to this jewellery party at this house, where there were fourteen scantily clad women. Now, you can't sell to all fourteen in one go, especially because they were all new to credit. So I had them in three at a time in the kitchen. I'd already sold a grand's worth of stuff, when this eighty six quid gold chain suddenly went missing. One of the birds had obviously tried it on, and then let it drop down her bra. What could I do? I couldn't very well line them all up for a strip search, now could I? Even if I'd wanted to. I've always believed, by the way, that you should never get involved with customers like that – even when I used to sell sheets and bedding. Business comes first, you have to remember that. Some of the reps that I've known haven't been as disciplined as me. There was one rep that I used to work with, who had five kids in five different houses on the same estate. Straight up. But I've always put the sale first. My old boss used to say 'never get your fishing tackle out when you're trying to make a sale', and I think that's a good philosophy of life. So I wasn't interested in any strip search at this jewellery party. So I played on their sympathies instead.

'I told them that it was a hundred quid chain, and that the money would be coming out of my commission. Then I watched their reactions. One bird asked if it really was worth as much as that. You see that gives you a clue – she must have seen the price on the ticket by that stage. Then the same bird asked 'Aren't you insured?' That gives you another bloody clue. So I say 'For the whole case, madam, not for a single item. So who wants to hit me on the head and take the whole bloody lot?' You see I'm still working on their sympathies. And it worked. One of the husbands, who had turned up by this stage, then ordered a three hundred quid chain. So I'm in profit, even if I have lost a chain.

'But this is small-time thieving. It's a dangerous game walking around some of these places with thirty six grand's worth of stuff in an attaché case. I can tell you. I've had a few near misses over the years. I was in this block of flats in Birmingham one time, and I was the only white face to be seen. My heart's pounding, and I'm gripping my case. There are these four big black guys in the lift with me, and I'm already thinking that I've been set up. There had been a single order, you see, from one of the flats on the top floor. So this big, black guy turns to me and says 'Which floor are you going to, doctor?' You see I was wearing a pinstriped suit, a collar and tie, and was carrying this attaché case. So I played along with it.'

A close friend of Bob's, however, who also worked for the same company, was not so lucky. He had been mugged in Moss Side in Manchester. As he emerged from one house, he was hit over the head with an iron bar, and knocked unconscious. He was off work for a fortnight. 'And the worst thing about it', said Bob – 'was that he was treated like a bloody criminal by the police for a fortnight. The police always seem to assume that it's an inside job, even if you're lying in the gutter with your brains smashed in. They think that you were involved in it somehow or other. My pal's carried all his jewellery in a sports holdall, rather than an attaché case, since the mugging.'

Bob had a theory about the violence that goes along with such robbery – 'The problem with muggings, is that the people who do them always get so hyped up beforehand. They think that they're going to have to do you, so even if you offer to hand over the case of jewellery, they end up doing you just the same. If anyone tried to mug me, I'd hurt them, for the simple reason that I know that they'd end up doing me anyway, so I might as well leave my mark on them. That way, they'd have to go to hospital sooner or later, and you stand at least some chance of getting your gear back. If you end up losing your gear, then you know that you're going to be the number one suspect, and that's not very pleasant, believe me. That's the negative side of the business, but on the plus side there's the thrill of selling, although you have to have a sense of humour for this job.

'I've got a joke for every occasion. Okay try this one – 'What do ostriches, pelicans and poll tax collectors have in common? . . . They can all shove their bills up their ass.' I've been using this joke on some of the estates where the poll tax isn't too popular. Or did you hear the one about this fellow who went to the ticket station at the train station, and said 'Two tickets to Nottingham please' (in that very nasal, blocked-up voice – from the TV advert). . . . So the guy from the ticket office says 'What you need is some Tunes'. And the other guy says 'Why do they cure cerebral palsy?' I use this joke all over the place. You need a good sense of humour in this business.'

Bob has spent a lifetime in direct selling, and telling jokes – it has not always been jewellery, although he reckons jewellery is easy. 'The basic argument with jewellery is that you have it forever. It will give you years of pleasure, even after you've forgotten what you've paid for it. You buy it now and you even get two years to pay it off, so it's cheaper than it would be in two years time. You get a new jacket, on the other hand, and the same time next year, it's out of fashion. I've sold everything. I used to sell Calor gas heaters – they produced so much condensation that one woman rang the Water Board, because she thought she'd got a leak. Then it was fitted suits. You should have seen the state of some of those suits – hanging right off the poor bastards who ordered them. One salesmen couldn't fill in the forms correctly with all the details. I put it to him 'Have you ever seen someone with a 56 inch waist, and a 40 inch chest?' Then it was safety rings for children to wear in the water, which came in the shape of ducks. With these particular rings, when the kids went into the water, the ring turned over. There were all these complaints from parents that their children had been nearly killed with these ducks. Then it was furniture, now it's jewellery. It's all the same to me to be honest. But the truth is with the jewellery we get a lot of respect from the police for carrying this much jewellery around with us. I was in an accident last year, when my car went down a ditch. You should have seen this copper's face when I told him what was in my attaché case. He climbed down and got it for me. When I told him where I'd been with the gear, he told me that I deserved a medal. Well, it's all a service to the public, I told him. Somebody has to be prepared to do it.'

August 1990

The dolemites

Pippy's is a landmark in Sheffield. Just ask any hippy throwback, Ozzy Osborne fan or heavy-metal kid-about-town. It's right on, it's far out, it's twenty years behind the times. But it's successful. It sells all the paraphernalia of a bygone age: Spiritual Sky joss-sticks, hookahs, American-flag cigarette papers and the authentic ethnic garb to go with it – woven Afghan sweaters, Indian cotton blouses, Chinese silk shirts (all mass-produced today). These are mixed in with the newer arrivals, the paraphernalia of newer youth cults and movements: Ozzy 'Bark at the Moon' T-shirts and Iron Maiden vests for £3.99, leopard-skin jump-suits, also for £3.99, studded belts, leather jackets and leather bullwhips.

They start at £1.99. 'They're a lot more expensive in sex shops,' said Pip the proprietor ruefully, 'but I can still make a profit selling them at £1.99. They can't cost much to make or they don't pay the workers too much. They're usually bought by guys 'for a friend'. I suppose just for a joke – you don't know, of course.'

It's a rag-bag shop with no obvious unifying theme. Peace and love gave way to coolness years ago, then the 'We hate the humans' philosophy grew and grew and this is reflected in the ware on sale in the shop. Peace and love joss-sticks, studded belts, kaftans and bull whips, cotton tops and leather jackets with 'We are the damned' on the back.

'Let's just say it's an alternative clothing shop,' said Pip speaking quietly in the corner. The thongs from a studded belt hung down from the ceiling and gently stroked his grey, curly hair – the thongs for all the world resembled the long dark fingers of some docile and decidedly ethnic servant. Not so docile as it turned out; one of the belts slipped on to his head. He jumped up displaying his considerable size and his large exposed chest covered in gold chains and gold medallions. The medallions looked somewhat out of place behind the joss sticks. He resumed his seat. Peace was restored. His voice was soothing, as if it had been through a thousand mantras. His gold jewellery still winked at me though.

'I sell alternative clothing for the dolemites.'

Dolomites?

'No, not Dolomites – *dolemites*. They're my customers – kids on the dole. If the unemployment figures double, my profits double. Simple as that. At least 50 per cent of my customers are unemployed: second-generation hippies, punks, kids with shaved heads. They all seem very different, but they go for the same things: belts with studs, black Afghan shirts with tassles – my most popular product, it sells for £8.99 – and little pipes for you know what. When I buy anything, I buy three of a colour and twelve of black. Well, the heavy-metal kids like black, so do the punks, so do the present lot. No, I don't know what they're called. They're just dolemites to me. But dressing up is import-ant to them. It's more than important, it's everything. When they get their supplementary benefit, I can see them leaving out £10 for the rent, £10 for food and £7 to spend here on a Saturday. It's a good-value shop, their money goes far here. It's not just a case of buying some gladrags – this is their whole way of life. I cater for the alternative person.'

Pip, a.k.a. Philip Hayman, was forty-eight years old and had been running Pippy's for some fifteen years. Until a year previously he had also owned and run a bookmaker's. He'd been doing that for twenty-four years. His business ventures spanned Sheffield society. How could a successful bookie run a shop for hippies and alternative people?

'It's not as difficult as it sounds, you know. My family have been in business a long time in Sheffield. My grandfather had a dress shop; my parents sold ladies' wear for fifty years. I can remember a lady coming in for a wedding dress for her daughter: 'I want it pink and a bit on the big side.' We all knew what that meant – the girl had got herself into trouble. A fortnight later she was in again. 'Could you reduce the waist now and could you do it in white – she's had a miscarriage.' That was the attitude then – because she's had a

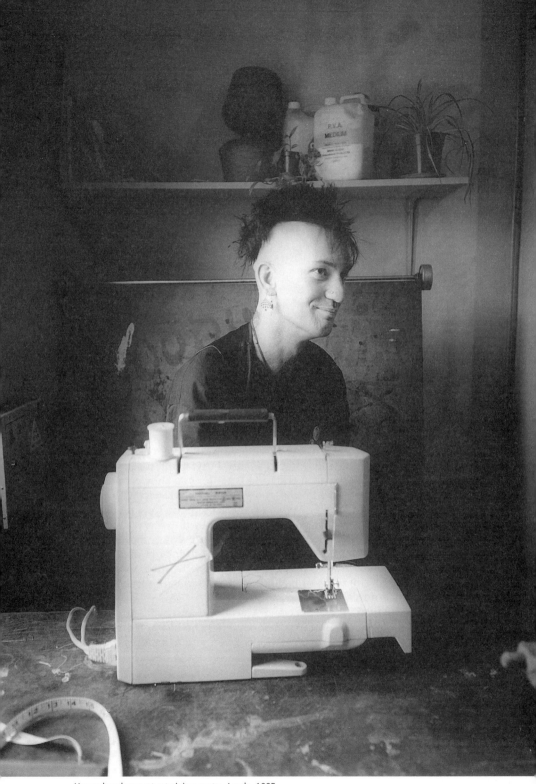

Unemployed man at retraining centre, Leeds, 1985

miscarriage, she was pure again. I went to public school – Worksop College – and after National Service I ran my parents' business, a chain of dress shops and a hairdresser's.

'I opened the original Pippy's in 1957, selling what used to be called 'separates'. I suppose you'd call them co-ordinates now. The rent was only £1.50 a week but it was still a struggle to make money. I clashed with my father about how to run a business. He was living in the past – he did everything on a cash basis. He would buy petrol out of his own pocket. He couldn't understand that it's a business expense and that you can run a business on expenses. There was a clash and I needed to make my own way in the world. The separates shop wasn't profitable enough. It was my uncle who had the bright idea of converting it into a bookmaker's. He was one himself and I'd always been keen on bookmaking. I ran a book at school when I was fourteen. I used to take all the boys' 1s 6d pocket money and pay out at half the publicised odds. I wish I could do that now. I set up the bookmaker's in 1960 – we got the *crème de la crème* of Sheffield society in, all the gangsters and prostitutes. It did very well. It was the only downstairs premises in the middle of Sheffield and my uncle had a good reputation as a bookie. And of course the punters wanted to get their hands on Hayman money. Everybody wanted a share of Hayman money. The only problem with the bookie's was the swearing – I wasn't used to it. It used to really upset me. I hadn't heard any at school. So I had this brainwave – why not employ ladies! Gentlemen won't swear in front of ladies, so I got some very attractive clerks to work here in little short skirts. They used to write up the odds up there in their tiny miniskirts. It did the trick all right, the swearing stopped and custom increased.

'We got all the notorious criminals in here. I would be terrified of them, but you could never show fear. Once you showed fear that was it – they'd have you. One bloke in particular who was particularly tasty – you know what I mean – gave me a lot of hassle. I bought this Alsatian and kept it in the shop with me. I knew he was terrified of dogs. Every time he banged the counter, Zak used to growl at him. It scared the life out of him and it soon put him off. I wouldn't have wanted to back him against the dog. You had to be respectful to the heavy mob, though. There was one guy in particular – the hardest man in Sheffield – he owed me £200. Who could you send to collect a debt off him, for goodness' sake? So I didn't bother. I just left it. He was put away for a few years. When he got out he won five grand in my other bookie's. The first thing he did was slap £200 down on the counter and say, 'That's what I owe you.' And that was twelve years later. This hard man is still about, but do you know something – he's shrunk, he's got a lot smaller. Age is a great equaliser, you know.

'I had a good rapport with all the criminal elements. There was mutual respect. Occasionally we got the odd drunk or lunatic in. I had a bouncer in the betting office and I kept a set of handcuffs just in case. If there was any trouble we'd handcuff them to the rail outside. The police didn't like it much because I'd been given the handcuffs by a policeman friend. But what can you do?

'I know it sounds a bit silly, but they were honest criminals in those days. You could trust them. There was one regular who'd lose £100 every Saturday

– without fail – like clockwork. Every Tuesday he'd come in and pay the debt off. Of course, I knew that sooner or later he wouldn't show. And sure enough one Tuesday there was no sign of him. I thought to myself, 'Goodbye, one hundred nicker.' The next thing I heard was that he'd been put away for embezzling four grand. He got three years for it. And would you believe the first Tuesday he got out he was in the shop and there was the £100. An honest criminal and no mistake. I could trust men like that – not like the dolemites today. Leave the shop unattended and they'd have it emptied. There was honour among thieves in those days, although of course I wasn't one of them.

'Of course, we had the odd spot of trouble. Three coloured lads raided the bookie's shop once – the manager needed fifty-four stitches in his head. They got caught and sent away for it. On another occasion, one guy came in with a meat cleaver and offered to chop one of the clerks' heads off. He wanted to put 50p on a dog but they'd started running already. He just couldn't accept it. He went home and got the meat cleaver. We talked him out of it, though. Another guy came in one day with a knife and demanded £500. He said it was either us or the shop next door that had to pay or he'd have us. We sent him next door – and we phoned the police. He got eight years.

'Things changed when my father died in 1966. I'd been a right stuck-up bastard; my father's death turned me into a better bastard. There I was, seventeen stone, bowler hat, rolled umbrella, the works. I drove a Jag. If you weren't somebody, I didn't want to talk to you. When my father died my attitude changed. I lost three stone in weight and started growing my hair and growing a beard. It was the flower-power era. I became Hippy Pippy. The punters didn't recognise me, my friends didn't recognise me. I changed the bookie's into 'Pippy's' in 1970. I kept the other bookie's going though. I recognised that there was money to be made in selling hippy clobber. I ordered kaftans from Carnaby Street and marked them up sometimes 100 per cent for the Sheffield market. I used to import some of my clothes direct from Spain. The stuff never went out of fashion – in twenty years I've never had a sale. Youth fashions come and go but they still go for this stuff. I sell and, I have to be honest, I sell to a very unclean section of society. We have to keep the joss sticks lit all the time. I was hoping that that hippy convoy you hear about would come Sheffield's way – there's a few scruffs among that lot. They come for cigarette papers, joss sticks, pipes – all the paraphernalia of 'high' society and the gear to go with it. No, I've never ever been tempted to sell drugs. We always get asked, 'Have you got anything to put in the pipe, man?' I just say, 'Go round to the tobacconist at the corner of the street.' I have sold poppers though – amyl nitrate. I never knew it was dangerous – not until the Sheffield *Star* did their investigation and told me. Honest. I thought they were air-fresheners. As soon as I heard I stopped selling them, even though it is legal and very profitable.

'All the time I was a hippy, I still ran the other bookie's. No, the punters accepted me, but you have to display wealth. There's no point at all in looking like a poor hippy. I always had a big cigar and a big American car. The punters thought I was a real character and they still wanted to get their hands on the Hayman money – good Jewish money.

'The truth is, the young people today are the most frightening people I've come across. They're so desperate. The punters from twenty years ago might have been addicted to gambling; but the kids I get in this shop now are just as addicted – no, not to drugs, despite all the Rizla papers and joss sticks. It's not drugs they're addicted to. It's money. They're money mad. They want things all the time. We have to chain every leather jacket up. They'd clear the shop if you let them. I caught one thief last week – a few days later he was in again. I heard him say, 'Let's go round the corner, we'll get nothing here.' Eight-year-old kids come nicking because they know they can't be prosecuted – they'll just get a free ride home in a police car. I've felt guilty about being a bookie in the past – guys coming in with their paypackets before they'd been home to give their wife their housekeeping. And of course I've taken their money and gladly. But you do feel guilty sometimes. But it was better then. Things weren't so desperate. You always knew they could go out and make a few bob again. It wasn't their last paypacket. But today – well it's a bit different. There's no paypacket. All the dolemites have is their little bit of posing as ace heavy-metal fan or whatever and they need money to buy the gear. That or steal the stuff, of course.

'To be honest, my handcuffs have never had so much use.'

September 1987

Moving up

The English language is permeated by the one idea that dominates the waking hours of the bourgeoisie. People are 'valued' in terms of hard cash. They say of a man: 'he is worth £10,000', and by that they mean that he possesses that sum. Anyone who has money is 'respectable'. He belongs to 'the better sort of people'. He is said to be 'influential', which means that what he says carried weight in the circles in which he moves. (Friedrich Engels, *The Conditions of the Working Class in England*, 1845)

Space invaders and fish and chips

Tommy Toumasos always wanted to be a teenage millionaire. There's nothing unusual in that. Tommy was a little different because he nearly did it.

'When I think about those days,' he said, 'oh boy, I was so close I feel so sick about it.' Tommy was now twenty-six – a very old twenty-six, in his own words. 'I've learned a lot – sometimes I think too much. You learn more in business than you ever would at college about life or about people. I'm still trying to make my first million but I've just had to revise my time scale. When I hadn't made it by twenty, I gave myself five more years. Now I'm trying to make it big before I'm thirty.' He fixed my regard with his handsome dark-brown eyes slightly discoloured by hangover. 'Champagne and brandy I'm afraid', and I could tell this was from the heart. Hitting the big time obviously meant a lot to him.

Tommy was a Greek Cypriot from Birmingham. His father had come to this country from Larnaca thirty-five years earlier because there was a shortage of work in Cyprus. His grandfather had been a silk merchant but his father wanted to turn his back on all that. 'My father always wanted to be a Greek Orthodox priest – he lived in a monastery between the ages of nine and eighteen – it was a bit of a joke in our family. He didn't want to be a merchant or get involved in business, despite this being the natural way for Cypriots. "Dirty work" he thought. But he found himself in England raising a family – a very large family – he didn't believe in contraception. He worked during the day in a bakery and at night as a waiter in a friend's restaurant to support us. My mother used to take in washing from neighbours, honestly. I know it's a cliché but it's true. They had six daughters and three sons. The problem for Greek Cypriots is that you must give a dowry when a daughter marries. The going rate is about thirty grand for reasonably well-off families. My father realised that he had reared an expensive family. He'd no choice really but to go into business. He opened some steak bars – he had three at one time. They were very successful. If he hadn't had any daughters he'd have been a millionaire. The financial commitment to daughters doesn't stop with the dowry: if ever a son-in-law of my father gets into financial trouble it would be his responsibility to bale the son-in-law out. This has happened a number of times. My father was only interested in making money for his family.

'His heart was never in business – it was in the church. Every year he'd go to Cyprus and spend a month in a monastery there. He always said that one day he'd enter the church. And then suddenly one summer – I was eleven at the time – while he was away there was a phone call for my mother. I can remember her screaming. I thought my father had been killed. It was a worse shock than that – he was just about to be ordained as a Greek Orthodox priest. To become a priest he had to spend three days in a church without food or water. He rang my mother – to tell her that he was on his way. My mother wanted to get on the next plane and talk him out of it. I was used to seeing my father as a successful businessman in a three-piece suit and driving a Merc – a smart Merc at that. I wasn't prepared for the transformation. I always thought religion was his hobby, not a way of life for him. Three months later he returned to Birmingham – black robes, black hat, long beard and hair right down his back. It was a big shock. The family was split on it. It was very hard to get used to it all. His new career restricted my mother's social life; they couldn't really go to parties any longer. And he didn't want to continue running his business. It would have looked a bit strange: a Greek Orthodox priest running a chain of steak bars in Birmingham. He got rid of two of the restaurants and the Merc immediately and sold the third restaurant a bit later. He also sold the house in Sutton Coldfield, which was a bit grand, and moved to a more modest abode in Great Bar in Birmingham. The new house was close to his church. My father lived on the profit from the restaurants. He also divided up his land – land that he owned in Cyprus – between his three sons. It was worth about 150 grand in total. Fifty grand each. Because of this we all chipped in something when necessary to help our parents pay their bills.

'My father, despite giving up business himself for religion, didn't try to put me off a career in business. It comes naturally to Greek Cypriots. People always say Jews are the natural businessmen. They had to do it for centuries out of necessity. There were no other careers open to them. Greek Cypriots on the other hand are born businessmen – they do it even when there are alternative careers. In Cyprus, even in the poorest village, the peasants work out ways of getting into business – making lace or tiles or little pipes to smoke from. They're always thinking of ways of making money. If an Englishman won the *Sun* bingo he'd put an extension on his house; a Greek Cypriot would try to use it to finance a business to make more money.

'I got into business young. I set up a takeaway food business when I was seventeen. It was like a man going to make love when he didn't have any pubic growth. Talk about being thrown in at the deep end. It was in Handsworth in Birmingham – famous now, but always a rough area. So much hassle, it was a joke. My father had the property and I got the shop rent-free. I sold mainly chicken, about three or four hundred a week with chips. I also wanted to get into goat meat but it's difficult to buy from the market. I'd gone to school in Handsworth – a grammar school that had become a comprehensive. Eighty per cent of the pupils were black or Asian. Most of my friends that weren't Greek Cypriots were black. I was making about £400 a week. It was easier then; there was no VAT on food and no heavy rates. I was making a fair bit but I was spending an awful lot. I bought a sports car and went out to nightclubs most nights. My close friends were all Greek Cypriots in similar social and financial positions to myself. We were all young and in business and weren't afraid to show the world we were wealthy. The English are very discreet about their money; Greek Cypriots don't hide it. We'd all drink Buck's Fizz in nightclubs – I actually liked it. It was a good time in Birmingham – the Duranies use to hang about the clubs as well. There were a lot of up-and-coming groups about.

'I sold the shop after eighteen months for twenty grand. I didn't owe any money so this was money I could invest in some new business venture. With a Greek Cypriot friend I got into the fruit-machine business. We started a business called M and S Automatics and put fruit machines into friends' shops – most of the friends were Greek Cypriots as well, running chip shops. Space

Invaders were just taking off. Within six months we had fifty sites earning us £40 a week each. What we did was, we went to a finance company and bought ten machines for £8,000. We were paying back the finance company at £60 per month but the machines were earning us £160 per month in rent from the shops so each machine gave us £100 per month profit. A nice simple, profitable business. Out of that we had to pay licence fees and pay for engineers on call. Within nine months we got up to 150 sites. We were into Space Invaders as well. Some shops would hire two or three machines off us. We had a turnover of four grand a week, our overheads were maybe £1,500 altogether. We moved a bit quickly in retrospect. We opened a show-room selling machines and just got bigger and bigger. We employed full-time engineers and secretaries. We had another year of exceptionally good business when we made maybe seventy grand each. We thought the money would never dry up and we thought we'd continue to grow. In a couple of years, we thought we'd be millionaires. But then – bang! The licensing department knew that people were making a lot of money out of fruit-machines and they put the licensing fees up from £40 a year to £350 a year. With 150 machines, we had to fork out over fifty grand a year in licensing fees. They also tightened up on licences – we started to have a bit of diffi-culty getting them. To get a licence they had to check on the shop – you had to have a table and chair, for example, before you could get a fruit-machine. We got a lot of hassle. So what we did was we started putting machines without licences into shops. We had to do it – we had repayments to make, bills to pay. We got away with it for a bit, but then we got raided. Every machine that wasn't licensed got confiscated with the money still in it. Fifty per cent of our sites were cut down in one stroke. We'd the same overheads, the same repayments and we'd now got the police on our backs. They took our gaming licence off us. We were in schtuck. We had a business potentially worth half a million but without a gaming licence it was worth very little. They had us by the balls. We weren't a limited company – if we had been we could have got away with fortunes. If we'd been a limited company, none of our personal possessions would have been touched. As it was we lost every-thing, including my flat. We had debts of eighty grand. We sold the business for 100 grand but saw nothing of that money. We were left with nothing. I had twenty grand stashed away and that was all. But I suppose I'd had a jet-setting lifestyle for a couple of years – holidays every three months in the Caribbean. And of course I'd gained some sharp experience of life and busi-ness – before I was 21.

'But my partner and I were both shattered by it all. We'd been whizzkids in Brum, we'd made a lot of money very early. We were very popular around town. My dad had this old saying, "Greek Cypriots are the first people to make friends with you but they're also the first to stab you in the back." The knives were really out now. Greek Cypriots are very materialistic – they were impressed by our success, by our money-making skills. When we went to a restaurant it was always "Get him a bottle," "Get him this," "Get him that," "Pay for his bill." After the crash, everybody's attitude to us changed. Our pride was hurt. It could have been worse though. I could have got eighteen months inside.

'After the crash, I went to Cyprus for three months. I wasn't going to give up. Business is in my blood. I bought two Wimpy-Bar-type places when I got back – one in Bakewell and one in Matlock (my sister has a chip shop in Matlock). My brother put a bit of money into the business. After six months I sold the one in Bakewell and made £15,000 on the sale and made another £9,000 profit out of it. I turned the Matlock place into a Greek restaurant, the Aphrodite. Then I sold that. That was no philosophy – a quick kill, in and out. I buy empty shops, do them up, get business going, then – out.

'In the last two years I've opened five places in Sheffield. All were Greek restaurants or chip shops. The chip shops were in Manor Top, Shirecliffe and Fulwood. Fulwood is the posh end of Sheffield. The other in Shirecliffe went down in a fire – I got the insurance and made quite a bit out of it. But I've still got the other two. There was a lot of opposition to the Fulwood shop – petitions, everything. Planning permission was difficult. I got a lot of abusive phone calls: " . . . a Greek peasant opening up a chip shop in the village – disgusting!" I said, "Stuff you!". 'I couldn't get any local staff. I had to bring staff from my Manor Top shop. Manor Top is very working class. I've got rid of it now anyway. It cost fifteen grand to do up. I sold it for forty-eight grand. A quick in and out and thirty-three grand profit.'

'I'm still working hard and playing hard, maybe spending too much on my social life. The management of clubs still won't give me a VIP pass or a free drink, though. They give passes and drink to people they like, not people who spend. Business isn't about dealing with people you like, and they don't seem to realise that. I was in a restaurant last week with two friends from Birmingham. The bill was 140 quid – we had two magnums of champagne. We were a bit noisy and this bouncer asked us to leave. Could you believe it? He actually picked up our champagne and asked us to leave. My friends said, "Jesus Christ, I don't believe this – the money we've spent in here, and they're treating us like this!"

'At the moment I'm a quarter of the way towards my goal – to be a millionaire, with chip shops and property abroad. I'm still looking for the big one, the big killing, and at the moment I've got my eyes on some premises right in the centre of Birmingham to turn into a wine-bar and nightclub complex. Business is in my blood – I don't understand how my father could give it all up for the church. I just don't understand.'

March 1987

Addicted to business

Barnsley is full of self-made men. Men who started out with nothing and got to – well, where they are today. Self-improvers, gritty, determined. Just look at Michael Parkinson. And they're not averse to showing the world that they've made it – the hard way. Rollers, minks, gold rings. Some of them go a bit over the top but who wants to be understated in Barnsley, for God's sake? They may do fry-ups in their Dallas-style kitchens but what's the matter with that?

Sue's Shop, Hyde Park Flats, Sheffield, 1987

A few years ago, you could see Alan driving along in his Bentley. He was certainly ostentatious. A suntan (in December), streaked hair, a pair of diamond rings. He got envious glances wherever he went in his car. He liked it. 'People always gave way in their cars,' he says. Sometimes the envy boiled over. He knew that every time he parked the Bentley on the street he risked a scratch. 'They'd do it so meticulously,' he said. 'They'd take real care to do it the whole way along.' When he stopped at pedestrian crossings he risked abuse. 'Affluent bastard,' they'd shout. He'd just look smug. This made them even more angry. Sometimes he'd flick his streaked hair. 'Fucking poseur,' they'd reply. By then, it was usually time to move off, quickly. One night this total stranger, quite overcome by envy, leapt on the bonnet of his Roller (Alan had got rid of the Bentley by then). Alan had to chase him off through the streets of Barnsley. 'Well, it was understandable,' Alan said in his normal understanding way. 'It was raining, and I passed this queue waiting for a taxi at half past two in the morning. There was I, dry, warm with this blonde beside me. What do you expect?'

The next day, Alan was back in his garage again in a little village near Rotherham. It was a proper garage forecourt, although the pumps, funnily enough, were not connected. He had space for about twenty cars. 'I was into collector cars in those days. For example, I had a 1932 Morris Minor with only 7,000 miles on the clock. The bloke who owned it previously had been packed off to a mental home. I picked the car up cheap but it took a bit of legwork. At the time I also had two hearses. I got them from an undertaker in Leeds. I paid four hundred quid for one and a hundred for the other. I got rid of one of the hearses to a guy who was doing school-meals deliveries – he had 'People are dying to eat my school dinners' painted on the side. Hearses do get you noticed after all. I was making quite a bit at the time. One week I sold seven cars and made £2,000 profit. I had the knack – I was always on the look-out for a bargain. You've got to stay on your toes. I took my wife and two kids to Jersey for their holidays in our car and before I'd been there for an hour I'd sold it for a nice profit. I had to hire a car for the rest of the week – not to take them about, but to drive round all the other motor dealers. My technique for buying and selling is simple. I would leave my Roller at home and take off my rings and put on an anorak. I'd just ask how much would they be prepared to sell the car for, to a poor man. It works – they always drop the price.'

'But don't all car dealers do just that?' I asked. 'Surely it doesn't work after a while?'

'You'd be surprised at how powerful appearance is – you react naturally to it. When you see me now – rings, gold – you react immediately and naturally in a different way. And don't forget, some dealers aren't prepared to dress like Steptoe to make a few bob – I was.'

The typical used-car salesman I hear you say. Pretending to be poor to fiddle the poor, but Alan's was, if anything, a double con. Alan was really a pipe inspector for Yorkshire Water Authority at the time. He did that for fifteen years. 'My job was to inspect pipes and water mains; if a pipe burst, I had to shut the mains off. To be frank, it was a nice cushy job. The hardest part of it was keeping out of the gaffer's way. We used to do a tour of all the colliery canteens in the area. We could usually fit in about seven or eight canteens in a day. Two nights a week I did a shift from 11.00 p.m. to 5.00 a.m. We used to sign in to working men's clubs when we were skiving and put the manager's name in the book. I started doing some part-time work when I worked for the Water Authority. One week I helped a mate rip his fireplace out. I got a job as a film extra in two films, Walt Disney's *The Pit Ponies* and Barry Hines's *Escape from the Dark*. I got £35 a day. I told the Water Authority I was sick at the time. But I've always been interested in cars. So I thought why not get a pitch and try selling a few. I got a pitch for £25 a week. It had flood lighting and everything. It all worked very smoothly. I'd go to the Water Authority at about half-seven in the morning, do a few jobs, then call in to the garage for a couple of hours. In the afternoon, I'd go back to the depot for a bit, do a few more jobs and then it was back to the garage. I'd have to park the Yorkshire Water Authority van a bit away from the garage and make sure I took off my uniform, but it all ran very smoothly. I was making about sixty quid a week from the Water Authority and about five hundred from the cars. I started driving to work at the Water Authority in a Lincoln Continental. That does about eight miles to the gallon so I was using about two gallons of petrol a day, just going to work. I had to start syphoning petrol out of the vans at work to help me along.

'Everything was going well until the garage ran into trouble. I wasn't making enough from the Water Authority to live on, so I had to pack it in. I took a Heavy Goods Vehicle driving course but I couldn't get a job because I'd got no experience. I was desperate. I got an articulated unit through some mates. I started giving tuition at £15 per hour.' But it didn't pay off. 'During this time my father died of cancer and I was spending most of my time down at my mother's. I had to get rid of the garage completely. So there I was, no garage and no Yorkshire Water Authority to fall back on. But I knew I'd got the entrepreneurial gift and the charm to get away with it. (Everyone says I've got a five-star smile – that's my octane rating.) So I just looked round to find something for which there was a ready market. It came to me in a flash – scaffolding clips. They need derusting, don't they?' I nodded tentatively. 'Well, they're always rusty, aren't they?' he added. I nodded, with more assurance this time. 'It wasn't entirely an original idea anyway – I'd got a friend who was in that line of business and he drove a brand new Ferrari.' ('But, Alan,' I was tempted to say, 'you were driving a Roller at the time.') 'Anyway,' Alan continued, 'I bought all the equipment – the tanks, the burners and the chemicals – for two thousand quid off my mate. I was ready for action. I rang about seventy building companies on the first day. Do you know what kind of uptake I got?' I shook my head. Alan's diamond ring winked up at me. 'Fifty per cent success rate?' I suggested. 'No, just one,' he said. 'I got two hundred pounds' worth of business and that was all. I had to ask the company to buy the gear back off me. I got a few hundred quid for it. The Roller had to go. My wife, in the meantime, had got a bit angry about my deals, by this stage, and my jet-set lifestyle. She vandalised the car. It knocked about three thousand quid off the price. The guy with the Ferrari is in the nick now for selling scaffolding. It wasn't his to sell,' Alan added, ruefully.

'After this fiasco, I got a job delivering computer paper for a couple of years, but I was desperate to be a success in business. So I went into the tarmacking business. A bit like *The Boys from the Black Stuff* really. The gear cost two grand. A mate and I reckoned there was really nothing to it. We did a garage forecourt first – in fact it was our only job. By the time we got the tarmac laid, it had gone off. The owner demanded that we lift it off again. We didn't know how to do that either. After that things got desperate. A friend told me that there was brass in cardboard. You can get quite a bit of money for cardboard if you know the dealers – about twenty quid a ton apparently. So I started going round all the supermarkets collecting cardboard. I did it for four weeks. All the girls knew me as "the cardboard man". I stored it in a big field next to my friend's house. We had this huge mountain of cardboard. I reckoned there was at least thirty tons there. A nice little earner, as Arthur Daley would say. And then this guy came to collect it. When he weighed it he found that there was just two tons – forty quid. For a full month's work. Hopeless. I spent more on petrol than I got from the cardboard. My mate said I was the only person he knew who buys retail and sells wholesale. After that I tried a different scheme to make some brass – collecting pig-meal bags. My brother kept pigs and it was him who put me on to it. A great idea, I thought. I finished up with about 2,000 – half a ton. Do you know what I got for them? Sixty quid, and it took me about four months to collect them all.

'I've always been into wheeling and dealing but it's never easy. And you never know who you can trust. After the pig bags I went back to cars and bought a JCB from a bloke. I left a ring worth nearly £2,000 and £2,000 cash as a deposit. He seemed perfectly genuine. The only problem was, the guy denied ever getting the ring or the money. I went to his house. I pleaded with him. No use.' Alan then opened his daunting briefcase – full, but not of invoices or orders; it was full of a voluminous legal correspondence about the ring. 'Some guys who wheel and deal go in for the odd bit of violence to oil the wheels of the transaction. I don't. I've never been in serious trouble with the police. I went straight to the police about the ring and look where it got me – solicitor's letters as thick as an encyclopaedia, no ring, no money and legal costs.

'At the moment it's my last chance. I was on the dole, then I got on to a government Enterprise Allowance Scheme – they pay you forty quid a week – and I've started a sandblasting business. I've got some orders at the moment – I've got a wall and some oak beams to do next month, but I'm really hoping that something like a church will come up – there's real money in churches. I've had a great idea about promotion. I do a bit of marathon running and in the past I've got about £70 sponsorship from Radiant Superglaze: I advertised the company on my shirt when I ran. This year I'm going to advertise myself and my sandblasting business. What do you think of that idea?'

Alan grew philosophical. Like a drowning man, his whole life was flashing before him and there wasn't much there. 'I've tried to make the big time, you know, but I suppose I've failed. I'm thirty-six and still living in the same terraced house – it used to look a bit funny anyway with a Roller parked outside. It's really difficult getting off the ground. I suppose I'm still on the runway but I love wheeling and dealing. It's in my blood, I suppose. I'd sell anything, or try to. Last week I sold a stone wall at the back of my house, for sixty quid. I think I'm addicted to business the way other people are addicted to drugs.'

February 1986

'I'm not a frigging monkey'

Wayne was the Moses of Manor Top. No, I don't mean that he floated down the River Don in a reed basket or even that his parentage was in doubt – although many people asserted that it was, in moments of anger. No, he'd seen the promised land, flowing with milk and honey, and he wanted to get there, desperately.

Wayne, you see, was just a body – just a massive pair of shoulders, a thick torso and a pair of knuckles with not so much on top, or so the punters thought. He was a bouncer, he collected debts, he intimidated, he minded, he protected. He was sixteen stone and twenty-five years old and thinking about his future, perhaps for the first time. 'I don't want to be doing this in ten years' time. I know that for a start. I want to be in business – a legit business, mind. Well, after all, crime doesn't pay, does it? A few short cuts maybe, but crime – where does it get you?'

Wayne was trying to get started in business using his contacts. He was keen to change his image. He hated the way people tried to stereotype him. 'Too many people see doormen as being a bit thick. Often we present ourselves that way, you know, because it's the best move you can make. You can get too involved with people verbally and things, talking to them. When you do this they often try to put one over on you. They think they can get personal and that they can start taking liberties all the time. It's not on. It's best to stay out of it, then they don't get personal. So we don't talk and they think, "Thick bastard." They look at you and I notice their mannerisms. All the time I notice their mannerisms and they think, "Knuckler, tattoo brigade," you know – Ughh! And there am I, saying nothing, the strong, silent type, I like to think – watching the bastards all the time, noticing their every move, seeing what's going through their devious little minds.'

Wayne did a lot of work for businessmen – 'All legit. I'm sent in to collect bad debts.'

Did he like this line of work?

'Well, it's a job. But you can just see them thinking, "Here we go, he's sent in the heavy." I go in polite – it's all on a business footing, but I do get annoyed. I tried getting this debt a few weeks ago and this guy turned round and said, "I haven't got the money, boss – honest." So I told him to cut it out. But he went on and on. He was irritating me. So I said, "If you don't pay me, I'm going to splat you all over this wall." And he says, "You don't dare." I don't dare. I don't dare indeed. He was getting up my nose. I get mad some-times, so I went to hit him. We were in his house. And I put my fist through the window. I couldn't believe it – I was right embarrassed. So I had to hit him then, didn't I? The guy was messing me about so he had to have it. So I told him I was coming back the next day for his car and I told him he was going to sign me a note saying that he'd given it to me. I told him he wasn't going to get no change neither. Whatever I make out of this car I'm going to keep.'

'Was this fair?' I asked.

'Fair? It was business – look at the aggro he was giving me. He was messing me about. He'd kept out of my way for weeks. Look at the time I'd wasted. I needed my bonus. I was on double time. So anyway a week later I visited him again and took his diving gear from his garage and his toolbox. It were a snap-on set – like eight hundred quid's worth of tools. I took his battery charger as well. I must have got a grand's worth of stuff altogether. Anyway, two days later he came up with a grand out of the money he owes – he was still two hundred short. He wanted his stuff back. I said, "No way – you've cost me too much time. We'll call it a draw." So he thinks I'm a bully and unreasonable. But I tried being polite. Where did it get me, eh? Eh!'

At that point I could imagine Wayne being a bit short-tempered.

'I've got loads of businessmen as friends and they all say they'll give me a leg-up – to get started, like. Some of the geezers I knock around with are millionaires. And what did they start with?'

'Brains?' I suggested.

'Brains? You've got to be joking. None of them are brain surgeons. A bit of savvy and a few good mates. That's what you need. I've got this pal who's right wealthy. He keeps buffaloes, no kidding. We're both a bit mental, playing practical jokes on each other. So I'm in his house one day and he threw a snake on me bed and I went potty. I've never seen a snake up close before and I got out of bed like a shot. It were only a common or garden grass snake but I didn't know. So anyway I went one better. I got this tarantula for forty-five quid, in town. Now I'm told they're not poisonous you see. I put it in his car. He sees this tarantula like and he goes bananas, screaming and everything. So he has to get his own back. So he gets this other tarantula – they're brown you see, and he sprays it black so it looked like a Black Widow and he wakes me up in bed and he throws it at me. I went berserk. I really thought it were this Black Widow. He says, "Look, I found this Black Widow, but they're not poisonous either." Me, I know they are. I get up. Did you see that James Bond film, eh, with the aerosol? So, I got this aerosol and I set it alight. Anyway I got this aerosol going but it wouldn't go out and I thought it were going to blow up. And the spider's still alive – it hadn't hurt the spider. Oh, it were terrible. That James Bond film must have been a load of crap.

'He was always into practical jokes this millionaire. He owned this farm, so one night he says, "Park the car in the garage – you'll be all right. Get your car out of the way 'cause we're bringing cows through." So I parked up and slammed door shut. I thought, God, what's going off now? So I stayed in me car and I switched all lights on and I couldn't see anything. I looked round and I saw this bale of straw and I thought, there's nothing here. You know how you do. So I get out of the car then a buzzer goes and as I got out of the car there was this God-almighty scream and something jumped on me. I were frightened to death honestly – I didn't know what were going off. And it were hairy. And I've got hold of this head, honestly, and I'm trying to drag it off me. I thought it was a giant rat. The more I tried to drag it off, the more it got hold of me and I'm banging away. And anyway, it let go and I threw it and it were in the headlights and I still didn't know what it were. And I got in me car and I got this shotgun out and I blasted it to bits. Me bottle had completely gone. I didn't know what to do. I shot it. Horrible. I reversed the car out of the garage – bust all his door open. I called him all the names under the sun. I didn't know what it was you see. Oh Christ. Do you know what it was – a monkey, a poor bastard monkey. When I think about it now.'

'What kind of monkey was it?' I enquired gingerly.

'Only a little thing – them that pisses all over everything. Not a chimp; that other type. Oh God, when I think about it. I were frightened honestly. But it were just a ball, you see, on the floor in the lights and shot – bump. You know I felt sick afterwards. I did honestly. But my pal can afford that kind of stunt, through having all that brass.'

And at that point I didn't know whether to feel more sorry for the monkey, Wayne or his sick friend who liked to demonstrate what money can buy, and where legit business can get you, by dealing in expendables. The spider was one, the monkey was another. I'd got this awful feeling that Wayne was next in line. He looked as if he knew it as well. His fate wasn't to be lit by an aerosol but he looked as if he might be destined to go up in a puff of smoke nonetheless.

But Wayne had seen the promised land from the mount and he was desperately clambering down the slag heaps to get there. He wanted the freedom that went with money. He didn't want to be a knuckler any more, or one of life's expendables. He wanted to be calling the shots, not taking them.

'I've a pal who's a bouncer,' Wayne continued. 'He's in his fifties. His eyes are going – he can't see who to let in to the club and who not to anymore. I don't want to be like that.' But what line of legit business could Wayne get himself involved in? That was the 64,000 dollar question.

'Well, I've tried a few lines of business already', he said. 'CBS before they became legal – that's not really legit, I suppose, but it doesn't harm anybody. Videos, property – the usual. I was into CBS in a big way, as a user, and a pal got me involved in the business side. What I used to do was fetch these CBS from London at £60 apiece, bring them back to Sheffield and my mate used to sell 'em for £120. So we started from there. We used to buy more and more and plough the profits back into the business. If I only bought one at £60 then I could buy two next time. And it went on from there. I didn't have any money at the time but my partner did. He used to buy more and more and eventually he opened a shop selling CB accessories. CBS were illegal but he used to have the shop full of them – daft, wasn't it? He got away with it. They weren't doing anybody any harm you see. In fact, they even helped out on a few occasions: somebody got lost at Ringinglow, two CB-ers found her. You could like say, "Oh I've just passed a bloke that's had an accident, can you ring the police up 'cause they're out of the way in the country." We were doing everybody a good turn. But eventually I got caught with the CBS by the Customs and Excise. They did us for fifty-two grand. We'd both put up half the money but the deal was this – I took 40 per cent of the profit and he took 60 and if there was any trouble, it was all down to him. It was his suggestion, this. So I said, "Fair enough." But when we got caught, they took the lot off us – we'd just bought 'em as well. So it wiped me out and it wiped him out, but he took the fall for it – it was a civil offence not a criminal offence, you see; that's why we didn't do any time, but I was skint. It was a big gamble really.

'I had a couple of near misses before that, anyway. I was travelling around a lot. I used to go to Blackpool and Skegness, and all the coastal places then

down to Manchester and Liverpool, all these places selling CBS you see. I'd
got these CBS delivered and I put them in Ravenhead glass cases. I had some
Ravenhead glass anyway because me mother likes them and so do a few of
me friends that have got shops. Anyway, police stopped me one night coming out of a motorway car-park. They wanted to know who I was and what
I'd got in the back. I suppose I looked a bit sus. I said I was a market trader
and it was all glass in the back, so they said, "Can we have a look?" So I said,
"Christ, I'm tired – I've driven all the way from Liverpool, I want to go home.
Look, here's me receipt – it's glass. Why are you messing me about?" and I
pretend to lose my temper, you see. So I shot out. I said, "Right, if you want
to have a look I'll show you what's in the back." And I slammed door open,
like you do, with a big bang, and I got hold of this box and I threw it on't
floor and I said, "Look, if you want to see what's in it – look, that's what's
there." And they're all doing their nuts. The police thought they'd got a
madman on the loose. I says, "Look, I'll give you another box, here," and
they're saying, "No, no, no more." I says, "You're gonna have one anyway,"
and they go, "No, put it down, put it down." They say, "We'll give you a
hand to clear glass up," and I get back in't van and I go, "I can't believe it," I
says, "take the lot," and I sat down on the floor like this. I says, "I'm not
talking to you. I want to go home. I've been stopped three times" (I'd been
stopped once, as it happened). I said, "Look, I've got a ticket to produce my
documents." I said, "Others didn't give me any 'cause I'd been stopped already,
and you're harassing me. I'm being harassed." "We're not, we're not, you're
all right. On your way."

'Oh, it were so funny that. I've met some right nutters you know through
working on the doors of clubs – I'd got all their mannerisms just right. But a
few weeks after, we were busted – it weren't so funny then.

'After the CBS, I tried my hand in the video game. I've got a pal who's doing
very well in it. But there's too much competition in the video market. Everybody opened video shops with their redundancy money and now there's a
mysterious spate of fires when the business goes down. Funny that. I did
hardly any business. My mate with the videos rents out cameras and by
mistake this guy handed back a video of him and his wife plonking. At least I
think it was his wife. Anyway, my mate lets that video out on loan for £2 a
night – a bit special that one. Anyway this guy from the film goes back in the
shop to hire a film one day and this other guy recognises him. He can't
remember how he knows him though! It were hilarious, but there are too
many video shops. Only a few are getting by.

'The problem with legit business is that there are so few opportunities to
make a few bob. My best bet is to save money from my bouncing and my
debt-collecting in a building society and buy some property which I could
then rent out to students. Well, I'd have no trouble collecting the rent,' he
said, 'and everybody has to start somewhere.

'It's hard to make an honest few bob from most lines of business today.
You just get peanuts from most enterprises and I'm not a frigging monkey
after all, am I?'

I just didn't know what to say.

August 1986

Miss Gazette finalists, Sheffield, 1982

Moving into the glamour market

In what seems like a different and distant era, certain women achieved symbolic freedom by burning their bras – there was nothing in them. I met one Sheffield lass – let's call her Jane Smith – who achieved her freedom not by burning hers but by sporting frillier ones, filled that is, and basques and cami-knickers, in fact the full canopy of male-oriented titillation. She wore such things herself and sold them in her new shop. 'Naughty but nice,' she said, 'wouldn't you agree?' Jane had more prison walls to scramble over than most. At fifteen she was pregnant and labelled for life. ' "A right little gold-digger" they all said.'

'I was one of six. I was always considered the black sheep of the family,' she said. 'I thought I was the one with the get-up-and-go. There was a bit of truth in both descriptions I suppose, looking back on it. At fifteen, I was very naive. I became sick. I was off work for three days vomiting. The doctor came to examine me, he just examined my tummy. I couldn't understand why. He didn't say a word. He just stared through his pince-nez glasses in a very meaningful way and went downstairs to see my mum and dad. The next minute my dad was in the room – he really blew at first. He just shouted at me, "You've bloody done it this time." I couldn't believe it. My boyfriend and I had only done it three times. I thought you had to do it loads of times to get pregnant. Bloody Durex! When my boyfriend told his parents they kicked him out and took the car off him. They were a posh family all right. They owned this cavern in Derbyshire, all the mining rights to go with it and the shop to sell the stone in. With his car gone he had to come on his bicycle to see me. I wasn't allowed to see him. I met him, by the way, at a Joe Cocker concert – he was twenty. My mother was the cloakroom attendant. He was wearing a suit and he asked me for a dance – at a Joe Cocker concert, for goodness' sake. My friend asked me had I seen his house in Castleton. She was obviously impressed. I was fifteen years and two weeks old when I met him. His family was right posh but it was obvious how they made their money. I remember his grandmother – it was her who had all the money – she'd been bought two bunches of black grapes. They were sitting in a crystal fruit bowl. "Go on, take a grape – but only one," she said, "they have to last a long time." That summed up their whole attitude. I was seven months pregnant when I got married. His mother didn't want him to marry. She said to him, "Are you sure it's your baby?" when I was sitting there within earshot. I could have gone on the pill but I lived in Bamford – it's a tiny village. I was frightened to death of going to the doctor.

'When I was married I moved into grandma's house next door to the mother-in-law. In the first year of marriage I got out once. I was now John Renfrew's wife, not Jane Smith any longer – never just Jane, just Mr Renfrew's wife. John went out every night. I used to ring all the pubs and say, "Is my husband there?" He always came home, eventually, usually with bumps in the car. He had four jobs in quick succession – he kept getting the sack for his lack of punctuality. I was very lonely. The villagers didn't like me even though they were nice to my face. It took me four years to feel part of that village. I was very depressed.

'I started helping out at the family shop on high days and holidays. It got me out of the house. Then came a big change in my life. I had a daughter when I was twenty-two. I'd had three miscarriages in the meantime. I was obsessed with having a girl, really obsessed. You can pretty girls up with frilly knickers and things like that and they don't grow away from you like boys. Girls are all basically stay-at-home birds. John was at the birth – it was wonderful. It was totally different to my first birth. When I had my first there was such hostility. I was treated like dirt. I had no guidance from the nurses. This time it was different. The sister remembered me. She said I'd been such a pathetic little thing first time around. This time the nurses were really marvellous. And when I had the first baby I got no presents; this time the doorbell didn't stop ringing. My husband started working in the family craft shop – he settled down a bit. I used to go and open it up – he still couldn't get up in the morning. The marriage was revitalised. He moderated his drinking and gave up darts. He'd been the captain of the darts team before. We went out together for really the first time. It was wonderful.

'It didn't last. I had to go to the doctor and he found a growth that shouldn't be there. I had a hysterectomy. It's horrible what it does to your body. Mentally you're so alert but your body wouldn't allow you to do so much as put a kettle on. Unless you've been through it you can't imagine the trauma. I had a daily help. The operation changed my personality. I was determined to get as much out of life as possible. I wanted more than I was getting. I went on a cruise on the QE2 for a holiday – my mother-in-law paid for the holiday and John gave me my spending money.

'The cruise was a turning-point in my life. What happened was this particular officer paid me a lot of attention. I was flattered and to be honest I was tempted. It stirred something inside me, it unsettled me. He took me to places in the ship where nobody else could go, to see the tugs. He worked in the boiler room. It was just a friendship but I was still really unsettled when I got home. John had filled the house with flowers, but I couldn't stop thinking about this QE2 officer. And the first thing that happened to me when I got back was I had an argument with the mother-in-law. She rang me to ask why I wasn't opening the shop. I said the cat was stuck in the loft. I asked her if she could do it. She got really cross. I said, "Oh shit," and put the phone down. She rang me and said, "Don't you ever swear at me, young lady." After I'd rescued the cat I went to the shop but the staff ignored me. She'd told them to ostracise me. She'd decided she didn't want me to work there any longer and she demanded the company car back. John packed in his job as well. He said, "If Jane's not working, neither am I. You can stuff your job." The only difference was she sent *his* wages round every week.

'The officer from the QE2 kept ringing me up. He told me to get out of the whole situation and do something different. He was the trigger, you know. So I decided to break free – from the family business, from everything. I decided to make my own way.

'I had a mentally handicapped brother who I visited regularly. It was the sister who suggested nursing to me. I had no O-levels so I tried for a job as a nursing auxiliary in a geriatric ward. This was a bit different from being the boss's wife, and cleaning faeces was a bit different from selling stone from the cavern. The rift between me and my husband was growing. After a hard day cleaning muck I didn't want to be bothered with dinner parties. There were a lot of arguments and I moved out to my mother's. While I was there John had a girl to stay with him – a right gold-digger as well, or so the locals said,' Jane laughed, 'although of course that's what they used to say about me. When I came back to the house she'd got five pairs of knickers in my drawer and dresses in the wardrobe. She was intent on moving in. John turned nasty. He showed his nasty side to me for the first time. He criticised my body. I remember him saying, "Your tits are bloody pathetic. Michelle's are just right." It was very hurtful. I wanted to stay on in the house – he said he'd get me out. The tension got worse and worse. The mother-in-law demanded a proper rent from me. Up to then we'd just paid a nominal sum. She also dictated to me where I had to park my car. Little things like that, but it was getting me down. She accused me of having an affair with the QE2 officer – I wish I bloody well had, I can tell you. It was the worst time of my life – I was terrified of losing the children. John said he'd fight me for custody. I tried ringing my QE2 officer. He was never in, or so he said. Once I actually spoke to him on the phone. I knew it was him but he pretended to be his own cousin. I was getting very depressed so I moved out and John started living with his girlfriend – within a few weeks of me leaving, would you believe. I was alone in a little flat that I rented, in a box room. I worked as a geriatric nurse and the kids came to stay with me on my days off. We all slept in a single bed or on the floor. It was quite a come-down. I used to spend all my nights in a local nightclub, Josephine's. I lived in the place.

'The divorce came through eventually. His solicitor was very shrewd – he's been on *Mastermind* actually – mine was a bloody chuff. But I did get a reasonable maintenance eventually, after a very long fight. I got a little house in Stannington in the end – I called it my doll's house. I had nothing to put in it. I asked John to bring some stuff round. He gave me cooking pots covered in rust and some bedding that I used to let the kids play in the garden with. But I was surviving. I used to go to the nightclub with the nurses from work. We'd get off duty at ten o'clock, by eleven we'd be at the club. At ten o'clock I'd be cleaning up faeces – at twelve I was running my fingers through some guy's hair. It was a standing joke among us. After the club we'd go on to a casino for breakfast and then sit up and go to work at 5.30. John had always told me I'd be in the bloody gutter without him but I bloody well wasn't, I was surviving. I needed a good night's sleep though. I had a nanny who lived in now and I wouldn't go out until the kids were in bed. I tried ringing my QE2 man again and again – he still wasn't there or so he kept telling me. I was naive enough at the time of the cruise to believe that there might be something in our relationship. It was probably just a game to him.

'But things eventually got better. I met my present husband, Roy, at the nightclub. He's unbelievable. When I was working in the mornings he'd get up at 5 a.m. and clear the snow from my car, put on the car heater and run a bath for me. There's not many men like that. He was a divorcee. I qualified as a nurse and married him and then I started doing psychiatric nursing. I worked in a psychiatric hospital in Sheffield in a long-stay ward for highly disturbed patients. The only problem was they were saying the kinds of things that I was feeling all the time. It was difficult to be neutral with the patients. I just think everything got to me in the end. I had a breakdown and was off work for quite a while. I had three operations for growths in my breast at about that time as well.

'I felt I couldn't handle full-time work after my breakdown so I got a job in a jeweller's part-time, then in a Post Office. I wanted to be with Melanie my daughter more of the time, so I got a part-time job as a private nurse with Medicare.

'But then one night I went to an Ann Summers' party – you know where they sell naughty undies and sex aids. A friend invited me along, for a bit of a giggle. I was expecting a real stunner to be the demonstrator but she turned out to be very ordinary – in fact she looked like a school-marm. I couldn't get over it. I thought to myself, "I could do this – no problem. No more standing for long hours at a Post Office counter or anywhere else, that's for sure." It's just a laugh really, for the girls on a night out. I did it three nights a week in different houses. I got 20 per cent of what I sold. I never earned less than £10 night, which isn't bad money. The hostess gets 10 per cent and a free gift. No, I won't tell you what they usually take. But I can tell you I sold as much of the naughty bits as the lingerie. The most popular was a special cream – for men and women both, if you must know. I had to learn to use a "naughty-but-nice" type of dialogue. I didn't want to be crude. You know – when I passed round the crotchless knickers I'd say if you're ashamed of hanging it out on the line when you've washed it, ladies, just turn it upside down and it looks like a little top – that sort of thing.

Miss Gazette contestant, Sheffield, 1982

Women were intrigued to find out what was on offer. You have to have an open mind at these parties.

'I started arranging Ann Summers's shows at nightclubs. I used to have the models pose in some of the naughtiest items.'

Jane pulled out a wad of black and white photos and I couldn't help noticing the leather gear and Nazi hats interwoven with the micro nurses's uniforms of a kind you wouldn't have seen in any hospital. Leather straps, which covered the nipples and nearly covered the crotch, seemed very popular. It was a bit disconcerting, though, to see the barmaid from my local modelling some of the gear. 'Oh yes, I employ a lot of amateur models,' said Jane.

'Anyway,' said Jane, removing the pictures and continuing regardless, 'I thought to myself, "If I can sell it in nightclubs and party nights why not in a shop?" It was a big gamble though – the rent and rates in Sheffield are very high. I've had a shop for four months. I sell everything from Cupid panties with a cotton gusset at 90p to pure silk Janet Reger nighties for £540. Just look at the detail in the work. That's why I love lingerie – the perfection in the workmanship. Also, it makes a woman more confident. It's like make-up really. It makes girls feel delicate and feminine. Some lingerie can also redefine the shape of the body. I sell a sexy corselet. They're very useful for holding the tummy in. The English are supposed to be pear-shaped, with more down below than above. I myself am an English pear. But I'm amazed how many girls have big busts. Our reps all say that busts are getting bigger in England. I suppose it's the pill.

'At the moment, I'm trying to move over from the "glamour" end of the market to the more sophisticated end but I still do some "glamour" products. I have to keep some of them out of sight in my shop! But I want to concentrate more on the Margarita Freeman type of stuff – £78 for pure silk cami boxer basque and knickers – and Janet Reger – £54 for French knickers. I bought a lot of Janet Reger stock. You can get it much cheaper here than in London.

'Without the "glamour" wear I'd never have got started though, and I suppose if it hadn't been for the hysterectomy and my husband's taunts about my tits, I'd never have had the courage to move over to this line of business. I used to sell penis extensions for men in my Ann Summers' party plan – I wish I'd had one myself in the old days! It makes me laugh now to think how that must make men feel when they get presented with one and all their neighbours, who are at the party, know. I suppose it's a way of getting even in the end.'

January 1987

An American dream

America, the land of hope, promise and opportunity, is full. A lot of media attention has been given to the Mexicans who in their thousands risk the swim across the Rio Grande and work illegally in the southern states of the USA. But not all illegal immigrants in America are of Mexican origin, of course. Take Martin, for example – ex-Sheffield steel worker, ex-Sheffield entrepreneur.

'I've just got back after working there for five years illegally – without a work permit,' he said. 'But I never meant to go as a worker anyway – I've always been an entrepreneur. I went to America for the big-time. I started at the bottom and stayed there, but it was still the best time of my life. I had a real good time,' said Martin, shifting into the American vernacular.

Martin was the kind of man who you could tell has been around. 'Put it this way. I've worked in thirty-two different markets in the North of England,' he said proudly. 'I learned how to pitch and sell pans or miracle cleaning fluid or whatever you fancy when I was still a lad. That's how I started and you've either got the gift of the gab or you haven't, and I've certainly got it.' After working as a universal miller in a Sheffield steel mill, Martin was nicely set up with a stall selling ladies' fashion-wear in Sheffield market; a shop in a pub – 'I know it sounds funny but it did good business. The pub was in a courtyard and the shop was in one corner'; and a shop in Doncaster. 'Nicely set up, I'd say,' said Martin, 'nice middle-of-the-road prices – nice and steady.'

'Then came the recession,' said Martin. 'I could see it coming. Doncaster was hit first – business took a terrible dive. It was all quite sudden really, looking back. I came home one day and I just thought to myself, "I've had it up to here with this bloody country – unemployment, 15 per cent VAT – I'm off." I'd got friends in Las Vegas. I just said to my wife Gill, "Let's get over there. It's got to be better than here." We're young, adaptable, I thought, let's give it a go. So we set off to Nevada on holiday to look for a business. We were prepared to be very flexible – we looked at fashion shops, slot-machine arcades, mom-and-pop-type restaurants. And within a couple of days we'd found this little restaurant in one of the rougher parts of Las Vegas. So we bought it. The asking price was $45,000 and we put $1,000 deposit on it. We got ourselves an attorney – that cost $150 as well. He told us that if we invested between $30,000 and $40,000 in a business, we'd be okay for an E2 on our passport, which would allow us to work in America. We were over the bleedin' moon. We came back to Sheffield and sold up – our house, our shops, our market stall, everything. We got about sixty-five grand in all.

'We went back to the Embassy in London and told them we'd bought a café in Las Vegas and we'd need an E2 on our passport. They said, "Where's your green card? You can't work there without a green card." I told them I wasn't going to be working – I was going to be the gaffer. He said if you're taking money out of the till, you're working. He asked us for our passports but I just said "Bugger this!" You see I didn't want him to stamp anything on it. We just walked out. So I said to the wife, "We're either going in dead straight or dead bent, and it looks as if it's going to have to be dead bent." So we did. I had this friend who explained to me all the ins and outs of going in illegal. We went in as visitors. We told the immigration we were staying in the Holiday Inn, Santa Monica – it sounded posh enough. We moved into the café and paid cash on the nail. In America there are two things you need – ID and a social security number. To get a social security number you need a green card. But my mate had told me you can get a social security number if you tell them you want to open a bank account. So I just went to this place – the equivalent of a town hall – and filled a form in. I showed my British passport for identification and gave them our real estate agent's address – he was bent, by the way. Six weeks later the social security number arrives. We were off. We worked as a couple in the café and we employed one girl. It was a struggle right from the start. The café was on the industrial side of Las Vegas, catering for people who were basically broke. We'd open every morning at 5.00 a.m. and serve breakfast to these cowboys, and I use the word carefully, from the Teamsters Union. Then one day this official came in and asked to see our beer and wine licence. Of course we hadn't got one because we were illegal. That was it – we had to stop serving drinks and our takings took a real dive.

'We knew we had to do something – the café was losing money – but it had to be real gentle because we were there illegal. I'd got my brother-in-law over by now as well. So we decided to set up a side-line – a little window-cleaning outfit. We called ourselves "Lovely Windows" and we got these flyers printed: "Two English guys from Sheffield, England, will make your windows beautiful". We distributed them all around these beautiful homes and we put the number of the café on the flyer. We charged $25 a house inside and out. We gave them a bit of fanny – you know, all the chat. It was bloody hard work. No sooner had you put the water on than it would be dry; we'd have to go out before the sun got real hot. We'd be out at six o'clock in the morning cleaning bloody windows. But we ended up doing about four a day and making about $100 a day and about $500 dollars a week from the café. But we were still barely getting by – after we'd paid the rent on the café and our waitress's salary. We were desperate and we couldn't go on social security – we were aliens after all. We had to try something else. The brother-in-law managed to get a job in Caesar's Palace – as a lifeguard in one of their pools. That was done through a friend.

'Things weren't working out. We put the café up for sale. I paid $45,000 for it. I sold it for $15,000 and only managed to get $10,000 off the guy. Talk about a bloody riches to rags tale. But just before I moved out of it I met this old man who told me he owned a gold mine in Nelson, about an hour's drive from Las Vegas. He said, "Why don't you come in with me as a partner?" So I bought myself in – for $1,200. When I got there I couldn't believe it. I thought to myself, "I'm nearer the bleedin' moon here than I am to Sheffield." It was the middle of the desert, there were no shops, nothing. And I saw rattle-snakes, giant spiders, you name it. It was 120 degrees. We tried a different kind of gold mining where you bulldoze off the top soil and put it through a sluice. Did we find any gold? You must be joking. We never got that far. I could never get the bulldozer fixed. I used to borrow this crane from these guys – we'd no money so we used to pay them in crates of Budweiser. They were all alcoholics – there was nothing else to do in the middle of the desert. My partner used to eat rattlesnakes. I thought I'd go nuts there. I grew to hate that guy. I was just sitting there in this desert one night, in the middle of nowhere, it was like the moon – honest to God – it was just like being stranded on the moon, and I thought to myself, "I'd give anything to be back in the Crosspool Tavern in Sheffield with a pint of Stones bitter." I'd be at the gold mine five days a week and then back window-cleaning two days a week. It was unreal.

'I knew I had to do something else and I knew I'd need a driving licence. There was no way I was going to get one in Nevada – I'd need a green card – but my pal told me if I told a few stories I'd be able to get one in California. So Gill and me drove 260 miles to Barstow in California. We had to take a driving test but it was dead easy. We gave as our home address my cousin's in San Francisco. My cousin sent the licences to us in Las Vegas. So we went down to the Nevada licensing authority with this California driving licence and told them we wanted a Nevada licence. I told them I was an American citizen and I'd been born in Boston, Massachusetts – there's a lot of Paddies there. My wife told them she was born in Florida. We gave my cousin's San Francisco address again. I even put on the accent – it's a hell of an accent to imitate but they fell for it. So there we were with Nevada licences as ID. Gill got a job with a doctor as a receptionist with her driving licence with the social security number on it. She told them she was an American citizen and her dad was a GI who brought her mum from England. We were getting awfully good at lying at this point!

'I had to get out of the gold mine and window-cleaning business so I met this guy from an Irish show band at a party. I said to him, "You work all the big casinos. You must know some casino people." So he said to me, "Can you deal blackjack?" I've got a friend who runs some casinos in England and he'd taught me a little before I left – just in case the café fell through. Anyway I went to this dealing school and got hired by the Sundance Hotel. This is one of the poor hotels in Las Vegas – not very many high rollers there. All dealers want to end up on the strip at MGM, Caesar's Palace, the Tropicana, the Dunes, the Flamingo, the Sands, the Desert Inn or something like that. The Sundance is downtown. I told them I was an American citizen. They always asked, "How come you've got an English accent, Marty" I told them I'd been living in England for thirty years. The only problem with being a croupier was that you need a sheriff's card and I thought to myself, "I'm here illegal – how the hell am I going to get a sheriff's card?" Anyway I went along with my social security number and my driving licence as ID and I got it – a sheriff's licence with my photo on it. Extra ID! I was over the moon, and I was picking up $30 a day wages and $35 a day tips from the casino. I was there eight months and through my Irish show band connection, I got a job at the Stardust Casino after working for a while at its sister hotel, the Freemount.

'This was the big-time, dealing to the big action, although they say it's run by the Mafia. I worked there three and a half years – and what an eye-opener. We had guys just run in and grab handfuls of hundred-dollar chips and run out again. Prostitutes would be in the bar at nights. They'd say, "Hey, any of you guys looking for a tune up?" They just loved my accent. One girl who used to play my table used to wear a bleeper – she used to fix housewives up with clients in the afternoon. The vice was real organised. And being a croupier was very hard work – in America you can handle the cards in blackjack, unlike England, so you're always watching out for punters to mark the cards with their fingernails or whatever. And it was often these old women, old retired dears, professional sharks, who'd be up to it. Everybody there is chasing for the mighty dollar in whatever way they can. I was on $45 a day and $100 a day tips. They're a big tipping nation – it keeps you on your toes. Even unskilled workers can pick up a fortune in tips. Gill was picking up $600 a week working as a receptionist as well. We were smiling – it was the time of our lives. Fantastic – the wealth, the suntan, the barbecues. I did everything. I've been and seen all the top stars – Sinatra, Rod Stewart.

'But I really missed Sheffield, I really missed the sense of humour – it's crazy really. The Americans just didn't understand a good old-fashioned Yorkshire double meaning. I'd say to some guy with a horrible check suit, "Are you wearing that for a bet?" and it would go straight over his head. They're a nation that loves to listen, but they've no sense of humour. I taught them all Cockney rhyming slang – they loved that. All the croupiers would be saying "Look at the Bristols on her, Marty." They loved my saying "birds" as well. They used to say, "why can't you call them 'broads' like everyone else?" I lived real well in America but I'd gone to make my fortune and hadn't. When you lose a lot of money it knocks something out of you. I had to come home.' He paused for a moment. 'So here I am.'

Martin now ran a pub – in Sheffield. He'd been back six months. He got the pub with the help of his father-in-law who works for a brewery. 'We were very grateful but the hardest thing around here is getting the glasses off the customers. It's their second home and nobody wants to go to their real home and they're not the sort you can push around. There's not a lot of fun around here to be honest – there's a lot of unemployment and a lot of crime. There's a lot of thieves and vagabonds who come here who like to keep themselves to themselves but they're basically good people. Good people in hard times. Of course, I talk about the States all the time, and I've got a few mementos just to prove it wasn't a dream.'

He pointed up at the wall. And there he was – tanned with shades, barely recognisable. 'That's me and Bob Geldof at the McGuigan fight. I got a priest to take the picture; and there's Bob and Paula Yates and me and Bomber Graham and Brendan Ingle in Las Vegas. One customer last night told me he was sure it was just a cardboard cut-out of Bob Geldof like they have on Brighton Pier. I told him he was barred.'

Nostalgia flooded in. 'My wife and I would have given anything for that green card, you know, so that we could have stayed there and made a better go of things. We'd still love it today. America is a great country – just ask Gill.

'My daughter's just gone back to the States. Her boyfriend, who's real rich, rang up last night and said, "I want to come and see you in your quaint little pub in Sheffield, England." When he gets to Sheffield he'll think the town hall clock has fallen on his head. He'll shit himself when he sees the place. They think they've got unemployment there, and a recession. Wait until he comes here. We were bottom of the heap there and it's still like a bleedin' dream to the people round here.'

February 1987

Moving down

It forbade all outdoor relief in money or food. The only relief offered to the poor was admission to the new workhouses which were promptly erected all over the country . . . The food is worse than that enjoyed by the poorest labourer in employment. In return the pauper is forced to work harder than he would in a normal job . . . Their diet generally consists of potatoes, very bad bread, gruel, and little or no beer . . . The pauper who fails to do the work allocated to him has to go without food. The pauper who wants to go outside must ask the workhouse master for permission . . . The men are engaged in stone-breaking . . . Women, children and old folk pick oakum . . . Pauper families are separated in the workhouse so as to stop the 'superfluous' population from breeding and to save the children from the 'demoralizing' influence of their parents. Fathers, mothers and children are housed in different wings of the workhouse and are allowed to see each other only at fixed, rare intervals and then only if – in the opinion of the workhouse officials – their conduct has been exemplary. (Friedrich Engels, *The Conditions of the Working Class in England*, 1845)

The telly for company

My directions had been extremely precise: 'Just opposite the gasworks in Garston in Liverpool. The flats that used to be lovely before the cockroaches came. Just ask anybody, everybody knows the flats, and the cockroaches. When you get to the flats, it's number . . . You have to ring the bell outside, Lizzie will be expecting you.'

Lizzie's daughter-in-law had given me the directions. The daughter-in-law was sixty-six. My anxieties had started even then. Who's going to believe an article about an old-age pensioner living alone, when her flat is situated opposite a gasworks, for goodness' sake? It's too much of a cliché. But it was a good landmark for direction finding, if not scene setting.

I approached the front door of the flats' complex, being careful not to step on any cockroaches. I read the large yellow sign – 'Beware. During the hours of darkness, these premises are patrolled by guard dogs.' There was no sign of the guard dogs, or the cockroaches for that matter. An old grey-haired lady watched me approach from a window on the first floor. She was staring at me in a kind of vacant way, as if she stood there all day staring at the strangers come to visit. Always waiting expectantly. Always standing there, just in case. A look of very mild expectation laced with resignation etched on her face. It reminded me of the look you get from those old ladies you see in hospital during visiting time, the old ladies that nobody ever visits. The creatures that time forgot. They watch the daffodils and the grapes being carried to all the other beds. They pretend not to mind.

I pressed the combination of keys corresponding to Lizzie's number and waited for the voice to come over the intercom and the front door to open. But they didn't. I tried once again and then again. The old grey-haired lady, from the first-floor window, stared harder now, and suddenly her body jolted into movement. It shuddered as she started to hobble down in my direction. Many minutes later, the front door opened. There stood the old lady with that same vacant look on her face. 'If you're looking for Lizzie, she's gone out – hours ago. It's such a lovely day to go out into the country. Her son took her out. It's such a lovely day to be out and about.' I asked if I could check Lizzie's flat just in case. And for the first time the face of the old lady showed some real undiluted emotion – fear. The security of the flats complex had been increased recently, even she knew that. I had been told that previously you could just walk straight into the flats. The only problem was that burglars were doing just that, and removing anything that wasn't nailed down, and several things that were, including the coinbox of the public telephone, the clock on the wall and most of the prints used to decorate the place. So what had I come for? The old lady's expression said it all. She stepped back as I seemed to push in past her. I passed one print on the wall – that dark swarthy girl with the big watery eyes and the strangely Caucasian features that they used to sell in Woolies. Her big doleful eyes seemed to follow me as I made my way on to the first floor with the old lady hobbling behind me, trying to keep up with me to see what mischief I might be getting up to.

I rang Lizzie's door, and I could just about make out this very quiet shuf-fling noise coming from behind it. The old grey-haired lady could hear it too, and she hobbled off, talking to herself as she went – back to her watch-tower, back to her lonely vigil. Lizzie opened the door about a minute later. The first thing I noticed was her eyes, they had this sparkle in them. They were the eyes of a young girl, and a very mischievous young girl at that. They weren't like the eyes of the old lady that had seen me to the door. 'You're an hour and five minutes late,' she said. 'Is that how you do things these days?' Having put me firmly in my place, for I was indeed exactly one hour and five minutes late, she motioned me into the living room. She walked in front and you could see that she could only move with the greatest difficulty, using a stick. Her body had been bowed by her eighty-six years until it looked ready to snap, like a bow that had been put under too much strain. But when she sat down, she sat upright, and her eyes dominated the conversation once again.

I looked around the flat. The living room had a curtain at one side of the room which covered her bed. You could just about make out her pink nightie folded neatly on one side of it. 'Not far to go to retire for the evening,' she said – 'just as well. The nightie's see-through, by the way, if you're inter-ested.' And she squealed with laughter. 'I'm looking for a toyboy, at the moment.' I could see that Lizzie was going to be calling all the shots in this interview. 'Now what can I do you for?' she said.

I told her that I was doing a series about people in the North, and that I wanted to include an old-age pensioner living alone. She looked at me as if I and the rest of the world had gone mad. 'What's the matter, isn't there any news in the world anymore? Isn't anything happening out there?' she said. I asked her to humour me by telling me anyway.

'Well, I can't cook for myself anymore, ever since I scalded myself with the kettle, so my daughter comes around every day and makes me dinner, and cleans. I have one daughter and four sons still alive, and they come to visit me as does my daughter-in-law who lived with me for nearly eighteen years. We're more like sisters really, she's sixty-six, it keeps me young having young people about the place. But I'm one of the lucky ones, I had a big family, some of the old people here never have anyone to call on them. Never ever. You know, this place used to be a lovely place to live. I was on top of the world when I got this flat. But all the nice old people have gone. They've moved some old confused people into the flats, and to be honest they don't make very good neighbours. One of my neighbours called Billy comes and sits with me for an hour every weekday from five o'clock to six o'clock. He's one of the ones that isn't confused, as bright as a pin he is. But I don't invite many people into my flat. We like to keep ourselves to ourselves here, that's the way we all like it. But Billy is an exception – I'm trying to get him married off to my daughter-in-law, but I wouldn't want him. I'd want somebody that was a bit more capable, if you know what I mean.' And she squealed with laughter again.

'Apart from my family, I've got the telly for company.' The telly was on in the background, as we spoke. 'My favourite is the wrestling. I love the wrest-ling, particularly the big men. If Big Daddy was to lose a bit of weight, he'd

Miss Kath Sharples in her sheltered housing accommodation, Oldham, 1985

not be so bad, you know. But all women love the wrestling. It used to be on later on a Saturday afternoon. But they moved it to an earlier time and now I hear that they're going to take it off altogether. It's terrible news for the likes of us. When the wrestling was on later in the day, all the men would go off to the football, and all the women would settle down to the wrestling. I used to go and watch the wrestling at Garston baths. They'd cover the baths with floorboards. One night this big Canadian was wrestling. God, was he handsome. All the lights went out and he took his dressing gown off and you know what? He didn't have any trunks on underneath. I don't know whether it was an accident or not, but I had a good look. I'll tell you that for nothing. He was fighting Billy Pie that night. He's probably dead and buried as well now. I'll tell you what if I could walk without my stick or without my wheelchair, I'd liven up some of these young people about today.'

Her wheelchair sat in the corner of the room, Lizzie needs it to travel more than a few feet. But, rather unfortunately you might say, she lives on the first floor of the flats. There's no lift. She only gets out of the flat therefore when one of her sons comes to visit and physically carries her down the stairs. There's a public phone in the corridor of the flats so that she can keep in touch with her family, but Lizzie can't get the money into the coinbox any longer. She doesn't want to be moved to the groundfloor because the flats down there are infested with cockroaches. So she's stranded on the first floor, waiting for someone to arrive to allow her out. 'Billy is a little past carrying me and the chair, otherwise I'd be in clover,' she said with a great smile on her face. 'Now my nights, I go to bed every night at about 10 o'clock with my Ovaltine and my tablets. Ovaltine always does the trick and sends me off to sleep. I wake up at about 2.30 am to see what's going on. I always have a good look through the window. There's a good view of the gasworks from my window. During the war, the Germans, and I don't mean Stan Boardman's Germans, dropped a landmine on a little parachute that landed on the gasworks. If it had gone off, the whole area would have been devastated, me included. I can't look out without thinking of what has happened and what might have been. Such memories.

'After my little quiet think, it's time for bed again, and up at 6.30 am. I have to get up early, it takes me nearly two hours to get dressed in the morning. I have to have a little rest after I put on each item. But I'll do it if it kills me. I always say that I'll die getting myself washed. There's a bath in my flat, by the way, but I can't get into it myself anymore, so I have to wait for my daughter to come around on a Friday night to help me into the bath. There's also a shower down the corridor, but there's no shower rail to hang on to, so I can't use it. It's such a pity, because I bought a shower cap and everything.

'I've had a good life, the thing that I always loved, though, was the singing. People always told me that I had a lovely voice. And every Saturday night I'd be in the pub with the relatives for a sing-song. But I stopped singing when my oldest son John died seven years ago. No matter how old you are it breaks your heart losing a child.' And she motioned towards an old photograph on top of the cabinet where a big proud woman was surrounded by boys in caps and girls in smocks. The big, proud woman had the same fiery eyes as Lizzie. 'That's my John there, and that's him when he got back from Burma after the war. He got £16 for the six years he served in the army. His wife bought herself and me a blouse each with the money.' And her eyes started to sparkle a little bit more, with tears this time. All powerful emotions seem to light the eyes up – one way or another.

Up to that point my own background had been studiously ignored, but Lizzie began to focus in on my accent. 'What part of Belfast did you say you were from?' she enquired. 'My brother-in-law was in the Black-and-Tans, you know,' she told me. 'He met a neighbour from Woolton, the village where I grew up, when he was over in Ireland, and he was ready to kill him. It's a powerful thing religion. I have a neighbour from a few doors down that's turned her little flat into a chapel, with an altar in one corner. Billy says that he can hear her praying at nights. But I'm a Protestant, like yourself. You know we had religious trouble in Garston before there was trouble in Ireland, and we've always celebrated the twelfth of July. Every twelfth the Orange Lodge would go on a day trip to Southport, a bit better than just marching through the centre of Belfast, if you ask me. We used to follow the band and sing all those Orange songs.'

I asked Lizzie to sing me just one, but she just looked at the photo of John, as a young lad, and said that she couldn't. 'What's a mother got to sing about when she loses her son, tell me that?' I asked her to hum one of the

Gaynor, age 20, Sheffield, 1988

songs then instead, and tell me the words afterwards, if she liked. She broke into a half-singing, half-speaking voice – 'Billy came from Ireland/A Protestant to be/He brought with him a root/Of the good old Orange tree... We used to sing at the top of our voices as we passed the old chapel in Garston.' And her eyes sparkled once again, as she remembered the long nights of passion in those days. Passion that stirs the soul – be it love, hate or sheer bloody-mindedness. Passion in the days when Lizzie had to wait on no man.

And as I left her little flat I could still hear her humming above the noise of the television, and the old confused people still talking to themselves.

June 1988

No place to go

Wayne had worked in Tesco's. He had to get up at 7.30 to get there in the morning. His mates, he said, were out boozing at nights and they could have a lie-in. They were all on the dole. Wayne decided he was missing out, so he packed up work and stopped paying housekeeping to his mother. His father kicked him out. 'We never got on anyway', Wayne said, 'but I guess I deserved it. I lived in a park in Sheffield for four weeks – it was bloody cold – it was October. One of my friends used to bring me old newspapers to put down my trousers. One afternoon, I met one of my father's friends. He

Homeless men, Lancaster, Christmas 1996

brought me home for a cup of tea. While he was making it I nicked a fiver and a watch off his dresser. He got the police, but he didn't press charges. He just wanted his watch back. My father worked shifts so I used to nip home in the evenings for my tea and then out again. It was four weeks before a mate I hadn't seen for a long time told me about a night shelter in Sheffield. I moved in there.'

Lorraine was sixteen but looked much younger. The first tentative applications of make-up, inexpertly applied, made her look like a child dressing up, pretending to be an adult. She had a slight speech impediment and was shy and unsure of herself. Her parents had picked on her because of her stammer, she said. She became the family annoyance, the scapegoat. Her father battered her. She had to leave home. She was now in a hostel for homeless teenagers.

John was a trainee hairdresser. He was seventeen, young and trendy. His parents were very religious. They didn't approve of his choice of life style or his choice of career. There had been a lot of tension in the family as they had tried to make him conform to their values and standards. He was beaten by his father on a number of occasions, and arrived at a night shelter badly marked. 'He wouldn't take his shirt off at first,' said the warden. 'It took me a while to work out why.'

Homelessness is on the increase, especially among the young. We know a little of the reasons. The Department of the Environment produced a report in 1981 called 'Single and Homeless' based on a survey of seven different local authorities. Among the young, parental disputes and family break-up were identified as the principal reasons for their losing their last secure home. What was alarming about the report was the identification of cycles of homelessness, with the majority of the young single homeless living in a variety of temporary accommodations and insecure homes. Few had managed to set up independent homes successfully. Homelessness, like cancer, develops and spreads.

It is impossible to put a precise figure on the extent of the homelessness problem. Impossible because to get even an approximate figure one would have to trawl all the parks and derelict buildings for those sleeping rough (called 'skippering'), tour all the emergency night shelters and hostels for homeless people, visit all the dosshouses and bed-and-breakfast dives and, in addition, go around neighbourhoods interviewing people to determine who was putting friends up. Nevertheless, it is possible to spot potential trends from the figures that are available. Centrepoint, the emergency night shelter in Soho, reported a 40 per cent increase in requests for admission from 1978 to 1981. In Sheffield, the number of people who approached the Housing Department claiming to be homeless more than doubled in the same period. Roundabout, an emergency night shelter in Sheffield for young people between sixteen and twenty-one, which opened in 1977, reported 153 people using it a year later (102 male, 51 female), and 247 last year – a 61 per cent increase in a five-year period. The proportion of girls using the night shelter had more than doubled in the same period. The Sheffield branch of CHAR (the Campaign for the Homeless and Rootless) rang round all the night shelters and hostels in Sheffield on one particular night in February 1984. They discovered a total of 362 single homeless people and 33 families (which included 53 children). And that was just on one arbitrary night in the coldest month of the year in a city of half a million. It is a major problem and a growing one, especially among the young.

There are a number of specific problems for young people. Council accommodation is difficult for them to acquire because they are not considered vulnerable under the Housing (Homeless Persons) Act, 1977, and therefore are not viewed as a priority group on the Housing Department's waiting list. In addition, young people under eighteen can't get council accommodation and, until recently, couldn't put their name on a council waiting list (the age limit of eighteen has now been lowered to sixteen in Sheffield). Furniture and household equipment also take both time and money to acquire. Young homeless people usually have little of either of these valuable resources. Grants are available from the DHSS but these are difficult to get. The alternative to council housing – private accommodation – is often too expensive for young people, and landlords are very reluctant to accept tenants who are unemployed. Consequently, the young single homeless have to turn to night shelters, hostels and bed-and-breakfast dives or derelict houses.

So what kinds of accommodation is available to young homeless people? I visited one emergency night shelter in Sheffield, Roundabout, and the Granville Road project offering longer-term accommodation. Both deal with single homeless young people between sixteen and twenty-one. (Roundabout, in emergency cases, will allow a fifteen-year-old to stay.)

Roundabout is both an emergency night shelter, open from 8 pm to 9 am for people who present themselves at the door, and an adjoining house of eight bedsits. The night shelter can accommodate seven (four in one room, three in another), but the number can vary in practice between two and twelve (couches are available). It costs £4 for a bed for the night but Audrey Waters, the warden, stressed that 'no one would be refused admission if they had no money' (at least for three consecutive nights). The maximum stay in the night shelter is two weeks; in the bedsits, one year (the licence renewable on a quarterly basis). Roundabout provides detailed statistics of the young people who use their facilities. In 1983, for instance, 247 young people spent a total of 1,684 nights in the night shelter (the bedsits are in constant use and in great demand). The majority of people who use Roundabout hear about it through the grapevine or see Roundabout's adverts in youth centres. However, a proportion were also referred by the police, the Probation Service, the Family and Community Services Department, the Samaritans, the Salvation Army, even by British Rail. Nearly three-quarters of the boys who used Roundabout in 1983 were offenders, but only one third of the girls. If anyone is violent on the premises they are banned – for life, if necessary. (This has only happened twice since it opened.) Roundabout refuse admission to anyone under the influence of drink, drugs or, more commonly, glue. They are told to come back next day when they've sobered up. (I'm not sure what the correct expression is for glue here.)

When I visited the night shelter, it had five residents – four boys and one girl. Two of the lads had come to Roundabout after a period of 'skippering', after they'd left home because of rows. One lad had come straight to Roundabout after being thrown out of his home for getting into trouble with the police. The other lad had had a row with his family and then with the friends he'd moved in with. The girl had had a row with her mother and her new stepfather. So here they were. Belongings in Adidas sports bags or polythene carrier bags. There are no lock-up facilities at the shelter and petty pilfering, according to the warden, is rife. Belongings can, however, be left in polythene bags in the office. The shelter is locked all day, so the temporary residents have to find something to do all day long. As the warden pointed out, 'Sunday is a terrible day'. Tensions can also run high. One skinhead who stayed at the shelter, with HATE tattooed on the knuckles of his left hand and LOVE on the knuckes of his right hand, complained in a private moment about one of the drop-in centres in town. 'You play spot-the-white man in there.' The skinhead had moved from Plymouth to Sheffield. 'But I've only been in three fights since I came to Sheffield, which isn't bad really.' 'No,' I said, 'I suppose it isn't.' The lad in the bed next to his was a West Indian. You could see it wasn't going to be a comfortable night.

After the two weeks in Roundabout the trouble really begins. The lucky ones may get into one of the bedsits; the majority can't, of course. (A major role of the staff at Roundabout is to help them find some longer-term accommodation.) Only a fifth return home after their stay. The rest move in with friends, find a bedsit or a bed-and-breakfast place, get a council flat or leave Sheffield – sometimes to be homeless elsewhere. Roundabout's statistics have one note of optimism – only one person last year went back to sleeping rough after his stay.

The trouble isn't over for those who get bedsits or council accommodation. Betty Horton, from the Home Finding Unit of the Family and Community

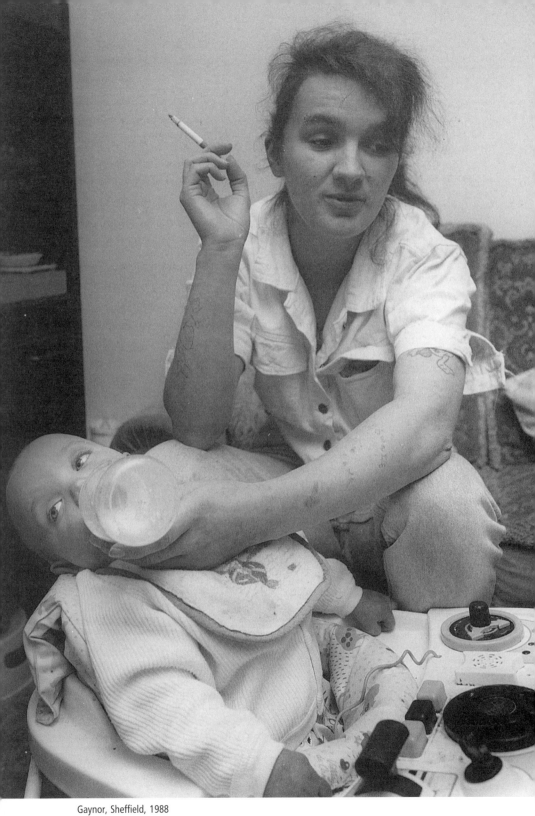

Gaynor, Sheffield, 1988

Services Department, said, 'It's one thing getting a young person a flat, it's another thing getting them to look after it, and themselves in it.' Living in a flat – cooking, cleaning, keeping it in order, paying the rent and finding the money for it, saving up for furniture, getting on with the other occupants and the neighbours – involves a set of skills which most of us take for granted. 'But,' Betty Horton said, 'many of these homeless youngsters haven't acquired them.' CHAR in Sheffield had been pushing for a 'homemaking' scheme for workers within the Housing Department to help young people settle into tenancies, to guide them through the Social Security maze and to assist them in setting up home. (A similar scheme was already working in Glasgow and in several other major cities.) Some people, however, don't see the problem or the need, Sheffield's *Morning Star* newspaper said in an editorial in April 1984, 'Young people do not need well-meaning snoopers telling them how to suck eggs.' It went on, 'Leaving home is a great experience for most young people.' It failed to see that for many, it isn't. Sucking eggs is one thing, understanding the Social Security system in order to get the money to buy them, being able to cook them and tidy away the shells afterwards is something else.

The Granville Road Homelessness Project is an attempt to smooth the transition from emergency night shelter to independent life in one's own accommodation. It offers accommodation for up to one year, mainly for teenagers between sixteen and eighteen. It has room for eight. The young people have a key to the front door and a key to their own bedroom. 'The aim of the project,' said Ruth Wallis, the warden, 'is to encourage and teach the youngsters to live independently but under some degree of supervision.' Ruth acted a lot like a surrogate mother – indeed some residents quite unselfconsciously called her 'mother'. 'It's easier than being their natural mother,' she said, 'you can view them more objectively.'

When I visited the project, it had four boys and four girls. Two of the boys came as dedicated glue-sniffers. Ruth had to play the role of counsellor. 'When Jason came he was right into sniffing glue so we talked a bit and he said he'd stop, but he still sniffed glue; so we talked a bit more and he still sniffed it. In the end, he did stop – he gets drunk now instead.' The glue-sniffers' parents (or foster parents in one case) couldn't tolerate them in the end. The other two lads – as were the four girls – were also there as a result of family breakdown. One girl had been ostracised by her family because she had a coloured boyfriend. Another was ostracised because of her speech impediment.

At Granville Road, they got the opportunity to learn some basic skills. One cupboard had holes punched in it after one resident had a temper tantrum. 'They have to learn to channel their aggression,' Ruth said. The kitchen had the remains of a pudding on the ceiling as a reminder of one resident's attempt at cooking. Ruth recognised the huge responsibility on her shoulders. For most of the kids, it's make-or-break time. Family life has failed them, or they have failed it. The easy options beckon. 'One lad used to flog stolen goods to the window cleaner. We couldn't do anything with him. He ended up in court.'

I heard that one girl when she came was on the fringe of prostitution. 'I don't know what it means, though' – Ruth laughed – 'whether you do it and don't get paid or you don't do it and you do get paid. We've had girls staying here physically pursued by pimps. I've told them to clear off.'

It's the last chance for many, in a different sort of family with the rules relaxed (residents can come and go as they please, and have a boyfriend or girlfriend staying with them for two consecutive nights in any one week). They need to develop new rules and standards about what is and isn't acceptable. 'They have to learn to live with others, to be considerate,' Ruth said, 'that blasting music in the middle of the night isn't on. On the other hand, some of them accept a bit too much – we've had a lot of trouble with girls being beaten up by their boyfriends. They've seen it at home and don't think too much of it. I have to persuade them that this isn't necessarily right or natural.'

Apart from the freedom, the teenagers often find themselves with money in their pockets for the first time. The vast majority are unemployed and they get a boarder's rate of £71 a week from Social Security; this leaves them £36 after the rent is paid. They have to feed themselves out of this, but it is still a lot of money for the average sixteen-year-old. Ruth stressed that they have to learn to spend it wisely, but some clearly don't. When I was there, the two glue-sniffers in their stretch denims and Wrangler T-shirts were joking to each other about how they behave when the Social Security money arrives. 'He's always acting the big man with the Hamlets and the whiskies,' one said. One girl asked for a cigarette and insisted on a Benson and Hedges. Paul Young leered down at them from a poster on the wall.

Time was also a problem. Ruth said that the majority didn't get up until the afternoon and complain about having to get up one morning a week to sign on the dole. I asked one girl what she did with her time. 'What did you do yesterday, for example?' I enquired. 'Oh, got some green spray and sprayed it all over my face and head with a friend. We had to get a taxi home because we didn't want anybody to see us.' The remains of the green spray were clearly visible on her neck beside a large love bite. Ruth added when she had left the room, 'You always know when she's got up – she plays her favourite record, "Words Don't Come Easy", over and over again.'

But Ruth had to cut through this superficial gloss – no matter how irritating and off-putting – to get right beneath the surface. 'You should see her in the middle of the night – frightened and alone. That's when it really hurts, being without a permanent home. And I do worry about the future for them. What future have some of them got? And what would they be doing if it wasn't for the project?'

November 1984

Kicked out of the house

Lee left home after a row with his dad. He slept rough for three weeks in a park in Sheffield. It was September. His friend used to bring him food from home. A social worker whom he met by accident in the park told him about an emergency night shelter in Sheffield – Roundabout. He went to

Roundabout, and got one of their bedsits for six months. At one point he tried moving to Yarmouth with another bloke and two girls. One of the girls gave him £200 for safe keeping. He left them all stranded. He got six months in Norwich prison. After he got out of prison, he moved back to Roundabout. He got a job as a glass collector in a nightclub and found some digs. Things were looking up. He was told by his employer that he would be considered for a trainee manager's position. But then he had an argument with his land-lord and he packed his digs up. He went to work as usual that day and, at the end of the night, got chatting to one of the regular customers. Lee told him about his predicament, and John said he would put him up. John lived in a terraced house in Crookes, in Sheffield – Lee noticed that John was visited a lot by a West Indian whom Lee just calls 'the Jamaican'.

'The Jamaican and John used always to have little silver packages on the table, but when I came into the room, they'd always gather them up very quickly. After a while they showed me what was in them – "Paki black" and "red Leb". John asked me if I'd be interested in taking four packets down to the Students' Union for a guy. He said he'd give me seven pounds. I said it sounded OK to me – not bad for an hour's work. After a while I used to go to Newcastle and Birmingham to fetch some – a 'weight' at a time. It cost £360. I used to get £30 a go profit. I was making three trips a week. It was worth quite a bit and I felt quite flash. But then one of the dealers got busted in the Students' Union. I thought things were getting a bit risky so one night I just buggered off with the float – £280. I went to my granddad's in Edinburgh for a couple of weeks. After about three weeks I came back to Sheffield, to Roundabout, but they said I'd been there enough so they sent me to Pat Moss House – a probation hostel which had some space. John, in the mean-time, had been going round pubs asking people if they knew where I was. He traced me to Pat Moss House – he'd got the address off a girl from the dole office – he said he was looking for a close friend and she gave him the address because she fancied him. John told me I had to leave Pat Moss House and come back and live with him. He told me I had to work the debt off. I did it in four months doing property repairs for Pakistanis in Tinsley. After I left John's I moved back to Roundabout. Then I met Carol, who's now my wife.'

Carol's history up to this point was very different. She had never been in trouble with the police. Her mother had kicked her out for coming in late. She was sixteen. She went to live with an aunt and an uncle. At the time she was working in a shop. But her aunt thought that Carol and her husband were having an affair, so she kicked her out. 'We weren't,' said Carol, 'we were just close – he didn't have any daughters.' Kicked out not in any meta-phorical sense – she was literally kicked out without her shoes and socks. She spent a week sleeping rough. 'I spent most of my time hanging about a bus stop,' she said. A friend told her to go to the Probation Service. 'I said "what for?" – I've never been in trouble.' But the Probation Service told her about Roundabout. There she met Lee. Together they got a council flat in Hyde Park Flats. Lee had made things up with his dad, and Carol and Lee started to set up house. They bought a suite, bedding, pots and pans, TV, fridge and so on. But one day Lee spotted the Jamaican at the flats.

'I couldn't go back,' he said. 'I was terrified – I hadn't paid him his half of the float.' So they sold some of their electrical equipment and gave the rest of their belongings to a friend for taking their key back to the council. They moved to King's Lynn. There they got lodgings. 'It was a disgrace,' said Carol, 'four blokes in one room – tramps and that – and there were bedbugs. Roundabout always had clean bedding.' They left King's Lynn because neither of them could get a job, and moved to Southampton. Things again improved. Lee got a job as a grill chef and Carol got two cleaning jobs (an hour a day each) and she was signing on. Lee was taking home £85 a week, Carol £24 from her cleaning jobs and she was getting Social Security. 'This was the best of times,' Lee said, 'we would go out for meals and everything. But the inevitable happened – Carol got pregnant.'

She wanted to go back to Sheffield but they had nowhere to stay so Carol moved in with her mother and Lee stayed at a friend's. But her mother threw her out again – 'We were always arguing about money,' Carol said. Together they moved to Roundabout before getting a council flat – their current home. They were married in 1982. They hated their present home. 'There's nowhere for the kid to play and there's loads of break-ins – we sold the music centre to buy an Alsatian.' (In the row of eight houses there are two Alsatians, two Dobermans and one mongrel.) They'd applied for a new house. 'I've told the Social this house is ruining our marriage,' Lee said. 'I can't stand this house and when I had a bit of drink inside me a couple of weeks back, I went berserk with a hammer – I smashed the colour TV, the cooker and the cocktail bar. I hit Carol as well, but not with the hammer – she called the police but when they got here they said there was nothing they could do – it was a family dispute. It feels like a prison here with that fence at the back. The factory behind us put it up because they said we were throwing rubbish over the wall. We weren't, though.' I asked what they did all day. Lee said he spent a lot of time redecorating – repairing the damage he did with the hammer. Carol kept the place tidy.

'I had an interview arranged for about a week ago,' Lee said, 'but I didn't go. I'm sure I would have got the job as well – it was a porter's job. I got all dressed up, but I didn't have any shoes. I've just got trainers. Carol said it wouldn't matter, but I told her everything matters in interviews. When I was in Pat Moss House, I got a £96 clothing grant but I haven't had any clothing money since. I can't afford any new shoes on what we get – £37.50 from the Social and £6.50 family allowance a week' (plus their rent, gas and electricity paid). I noticed that they both smoked Marlboro and I asked how much they spent on these a week. 'Oh, seven pounds between us,' Lee said, 'but it's our only pleasure.' As we finished talking, Lee complained about the system. 'It's all wrong,' he said. 'We've applied for a removal grant but they said we're not entitled to one – you have to be disabled or just out of hospital.' 'But couldn't your father help you move?' I enquired. 'He might be able to do it in his works van on a Saturday morning for us,' Lee said, 'but the Social should cough up.'

Kevin was their closest friend. He was also twenty-four. He had been put in a children's home when he was thirteen. He walked out on his foster parents in Chichester when he was seventeen, after an argument. He got a job as a trainee chef which was a live-in position. After six months, he got the sack. 'I didn't get on with the manager,' he said. He then got a job in a fair and travelled with it to London – to Croydon, where it was based in winter. He left it with a mate. They took £50 worth of tools, wires and bulbs with them. They slept in the YMCA for one night and then roughed it in Croydon for three weeks. They slept in multi-storey car parks, derelict houses and in the middle of roundabouts, under bushes. They didn't have any sleeping bags or blankets – just the clothes they walked around in. It was November and it snowed. Kevin said he knew nothing about Social Security at the time and so he nicked – cakes, biscuits and sandwiches – to survive. 'That's how I got into thieving,' he proclaimed (temporarily forgetting about the tools from the fair). During the day, he and his mate would walk around Croydon. 'It's a dump – like a smaller version of Sheffield. We'd look for somewhere good to kip – we'd wake up in the mornings with the bloody birds singing in our earholes.' He and his mate never made it into the centre of London.

Eventually, they met a lad from Mansfield who invited them to his house for a week. The police lifted them as soon as they arrived in Mansfield, but let them go. 'We were a bit scruffy,' said Kevin. He signed on for the first time in Mansfield but there were few jobs going, so he and his friend moved on to Chesterfield. They didn't have anywhere to stay for the first two nights but eventually they got a bedsit. In Chesterfield, they did some thieving. They were caught nicking a bottle of Blanc de Blancs from Marks and Spencer, and followed home by a store detective. 'I didn't even like it,' said Kevin. 'I had one mouthful and spat it out. I don't even drink. It's lucky the police didn't search the place, though. We had stolen clothes, radios and watches all over the place.' He got fined £30 for the wine, of which he paid £6. A few months later the police accused him of nicking lead from roofs. He insisted he didn't do it – 'I never do anything like that, I'm too big a coward' – but they warned him to leave town. He decided on Sheffield. Steel City – there's bound to be jobs there, he thought.

As soon as he got to Sheffield, he met a guy at the bus station who told him about Roundabout. 'It was right fantastic,' he said, 'but there were all kinds there – some were right snotty teenagers who didn't get on with their parents. Others were trying to get away from the law.' He got a job in a Wimpy bar as a pot washer and met a girl in Roundabout. She had the bedsit opposite his. She moved back home to her parents and he went with her. 'It was frightening,' he said, 'I never knew what to say or do. I got the sack from Wimpy for talking when I shouldn't have been, so I was signing on again. Her parents only charged me £10 a week for food and lodgings. This left me with £18 in my pocket. Eventually she went back with her old boyfriend so I had to move out and back to Roundabout.'

Here he met another girl and they got a bedsit together in Pitsmoor. 'And then the inevitable happened,' he said, 'she got sent down for seven months for fiddling the Social. She was two months pregnant at the time and she had the baby inside.

'When she got out, we moved in with her parents for two weeks, and then we got a council house. We got married – it lasted for two weeks. She found another bloke.' Kevin had his son Stephen living with him for a while but had to give him up. He's hoping to go to court to fight for custody of his child. In the meantime, he took his Alsatian, Sash, for long walks. He was unemployed. He was bitter about most things and critical of the system. 'People say we get too much money on the Social, but let them try it – I had to save up to go and see *Sudden Impact*. And the Queen is a right waste of money. Fair enough, she has to pay her own household bills. How much does she get now? Twice as much as the miners, I bet – at least two to three hundred quid a week for herself . . . The future doesn't look bright. Soon computers will be doing everything. One thing I do agree with, though, is cruise missiles – they're not wasting money. And the more missiles, the more people there'll be to guard them – the more jobs there'll be. Fair enough, it's only the army that guards them – but then the more people will be accepted in the army.'

And Kevin's strange logic gradually unfolded until his whole world view was laid out and tangled round my feet, and his. And as he got up I couldn't but notice the word HATE tattooed inexpertly on the back of his hand. He was the second person I'd seen that day with that tattoo.

November 1984

The night of the living dead

It was an old house out on its own. You could see the old woman who lived there out with her dog in all weathers. She would wave at me when I was out running. In the winter few pedestrians ever made it that far. On that grey and blurred landscape of running, the house was something of a landmark. It told you how far you had still to go. She was a landmark as well. That old grey-haired woman in the pelting Autumn rain. Just the two of you on the sticking, sodden leaves. She reminded you of all the sacrifices you were having to make. You could be tucked up somewhere snug and warm, not out on this wet mushy night. You the runner, and she the ghost of Rivelin Valley.

It was Paddy who took me to the house. Paddy was through with the gym. He had trained there once. I wasn't sure whether he had ever done any boxing in the past. 'I was just a scrapper at the best of times', he said, but you didn't know whether he meant in the ring or outside it. Now he was on the streets keeping an eye open for 'opportunities'. 'They keep coming my way, I can't complain.' He was running a security agency and a fleet of pubs. But he wasn't complacent. 'You need to keep your guard up, and your fucking eyes open.' I used to think that he had a chip on his shoulder. Everyone I knew thought he was just plain arrogant, but he described it differently. 'When you've seen the tricks they get up to . . .'

'They' were the privileged, the people in power, the church, the state, anyone, anywhere who can shit on you. He was always finding people to spend a day with, to prove his thesis, to keep his anger going. He took me to the house. It was just one of Paddy's little lessons. Just to show me life.

The house was in the damp hollow below the cemetery. This was Eileen Murphy's home. She had lived there all her life. Her father, William Joseph

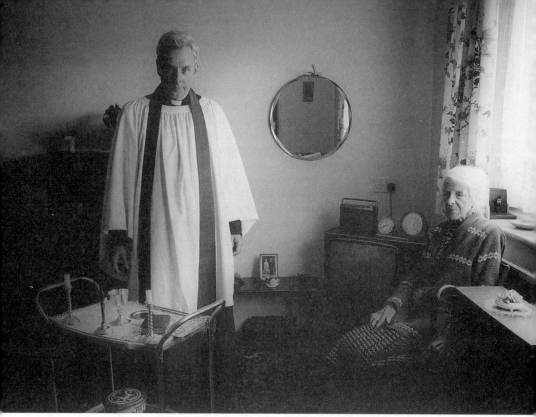

Father Quance, celebrating Mass in sheltered housing accommodation, Oldham, 1985

Murphy, was born there. His parents had decided to leave Ireland in search of a better life. So the Murphys had taken that great ride to prosperity across the Irish Sea in the middle of the nineteenth century, and that route had led here – to a damp little hollow just outside Sheffield. Her father had ten children, Eileen was the last surviving progeny. Her brother Eddie had died in 1978. Together they ran the cemetery, with Eileen keeping the books, and Eddie digging the graves and doing the stonework. Now she was all on her own. A man came in from outside to dig the graves.

She sat on a freezing November day huddled near the one bar on the electric fire that worked. She was watching an old black-and-white television that flickered in the corner. She had a colour television once, but then she had the first of her burglaries. There was an old photograph of her father to remind her of happier times, and a Christmas card of the Virgin Mary. A crucifix nestled in one corner at the top of a cracked mirror. Religious icons were everywhere, the whole house was dedicated to Jesus, and water and damp ran down the walls. A tray covered a hole in the wall, the plaster fell off in strips. Eileen lived in the front room with her dog Jenny and her cat Tom. Neither the dog nor the cat liked strangers. Eileen was the only person who could even approach the cat, the dog snarled at all strangers. Both had their reasons. Tom was thrown out through the window by the last set of burglars, Jenny was kicked. All three were now living in terror. A heavy lorry passing on the road outside blew the windows out recently. Eileen thought that the burglars had returned. She cried 'no, no', and pulled the curtains.

I walked around the house trying to imagine burglars stealing from a house like this. When you left the front room, it is hard to imagine this as a house even used for human habitation. The damp had stripped the wallpaper off the walls years ago, it stripped the plaster more recently, but that was still years ago. The grand piano in the backroom had mildew, and wouldn't play a note. Everywhere there was water and damp and great gaping holes where the plaster had given up the ghost. 'I used to play the piano', said Eileen, but that was a long time since.' There was a picture of her eldest sister above the piano. She was a nurse then, now she's up the hill', said Eileen pointing to the cemetery. Death hung over the house. Death and religion both, with the promise of eternal life, and the certainty of the dank wet grave.

But then water always runs downwards. The graves were up the hill. One member of the local congregation had described the cemetery as 'a marvellous place'. He had gone on to tell me that a Mass is held there on the first Monday of every month, and that 'there's a great feeling about the place. It's not at all like a cemetery. It really transcends time.' That it certainly did. Eileen looked up the hill in the autumn light. 'It's quite nice up there, quite homely', said Eileen, without any trace of irony.

She took me upstairs and I read the prayer to the Queen of this house – the blessed Virgin Mary. The damp had curled the ends of the prayer, as if it too was trying to get away from this environment. 'Dear Lady of perpetual succour, spotless mother of God, we choose thee as the mistress and lady of the house. Guard it dearest mother from pestilence, lightning, fire and tempest, from schisms and heresies, from air raids and the malice of enemies, protect those who dwell within.' The prayer reminded you of air raids and the pestilence of even older times. Things have moved on surely from tempest and schism and the malice of enemies, but not here. I entered her bedroom, and closed my eyes. This was not in prayer. It was done partly in shame and partly to help me imagine a human being living in these conditions. It was impossible.

There was, however, a good view of the cemetery from the bedroom window. 'That's where my family are now', she said. 'My father and mother are in the St Joseph's plot with Eddie my brother, my sister is in St Edward's, my grandfather and grandmother are in St Bridget's.' Eileen knew who was buried in every plot, in every square inch of that cemetery. She kept the register in her head. 'I'll join my brother Eddie up there one day. He was the gravedigger and stonemason. I miss him terribly. He rests up near the yew tree. We picked the spot before he died. I've nobody left, nobody except Jenny and Tom that is. Since the last burglary, the dog sleeps under the bed. I couldn't bear to be parted from her after what we've been through together.' The dog looked up at her. 'This is our family house. I can remember all the good times we had here. I think about my father and mother all the time. But I don't think they'd like to see what has happened to the house. I don't think that they'd like it at all.'

There was no electric light in the bedroom, the room was lit by the street light. She read by this light. At that time it was 'The Parson's Daughter' by Catherine Cookson. She retired every night at 10.00 pm. One religious icon dominated this room – one dedicated to 'St Francis, Lover of Creatures'. In winter the snow sometimes cuts Rivelin Valley off, but she still managed to get out of the house somehow every day. 'Jenny loves the snow. It's just as well', she added.

In 1989, at the age of 79, Eileen was retired from her job. Up to her retirement, the house went with the job, now she had to pay £30 a week rent for this damp festering hole. Sheffield City Council have declared the house unfit for human habitation, and detailed eight pages of work that need to be done to bring the house up to a necessary standard. The house basically needed rebuilding. The work should have been completed by June of this year. It had not yet been started. One problem was that Eileen did not want any alternative accommodation, where her dog and cat would not be allowed. She had been through too much with them. No suitable accommodation had been offered for the three of them, so there was stalemate.

The house was owned by the Trustees of the Sheffield Vincentian Trust, and one of the members of the congregation of St Vincent's Presbytery put it to me that the state of the house was partly Eileen fault. 'It's an attitude of mind, as well as money, you know. Some people have other priorities in life, apart from doing up a house. Stonemasons are self-employed businessmen after all. But the family were Irish, you see. What they did with their money is their business.' But there was no evidence that they had squandered any money, just that good old-fashioned belief that if you end up with a bum deal as bad as this one, then you must have somehow deserved it.

Another parishioner, a local solicitor, Vincent Hale, attempted to offer a different explanation of the situation from the church's point of view. He explained that in the past he personally has done everything he could for Eileen. When the toilet seat broke, it was him who replaced it. When Eileen was in dispute with the local priest over the occupancy of the house, he decided to act as the mediator. 'She had a burst pipe for four months in the middle of winter. The priest at the time took Eileen's refusal to move out of the house quite personally, and it led to a rather difficult situation. I told the priest that I would sort it out and that he didn't have to know anything about it. I sorted the plumber out. When her television was stolen, it was me who replaced it. I have enormous sympathy with Eileen, but it's a very difficult problem.'

He had started keeping the records of the cemetery. Eileen, he said, was not making a good job of it. 'Her grandfather's records were a work of art, her father's records weren't quite so good, but hers have always been absolutely hopeless. I've had to take over. When you pick up one of the books a piece comes off in your hands. I've had to photocopy the books, and at the moment I'm trying to computerise them. This is what's required in bookkeeping in cemeteries these days. Eileen couldn't really keep up with it. She should have been retired years ago. No other business concern would have done what we have done. They'd have had her out. I honestly think that the kindest thing is to let her see her time out in the house.'

But this was the church after all, and Eileen might not be ready to go up the hill, just yet. In fact, she was clearly not ready just yet – she was getting up at eight o'clock every day and taking her dog for a three-mile walk twice a day. Eileen was out there in all weathers. She rarely got colds. 'I hate doctors, me', she said – 'I try to stay away from them.'

In the meantime, she was left in a house that wasn't fit for an animal, with no apparent end in sight. It might be her family home, but she was now retired. She said that she wasn't going anywhere without Jenny and Tom, so there the three of them sit – suspicious, worried and very, very, cold.

But Eileen still had that spark of life in her. For someone who has spent her life beside a cemetery she knows that can be a problem. 'There are a lot of people hoping that I'll just die and that will be the end of it all. Then they can get somebody new in. They're just waiting for me to pass away. But I've a lot of life left in me yet. Every night I look out on where my parents and Eddie are buried. Death doesn't worry me the way that it worries some people, but the problem basically is that I'm just not ready yet. Don't worry, I'll let them all know when I am, but I might just take my time.'

December 1990

Wind of change

Adelle and Alistair were once the biggest things in the music business in South Africa, when that country was culturally isolated. Adelle First was top of the bill at the Swazi Spa, Alistair in his famous band, the Helicopters, filled open-air stadiums with screaming fans. In the days before change. Now they live in Brightside in Sheffield, in Alistair's home town, in a little terraced house on a steep slope down to the Lower Don Valley, dreaming of the pool and the Porsche, and the life that has gone forever.

Adelle was born in South Africa. 'My mother was registered "coloured", so I was – it was as simple as that. I've always thought that I looked white. Some of my ancestors came from Mauritius, I think. To be honest, I'm not very sure where they are from. But what I do know is that white South Africans would take one look at me and they could tell immediately that I was coloured. I've been kicked off park benches and out of trains. "Get off you stupid bushman", they would say to me. We probably suffered more than the blacks. When large companies invested in South Africa, they would use their social con-science budgets to build schools or playgrounds for the blacks, but they never did it for the coloureds. They didn't get the same recognition for doing this sort of thing for the coloureds, so they didn't bother.'

Adelle was discovered at seventeen at her gran's funeral. She says that she was the first coloured female singer on television in South Africa, so she became 'Adelle First'. Her manager argued that if she didn't change her surname from Fourie, then all the coloured people would think that she was an Afrikaner. In 1980 aged seventeen she recorded God Bless Africa. It went to number one on six black radio stations. Fame changed her life. 'We had press guys on the doorstep in our coloured area in Horseshoe in Johannes-burg. I was the only happening thing in South Africa. I was the baby of all the non-white press, – the *Sowetan*, the *Swazi Weekend Observer*, the *Drum*.

Adelle and Alistair, pop stars at home, Wincobank, Sheffield, 1995

I toured Lesotho, Swaziland, Transkeii, Botswana. I was on TV every Thursday. Basically, I was a superstar.'

Alistair, on the other hand, is Sheffield born and bred, and it shows. He went to South Africa in 1985 to Sun City with his group Radiation. 'It was loads of money for walking on stage and not doing very much. I took a nine-month contract out there. I had no qualms, I was a musician. What did I know about politics? Loads of people said to me "You can't go to a country like that." But don't forget I was the only white person in a lot of black bands in Britain. To be honest the situation there didn't mean a great deal to me. I knew that they had lots of problems out there, but so does everywhere else. I loved the place.'

Alistair talks in a broad Sheffield accent with every now and again a sort of mid-Atlantic twang coming from nowhere into his voice. 'The music biz over there was wide open at the time. They were isolated and fifty years behind the times. I was used to the hard graft of the music business in England. I went over there and just cleaned up. I knew exactly what to do. I put a band together – the Helicopters. They hadn't got to grips with all the hype over there, all the marketing and the stuff that we took for granted in England. I just went out there and pulled all the strokes that you do every day of the week in England.'

The mid-Atlantic twang was growing more noticeable, as he gave a long hard pull on his cigarette. 'Over there they would just make a record and send a hundred copies out to DJs and sit back and wait. We'd go around supermarket chains, giving things out, signing autographs. Just the usual publicity stunts. All of a sudden, South Africa had some superstars, that were behaving like superstars. We played to 50,000 people in open-air gigs. We were a bit like Duran Duran with the make-up and the whole works. We were the biggest rock group in the history of South Africa, and we appealed to all the different race groups. 1987 was the really big year for us. We had a double-page spread in the *South African Sunday Times*.'

Alistair has put on a bit of weight since returning from South Africa, the sparkling blue eyes have dulled a little. But they shone as he recalled how things were. 'I had a box full of panties and bras that chicks had thrown at me on stage. We used to create the whole hysteria thing. We used to have chicks taking their clothes off and flinging them at us. I suppose we were a bit raunchy. South Africa was deprived of our kind of performance at the time.'

Alistair and Adelle met when Adelle recorded an advertising jingle for him. 'Alistair didn't like me at first. He thought that I was basically a jumped-up superstar.' I asked innocently which of them was the biggest superstar at the time. They started to argue about it. They lived in a white area of Johannesburg with two and a half acres of land, a swimming pool, and three cars, but in constant fear because of Adelle's coloured status. 'We had the house burgled', explained Alistair 'and Adelle was very scared when we had to call the police, because this was not an area for "coloureds". The only advantage we had was that we were superstars, so they didn't touch us.'

But the wind of change was starting to blow over South Africa itself. The political changes happening in the country would end South Africa's less than splendid isolation. But closer to home, there were other changes which were equally significant. Adelle had a baby, Samantha. 'Samantha had to be registered at the Department of the Interior and she had to be registered as "coloured"', explained Adelle. 'We wanted to register her as "white", which is what she looked, or British. But they said that this was impossible. I knew what it was like to be brought up as a second-class citizen. I didn't want the same thing for her.'

So they left South Africa for a rented houses in Firth Park in Sheffield. 'For six months I didn't go out of the door', said Adelle. 'I was very depressed. It was awful. We took our last thirteen grand out with us. We had lots of contacts, but we didn't work for the first eighteen months, and we couldn't claim the dole. I couldn't believe what we had descended to. Al suggested to me that we should do Working Men's clubs. I couldn't believe it. Al had to hassle me to go back to work. We were nobody and nothing.'

Alistair took up the story. 'I put a show together, with me on keyboards and Adelle singing. I went out and bought a little van. Adelle couldn't grasp the concept of a Working Men's club. She was used to five-star hotels. She wasn't even used to carrying her own microphone. When we got to our first club this big fat, beer-bellied old guy said to her "Are tha' turn cock?' She thought he was being obscene. She was used to short sets in the most exclusive of surroundings, not two sets for ninety quid in some poky little hole. But we've had to stick at it, and now we've got quite a big following in Hull and Cleethorpes.

Meanwhile, South Africa has been transformed. Adelle sees the transformation a little differently to everyone else. 'There's been a big flip flop.

There used to be signs saying "whites only", now there are signs saying "blacks only". The TV and the entertainments business are dominated by blacks now. My family tell me that Johannesburg is very dirty now, and the country is so violent. And coloureds like me are still left out in the cold', she said.

'Even if you were a superstar', added Alistair. 'Once.'

May 1995

Little and large

I used to call them 'little' and 'large'. Two brothers, Tony and Mike originally from Jamaica, but brought up in Kilburn, trying to make it in the North of England. Tony was always in the shadow of Mike, always a few feet behind. Mike was huge. He would have blocked out the sun, if you had managed to catch him out in the daylight. Instead, he blocked out the glare from a string of fluorescent lights. His vital statistics were 48–29–20. The last measurement was his biceps, 'and getting bigger all the time', Tony would be keen to tell you. Mike looked as if he had been inflated with some giant foot pump, his massive frame billowing out, the muscles all bulbous and veiny. He looked as if he was ready to burst. He had a short temper. Little of it looked natural. Tony would stand back with his arms outstretched inviting you to behold this great spectacle. This was the eighties, and the years of enterprise culture. Mike and Tony had heard that the North of England was ripe for business opportunities. It was too cut throat down in London. Mike had served two years in Wormwood Scrubs for armed robbery. He was driving his own car on the job. He always swore that he didn't realise that his mates were going to carry out an armed robbery. He thought that they were just going to the butchers to pick something up. 'It was only when my mates got back into the car with loads of notes that I realised what was going on. Nobody believed my story.' He pumped iron with these mates. He trusted them. He survived prison because of his size. 'I was the strongest prisoner they ever had in the Scrubs. They put me in charge of all the weights. I could train to my heart's content. Everyone wanted to be my friend in prison because of my size. People would give me their dinners just so that I'd be friendly towards them. Others would give me tobacco or their gold chains so that I'd look after them.'

I was there the night Mike came runner up in the Mr Physique contest in Romeo and Juliet's nightclub in Sheffield. Mike was always accompanied by a small hard-core posse of hangers-on and fans. 'They like to be seen out with me', he always said. 'They like to be seen out with somebody my size.' The compere in the nightclub worked his way around Mike's magnificent frame. 'Traps and thighs' . . . 'front biceps' . . . 'back biceps . . .'. His fans were whooping with delight. Mike was sailing through the competition, before his calves let him down. They were not exactly puny, but they were just not in proportion to the rest of his body. Tony was still cheering from the front row, as always. One hundred and fifty pounds prize money. 'Not bad', said Mike. 'A start', said Tony – 'business capital.' Mike was happy with that. He was supplementing his prize money, by working on the doors of clubs and 'personal

Ducking and diving, Park Hill Flats, Sheffield, 1994. Tony is in the middle

protection work' for some Asian businessmen. 'They're shop-owners basically, and they needed a bodyguard because everybody hates their guts. They'd walk around the market and bump into people and if there was any trouble they'd ask me to sort it out. They liked me wearing just a T-shirt to show off my muscles.'

Mike could, however, see where the big money was. Robbing butcher's shops in your own car was a mug's game. In the mid-eighties he got into the kissogram business. 'For twenty five quid I strip off and give the birds a kiss on the cheek. It's easy money. Multiply that by ten and we're talking good money every night.' 'A nice little business opportunity', added Tony.

I took some photographs of Mike in the local YMCA, benchpressing what for him was a routine 380 lb, and finishing by blowing up those veiny bulbs of muscles with 440 lb. I met up with him a few nights later in the underground car park below a nightclub at the bottom of some concrete steps reeking of urine. Mike didn't like the photographs that I'd taken. He started to rip them to pieces and threw them into the pools of fresh urine at the bottom of the stairs. He had a very short fuse. I apologised for taking such unflattering photographs. He asked me if I was trying to damage his business opportunities. Tony had melted into the shadows of the underground bunker. He always stepped back when Mike had a fury like this.

But that was all before the recession, back in the days of optimism when one's body wasn't so much one's temple as one's enterprise zone. The fact that the whole thing had been blown up out of all proportion by artificial stimulants was neither here nor there. They were the years of thinking big. But it was always going to be a business founded on shaky principles. 'The steroids make him aggressive', explained Tony. 'You just have to keep out of his way.' Mike returned to London, Tony stayed in the North to ride the recession out. Tony was making his own way now. Occasionally, he would fetch a load of silk shirts out of a carrier bag in a nightclub and flog them at a fiver each. He was doing okay on his own, he always seemed to have enough to get by on, to get the drinks in with. But he was still always talking about Mike. Mike did this, Mike did that. Mike's pecs, Mike's lats. Mike was going to fix his calves one day and then there would be no stopping him. He would then come back to take up where he left off.

Mike had left a great impression on a provincial Northern town, and Tony knew it. He traded on it. 'Mike was big then, you should see him now. Fucking huge, fucking enormous.' Mike was being blown out of all proportion.

This week Mike was back, but the body had gone. I never realised before that Tony was actually taller than Mike. Normal maturational processes had made Tony bigger, Mike looked like a balloon which somebody had let the air out of. Tony walked through every door first. Mike tagged along, unsure of himself. His character had been so tied up with his size, that there were bound to be big changes inside as well as out. His whole personality had been shaped and determined by how others reacted to that bulk. Now the world around him – the world of interpersonal space and body buffer zones, the world of the micro-politics of social interaction, the world of respect and deference from total strangers – had been turned upside down and transformed out of all recognition. This was a parallel and strange universe, which Mike was negotiating with some unease. Tony was no longer the man in the shadows, but his guide. The aggression and the short temper had gone. He had got himself clean, but in the process had become mortal like the rest of us.

Mike was now polite to a fault. He asked me if I had managed to hang onto any of the old photographs of him pumping up, so that he could keep them as a memento of how things were in the good old days of plenty.

May 1994

Crime and vice

The clearest indication of the unbounded contempt of the workers for the existing social order is the wholesale manner in which they break its laws. If the demoralisation of the worker passes beyond a certain point then it is just as natural that he will turn into a criminal – as inevitably as water turns into steam at boiling point. Owing to the brutal and demoralising way in which he is treated by the bourgeoisie, the worker loses all will of his own and, like water, he is forced to follow blindly the laws of nature. There comes a point when the worker loses all power [to withstand temptation]. (Friedrich Engels, *The Conditions of the Working Class in England*, 1845)

Immorality among the young people of Sheffield appears to be worse than anywhere else . . . In Sheffield, on Sundays young people hang about the streets all day gambling by tossing coins or by organising dog fights. They frequent gin shops assiduously, where they sit with their girlfriends until late in the evening, when it is time for the couples to take their solitary walks. In one low beer shop visited by the Commissioner (J. C. Symons) forty to fifty young people of both sexes were sitting. Nearly all of them were under seventeen years of age and every youth had his girlfriend with him . . . Known prostitutes were among the company. (Friedrich Engels, *The Condition of the Working Class in England*, 1845)

'Jack the bloody Ripper doesn't get this treatment'

Danny, still only twenty but already a pro – he'd served his time at his chosen profession in more ways than one. (Several hundred burglaries in five years and two stretches in borstal and one in prison.) In official terms he's a recidivist. He put it bluntly: 'Money, clothes and having a good time is my life. If I got a job I'd have to change my whole life style. What would I do with £80 a week? I can spend that in one night. Burglary is the only real skill I've got.'

Danny's profession runs in the family (his father was at the time on the run for an armed robbery offence) but he said his family had nothing to do with it. It was his mates. He was fifteen, they were sixteen, he was their eager pupil. He started with a warehouse. 'We were careful to choose one without a burglar alarm. We got in through a ground-floor window. It was dead easy. We all had a look about and I found a cashbox in a drawer with a hundred quid in it. I couldn't believe it. It was money for old rope. We blew the money in two days on Indian meals, taxis and drinks. Then we went out again about three days later. We'd just get the bus a couple of miles down the road to the Moor or Bramall Lane and have a wander about.' Danny enjoyed his new pastime. 'Some nights we'd do three places in the one spot. Sometimes of course you'd find nothing but occasionally you'd hit the jackpot.'

Within six months Danny had graduated to houses. 'We'd usually get the bus to Gleadless, which was a good spot because it borders on a wood. Dead easy to get away. We'd go up in the afternoon and just pick a house that looked empty. My two mates would stay in the next street and I'd just go up and knock the door. If anyone answered I'd say, "Is Paul in, please?" Nobody was ever suspicious. They'd just say, "Sorry, you must be at the wrong house." If nobody answered I'd just go and get my mates and we'd go round the back and steam in. If the windows were locked we'd just put a coat up to the window and knock it in. When I was in, I'd head straight for the bedroom to look for the jewellery case. I'd also look under the mattress straight away. Then it was down to the kitchen. You'd be amazed how many people keep money in the oven, but I've even found money stashed in cornflakes boxes. We never made a mess, at least deliberately – some houses would look a bit untidy afterwards but that's because you're looking for things in a hurry. You haven't got all day. The most I ever got from a house when I was a kid was eight and a half grand in goods from a house in Lodge Moor – at least that's what the local paper said. Me and another kid only got a grand and a half for the jewellery and stuff. Our fence was a market stall holder – a friend put me in touch with him.'

'We also did quite a few electrical shops – well, some of them used to have eight videos in the window at the one time. The first time a mate of mine told me about this shop in the Ecclesall Road with eight in the window. We were in a nightclub at the time. So we get a taxi back to my house – I told the driver I had to get some stuff for work in the morning. Then we got the

Late afternoon, Park Hill Flats, Sheffield, 1994

taxi to the Ecclesall Road and we got let off about a hundred yards from the shop. It was about three in the morning. I just kicked the side window in – the shop didn't have an alarm. I climbed in and passed the videos out. We hid them on some wasteland nearby. Early the next morning we rang our fence and he came and picked them up. We got one hundred and fifty quid for each one. Nobody noticed the broken window until the shop opened. The display must have looked a bit bare, though.' Danny laughed. 'The only problem was that I cut my hand badly getting in through the window. I showed it to my mum and she was really concerned. She said I needed to go to the hospital. But I couldn't go in Sheffield. I must have dripped blood all over the shop. So I got the train to Hull with the Sheffield United supporters. The hospital in Hull is very close to the station so I went there and gave them a false name and told them my mum had locked me out, for coming home late, so I had to smash a window to get in. My hand needed fourteen stitches. I went on to the match, but Hull City won 3–2. But what happened next was that the lad I did the electrical shop with got caught on another job. He grassed on me. I got a £554 fine plus probation. Of course, the fine wasn't that bad. I'd made quite a lot by then. My mum had to pay the fine, though. I'd spent what I'd made.'

After his court appearance Danny eventually got on a Youth Opportunity scheme but was dismissed for fighting. He then got on a building course and landed a job on a building site. This time he was sacked for being late. He kept up with his burglary and explored new avenues of thieving. At away football matches when his friends were congregated in a pub, he'd nip upstairs to the private quarters to take what he could find. On one occasion he found

£600 in a cash box. But one lunchtime in York as he was trying to slip back into the pub, the landlady spotted him and grabbed him. 'I nearly crapped myself,' he said. 'I had to slip out of my coat and run off. Luckily my friends could see what was happening so they created a bit of a disturbance so that I could get away.'

At about this time another of his friends was arrested and the police started calling at his mum's. 'Just a few routine enquiries, madam.' Danny was off – to a little town in Wales. 'It was great,' he said, 'none of the jewellers or cigarette shops had alarms. They weren't used to crime. I was staying in the best hotels and coming back to Sheffield to sell the goods.' But on one visit home things went badly wrong. 'I'd arranged to meet this fence in a pub. He wasn't someone I'd ever done business with before – he was a friend of my dad's. So I sat there waiting, but he didn't show. The next minute the place is full of coppers – but they ran straight past me. You see, I used to have a perm but in the meantime I'd had my hair straightened and streaked. I also had a good tan from a sun bed. The coppers didn't let anybody out of the pub, though, and the landlord identified me. He said he didn't know I was on the run. The fence must have grassed on me – to do himself a favour with the coppers. At Sheffield Crown Court the judge said I was a professional burglar and if I'd been older I would have got five years. As it was I was sent to Everthorpe borstal. I did thirteen months.'

Danny went back to burglary within a week of getting out of borstal. 'I'd got even more bottle now,' he said. 'I went into this jeweller's in Sheffield and asked to see some gold chains. When the assistant went to get her calculator I just grabbed the tray and ran. She started shouting, "Stop thief!" I thought they only did this in films. She ran after me and so did three passers-by. I ran all the way to Park Hill Flats where a friend of mine lives. I lost the people chasing me in Pond Street. The chains came to £7600 and I sold them to a fence in Birmingham for £2800. When it eventually came to court, by the way, the jeweller claimed it was £10,000 worth of stuff. They're all bloody bent.

'The really funny thing was that they had all these eyewitnesses giving different descriptions. I had a really good suntan at the time and a customer in the shop swore I must have been a Paki. But the shop assistant gave them a good description and I was eventually spotted in a hairdresser's. They pulled the hairdresser in as well because I'd been talking to her and she had a big gold chain on. She started bawling. They asked me to go on an identity parade but I refused. The police kept saying that all they were interested in was getting the stuff back, which wasn't a hell of a lot of good because I'd sold the stuff and spent the money. But when I was in the nick, this old bloke gave me a bit of advice. He told me to tell the coppers that I'd take them to the stuff but do a runner instead. He said that if a fit young lad like me couldn't get away from two fat CID men, who could?

'So I told the coppers I'd do it, but I didn't want ten big CID blokes tramping up to my mate's house. So they said, "That's OK, Danny, there'll only be two." So they picked me up about nine o'clock and handcuffed me. I told them that I wanted to ring my friend from the telephone box on the corner to make sure he was in. So they undid one of my handcuffs. So I went into the telephone box and pretended to make the call. They let me walk to the house with one of them, a sergeant, holding the end of the cuffs. He said to me, "You're not going to try and do a runner or owt like that, are you?" I said, "Of course not." I told them the stuff was in the bin in the back garden. I knew that part of Sheffield really well, and as soon as I got to the garden I sprinted off across this wasteland. The sergeant was just standing there shouting, "Come back, you little bastard!" I ran straight to one of my friends' houses and he sawed the cuffs off. They sealed the whole area off and got dogs, Land Rovers, the lot. As my mum said, "It wasn't bloody fair, all this for one kid – Jack the bloody Ripper doesn't get this treatment." I sat up all night watching them search this wasteland from my friend's bedroom.

'In the morning the coppers called at my friend's at about eight o'clock. I was still in bed and his mum had to waken me up. I climbed out of the bedroom window with no shoes or socks on. It was December and it was bloody freezing. I was going to nip back in when they'd gone but some cleaners from a pub spotted me so I had to leg it. I saw this woman in her garden and told her my dog had run off and I was chasing after it so she loaned me some socks.' He hid with his cousin for a few days but the police went round all his friends and relations and Danny was eventually found hiding in her cubbyhole. 'The police told me I'd really done it this time. It was a really serious offence – what would have happened if the shop assistant had got hold of him? I was also charged with escaping from police custody and theft of handcuffs. Could you believe it? I was really crapping myself. Anyway the case eventually came to court and all I got was a "recall" to borstal – sixteen weeks. I'd been on remand for thirteen weeks so I only had three to do. My relatives in the public gallery all started clapping. The police weren't too happy about the sentence, and the two CID men who I'd escaped from got demoted to the shoplifting squad. I saw them last week – they gave me a real evil look.'

Danny went back to burglary within a few weeks of getting out of borstal. He started nicking Capo di Monte figures. 'Some people do collect them, you know.' Within two months he was back in remand. 'This time I got a really bad judge – I got fifteen months this time and spent the last eight in Armley prison in Leeds.'

Danny leaned back in his chair. 'It might seem to you that I haven't been that successful, but I've done hundreds of jobs and I've never actually been caught on the job. It's usually people wanting to do themselves a favour with the coppers. I know I've got the bottle and the skill. In ten years' time I'll either be doing a ten-year stretch or living it up. I'm not going to change my life style.'

And as he got up to go, suntan, streaked blond hair, expensive leather jacket – all the trimmings of the pop star – I asked him the question I've always wondered about, 'Do you ever think about your victims?' Danny doesn't think about this. 'Why should I? The people I burgle can afford it, and jewellers are all bent and bump up the insurance claims. Another thing, I never burgle poor people or old people.'

Danny was beginning to sound like Robin Hood. 'But just a minute, you've burgled council houses, isn't that right?'

'Yes,' Danny said, 'but loads of ordinary people have stacks of dough stashed away.'

'But do you really mean that if you went to all the trouble of breaking into a house and then discovered that it belonged to an old person, you wouldn't take anything?'

'Well, not nothing,' said Danny, 'but I wouldn't leave them broke.' And Robin Hood had, before my very eyes, started to metamorphose into the Sheriff of Nottingham – just enough left in the kitty to survive, when Danny's high demands were met.

October 1984

Shrinkage

There she stood, surrounded by a huge wall of belts. Belts of every description – red, green, white, leather, suede and shiny shiny plastic. All glittering, all beckoning. It was obviously too much for her. She was almost fourteen, fat and untidy. She selected one little leather number and ran her fingers along its machine-crafted seam. And then the buckle – chrome, real chrome. She lifted it down from the stand and started to try it on. 'Watch it disappear,' the store detective, Jenny, said. All eyes were on the belt and suddenly, like a float in water, it went under; it dipped under her voluminous coat. The fish had bitten.

But it resurfaced again; it didn't fit. She selected another from the glittering display – a larger one that might fit around her considerable girth.

'This time we'll get her,' Jenny said. We were waiting for a second bite. Jenny nodded to another store detective – Paul, dressed unobtrusively for the day in pink vest and pink socks – 'He's gay, you know,' said Jenny. 'The fat lady,' she whispered. Paul looked confused. 'You're standing beside her – fat girl, I mean,' she said, correcting herself. Paul started flicking through some scarves – just another gay boy out for some Saturday shopping in the ladies' department of a large store, or so it seemed. He stood right beside her. The fat girl, who was now trying on another belt, was visibly perspiring. But whether this was from the anxiety of an imminent bout of shoplifting or from the sheer effort of getting a belt around her large waist or even from the fact that an obvious member of Sheffield's gay community was violating her personal space was much less clear. Paul didn't take his eyes off the scarves. 'He's watching her every move, though,' said Jenny, and I started wondering about the exact properties of Paul's eyes.

The fat girl struggled with the belt before giving up in despair. She put it back on the rack, her reputation intact, just. Saved by modal fashion. We left Paul, still examining the scarves.

No one doubts that shoplifting is a serious and prevalent form of crime in Britain. Newspaper headlines insist that it's the equivalent of a Great Train Robbery every day, even allowing for inflation. But it's hard to put an exact figure on it because 'shrinkage' in retail includes all the pilfering by everyone from the warehouse staff (through the delivery drivers, the sales assistants, the shelf-fillers, the managers) to the people who operate the tills. The customers play some role in 'shrinkage' but it's clearly not the whole story. It's nevertheless a sufficiently important part to warrant a boom in the growth of security services and store-detective agencies.

Jenny Brough and her partner Sylvia Woodland had operated a store detective agency (SYLJEN) in Sheffield for the past five years. They had about twenty employees, nearly all women, Jenny said that before the recession, men wouldn't really have been all that interested in spending an entire day in ladies' fashion. They had been billed as Sheffield's *Charlie's Angels* but without any hidden male master behind them. Store detecting is a cut-throat business, in more ways than one, and the only way to make a decent profit was to have a reasonable number of employees because they only charged shops around £3.85 an hour. SYLJEN operated in many of the large retail stores in Sheffield, Barnsley, Rotherham, Scarborough, even Lincoln.

I met one of their best store detectives, Ron Teskowski, twenty-six, an ex-miner. He'd been a store detective for the past five years. 'He's good,' said Jenny, 'he can blend in anywhere. I've seen shoplifters look straight past him.'

Ron interrupted. 'There have been loads of times when I've arrested a smart-looking lady and the police have been called. When they arrive they say, "Right, madam, tell us what he did." I have to say, "Hang on a minute, I'm the bloody store detective, she's the thief," and on one occasion I was standing next to this old lady in a chemist's and she slipped a bottle of shampoo into her bag and said, "Don't say owt, love, I'm a pensioner." I had to nick her, of course.'

Ron said store detecting was like a hobby to him. 'I've caught thirteen shoplifters in one day, if I don't catch anybody I feel really guilty. My thrill used to be in catching people nicking large amounts but it's the unusual ones I get a kick out of now – I get a real thrill out of catching a company director or a policeman.' All 'stops' were recorded in his little notebook and this register chronicled the full gamut of human greed, rapacity, weakness and folly. 'Here's a good one,' he said. 'I caught these four unemployed lads from Liverpool with £350 worth of stuff. They were coming out of a store as I was walking in, and I heard one say, "Let's do Burton's now." So I followed them there. Two of them just picked this rack up and ran out of the shop with it. Their mates just walked slowly out behind them. I followed them to this multi-storey car park. They put everything in black bags in the boot of this car and set off back to town. So I phoned the police and me and the police hid in the car park and we pounced on them when they got back. They had sixteen pairs of cords and seven shirts in the boot.' The bulk of this stuff came from Burton's, but Burton's still declined an offer of this agency's services.

'Or look at this one. I saw a bloke nick a small toy train from one shop so I followed him. He went into the next shop and nicked a portable television. We got the police. When they searched his house they found that his cellar was set out like a mail-order catalogue. He kept a book of all the things he'd stolen and there was more than £30,000 worth of stuff recorded.'

These cases contrast markedly with some others in Ron's book.

Girl aged 10. Stole 39p lip gloss. Slipped it into left-hand pocket of coat. Parents called.

Charge hand aged 64. Stole one pair of socks   99p
                              one plum   3p
                              ─────
                              TOTAL £1.02

Police called.

Some of the entries were just plain embarrassing. 'This woman said hello to me as I went into the chemist's. She lives on my estate. I saw her slip two packets of Durex into her purse. I had to stop her, but I let her off with a verbal caution. She can't look at me straight now.'

In some shops in which this agency works, calling the police is at the discretion of the store detectives – luckily for the woman with the Durex. In many others it isn't. If the shoplifter is under twelve, however, the parents are called instead. When they have discretion, what affects whether the police are called or not?

'Well,' said Jenny, 'if you're between say fifteen and sixty-five you've no chance unless you're on day release from Middlewood [a local mental hospital] or something like that. Between these ages we get the police. With kids or pensioners you like to give them a second chance. Some kids don't know any better, with pensioners they usually nick for attention because they're lonely. But you can't feel too sorry for pensioners – I haven't met one yet who has stolen out of necessity. And they've all got excuses, of course.' She showed me some letters written to her by people they'd apprehended, blaming the slight deviation from the straight and narrow on (variously) 'intestinal infections', 'sudden bereavement', 'high blood pressure', even 'flu'. 'Most people are very upset when you stop them, although some couldn't care a monkey's,' she said, 'and it's amazing how many women urinate on the spot when you stop them. One even pretended to have a heart attack. Five minutes later, though, she was asking me for a fag and pulling down her knickers to show me the scars of an operation she'd had. There's one pensioner in Barnsley who's seventy who we've caught loads of times. The last time I caught her she'd nicked two bottles of cough mixture. You'd probably think "poor old dear" but when I stopped her she ran off, and I had to chase after her through the middle of Barnsley. When I eventually caught her she thumped me with her shopping bag. She's tough as an old boot – she's been in Holloway three times.

'Shoplifters are definitely getting more violent,' said Jenny. She was just getting over a badly bruised face. 'I stopped this lad going out of a shop with a stolen ski jacket on under his own coat. He tried to get away so I grabbed his arm and we fell to the floor. He had three mates and they doubled back and gave me a good kicking while I was down.'

Jenny did not underestimate the seriousness of being caught shoplifting, but, she said, 'If people want to risk it, that's their business. I caught a lawyer nicking a packet of disposable razor blades from a chemist's. He'd even nicked two tins of dye and a book from an Oxfam shop. The police searched his house and found more stolen property. Ron caught a Bradford policeman who had been in the force for thirteen years nicking a brass switch plate worth £5.28 from a DIY store. He had to resign. A Sheffield Crown Court judge, Mr James Pickles, even admitted in a court case in Sheffield that he had once, earlier in his career, walked away from a souvenir shop without paying for some postcards. When he suddenly realised what he'd done he went back immediately to pay for them. But he says he's had considerable anxiety over the years about feeling a hand on his shoulder when he's in some stores. What occasioned the confession was his instructing a jury to find a manager not guilty of stealing some batteries. The judge knew how easy it was to absent-mindedly leave without paying.'

But what about Jenny – had she ever shoplifted? 'Well, I once tried to nick some Snowdrops perfume from Woolies when I was about ten. But I panicked and dumped it in a woman's shopping bag.' Panic had kept her record clean.

John, another store detective, knew what it feels like to have a slightly soiled past. His nose had been rubbed in it enough times. He'd been a store detective for three years and by all accounts a very good one. When he got the job he didn't mention his 'criminal record'. When he was eleven, he and a group of friends threw stones at some greenhouse windows. Some windows broke. 'I don't even know if my stone broke a window,' he said. He was fined two pounds. Two years later he nicked a Mars bar, and got a verbal caution from an inspector. When he was fourteen a friend (also fourteen) gave him a lift in his dad's Reliant Robin. They got stopped by the police. They had to say that the father hadn't given them permission, even though he had. Again a verbal caution.

Hardly notorious form, and all at least twelve years ago, but it was still on file. 'I caught a retired policeman who was seventy-two in Barnsley nicking. I got the police and went with them to the station to make a statement. When I was just about to sign it the station officer suddenly said to me, "Have you ever been in trouble yourself, lad?" I just said "Why?" and he said, "Well, I'm just asking you a question, have you ever been in trouble?" Well, I wasn't really expecting him to say this so I said "no" at first. He got up and went out of the room and came back with this piece of paper and started reeling off my three convictions, one after the other. He'd checked me out, even though you're not supposed to do that unless you're suspected of being involved in a crime. All I'd done was catch a bloody ex-cop nicking. So I said, "I don't think you should bring this up," and he just said, "I don't think we'll be seeing you around Barnsley again." I just got up and walked out.' The statement was never signed.

The police then phoned Jenny and asked if she was aware that John had been convicted of shoplifting and criminal damage. 'We were flabbergasted,' said Jenny. 'We had him up in the office but when he explained how long ago it was, we stood by him. They'd no right to use this against him.'

John broke in: 'It's because of my brothers – they've been in trouble with the police quite a few times.' 'It's also because he's too good at his job,' said Jenny. 'John caught a superintendent's son who's thirteen nicking £57 worth of stuff. And would you believe it, a couple of months later we caught the same superintendent's dad shoplifting as well. Both got an instant verbal caution. That means nothing went on record. Neither file was processed. No criminal record, no blemishes on their character. No nothing. And who says crime doesn't run in families?'

January 1985

Doormen, Millionaires nightclub, Sheffield, 1995

Bare knuckles

The night before

I heard the word the night before in a nightclub. It was to be a fight, the like of which I hadn't seen before. Bare knuckles, anything goes, a fight to the bitter end. It was Big Steve who gave me the word. 'Bring your camera', if you like – 'You'll get a few good shots.' It was his older brother who was fighting. He wasn't with Steve in the club. 'He's in bed resting', explained Steve. 'What's it all about?' I asked. I was told not to worry about that. It was a grudge match. The nature of the grudge was never explained. 'But he's fighting a blackie', added one of Steve's entourage, trying to give it a bit of extra sparkle. 'Just remember to bring your camera', said Big Steve again. 'We want you there to record it for posterity. One of my pals is going to video record it for me. We'll have something to look at when we're old men, something to look back at when we're past it.' The venue and the time were whispered in my ear. I was a little bit surprised by both. I thought that he might be setting me up.

The morning after

It was a bright sunny, spring afternoon and the park in the posh west side of Sheffield was full of children, ducks, and lovers. The sunshine had drawn them all out. A circus tent had been erected in one corner of the park, and the children were congregating down that end. At the opposite end by the duck pond stood three men in their late twenties or early thirties. One wore shades and a bright yellow Levi jacket. He had the build of a bouncer. He and his friends were obviously waiting for something. It just wasn't clear what. They didn't look like the type to waste a few hours in a park, even on a sunny afternoon. They looked like the type who should be bobbing and weaving in some dark corner somewhere. The sort who don't get up until lunch time.

They sounded lost. 'Are you sure this is the right spot? It's the only needle thingamyjig in the park. It must be here. I bet your other man doesn't show, anyway.' The man in the yellow jacket with the size 52-inch chest seemed to be thinking aloud – 'This is going to be a right waste of time.' 'A right waste of bloody time', echoed his friend, as another young couple with their nice, neat middle-class children in tow walked past in search of the ducks. 'I've better things to do on a Saturday afternoon than this, you know', said the man with the huge chest and the shades. Suddenly a cavalcade of cars approached along the road at the side of the park. 'Eh up, something's happening', said the man in the shades. But you couldn't see his eyes to determine whether he thought that what was happening was positive or negative. A series of cars pulled in opposite and out of each one poured groups of men of the most unlikely shapes. One was at least six foot six, and twenty-two stone. None of the men looked far behind in terms of build. I could only guess at their occupations. They were clearly not men to mess with. Out of the last car emerged two females, with unlikely shapes of a different sort, and tight-fitting clothes which accentuated their shape. The men poured into the park, the females hung back gingerly.

Two men seemed to be leading the group. One was smaller and older than the other. 'He's ready', said the large one. It was Big Steve. He winked across at me. 'Fit and ready for the fight', he said again reassuringly. His older brother wore what looked like an old casual shirt, khaki-coloured combat trousers, and trainers. 'I came down this morning and swept the concrete slab where they'll fight', said Big Steve. 'I bet it'll be as slippy as fuck', said his brother. 'I'll be slipping all over the fucking place.' And at this point he performed a few mock slips, before going into a hand spring. 'He may be forty five and he may not have had a proper fight for fifteen years but he's as game as fuck', said the man in the yellow Levi jacket. And the bare-knuckle fighter stood in front of the assembled throng demonstrating his kick-boxing technique. 'Whamo', he said as he kicked the air. 'Whamo.' 'I may not have had a proper fight for all those years, but you never lose your ability. Isn't that right, brother?' Big Steve just nodded. 'My whole family have natural fighting talent, natural talent, none of this steroid crap', Big Steve added after a slight pause. 'I fucking hate steroids. You see all these bastards walking around full of them.' The man with the very large chest, indeed the unnaturally large chest, dressed in the yellow Levi jacket winced.

Steve's brother did another hand spring on the grass. I wasn't sure whether he was warming up or giving us all a demonstration. But a demonstration of what? A demonstration of the fact that although he was forty five years old he could still do hand springs on the grass? Or were these moves he was going to make in the fight, the fight where anything goes? Even hand springs.

We all waited patiently. Millsie had been one of the first to arrive. I just hadn't noticed him. He had been sitting on a memorial to Queen Victoria. He looked pleased to see me. 'I hope you've not come to fight in those clothes, Geoffrey. They might get a little bit dirty.' They were all laughing, including Big Steve's brother. I suppose that it was a way of relieving the tension. I just happened to be a convenient target, the fall guy. 'Things may get a little bit out of hand, and you're poncing about as if you're going out for the night. I mean black trousers and an orange bomber jacket. What the fuck do you think you're here to do?' It hadn't occurred to me that I might be involved in any of the fighting. My imagination did not stretch that far. They were all roaring with laughter, but they got bored quickly. It must have been the tension. I asked Millsie what he knew about it all. 'All I know is that it's a bare knuckle fist fight between our man and this black kid, who's twenty four. It's a bit of a grudge fight really. The dispute's been going on for months. It flared up again in a casino in the middle of the week. There was no way it was going to be settled amicably so they agreed to settle it here today at 2 o'clock. Big Steve asked us down here to show a bit of presence, to back him and his brother up. I came because you never know when it's going to be your turn to need some backing. Big Steve's well respected in this town, in fact, he's got the hardest reputation in the whole place. But it's his older brother who's involved today. The rest of the family will have to stay out of it, if the blacks do, that is. If they get involved it could be really dangerous, because some of them could be carrying – knives and that sort of gear. It could be a war down here today.'

It was now five minutes past two, and the seriousness of the occasion seemed to be lifting. The birds were singing, for goodness' sake. Big Steve's brother continued to loosen up with a series of kicks and hand springs. I thought that he might wear himself out. The hard men with the fifty inch chests continued to greet each other and remake old acquaintanceships. 'What time did he ring you at?' There was a certain pride in who had been contacted first. It was a measure of each individual's personal worth. Then it was time for other chit-chat – 'Did you have a lot of trouble on the door last night?' I overheard one boxer talking to his friend – 'I know somebody's who's put two hundred quid on the black kid not showing. My pal says he hasn't got the bottle for it, and look at all us mugs standing about here on a Saturday afternoon. I bet we look like a right circus.'

There was almost a party atmosphere, growing as every second past. The other kid was late. 'No bottle.' You would have had to be deaf not to have heard the whispers. 'No bottle.' But suddenly the whispers stopped. 'Just look down there. It's like something out of the film *Zulu*.' And sure enough across the park walked this large group, nearly all black. Just one white person with a shaved head and an Alsatian dog and girlfriend in tow. There were over thirty of them, nearly all big just like the other group. 'This is war', said one. 'Jesus, they've even brought their families for a day out', said another. The bare-knuckle fighter momentarily stopped his kick boxing, and stripped off his shirt. He wore a black singlet under the top. 'There's the black kid down there in what look like brightly coloured pyjamas.' And sure enough one well built black guy with a shaved head walked towards the concrete slab. 'Right, brother, you're on', said Big Steve. One of Big Steve's pals with a camcorder made his way down to the slab to record the whole thing for good measure.

The two fighters faced each other from opposite ends of the slab. There were no rules or seconds. This was a fight from a different era. They circled each other slowly. The white fighter appeared to be smiling ever so slightly. The other one looked extremely serious. This was after all a fight with no rules. This was a fight that nobody would stop. The large contingent of spectators would see to that. I noticed that some kids from the park had crowded in for a better view. One little girl with long blonde hair was playing with the toggle on her hooded sweatshirt. It seemed an age before any punch was thrown. The black fighter missed spectacularly with one. The white fighter smiled again. The crowd grew impatient. 'Go on, get stuck in, stop fannying about.' 'Go on, get stuck in.' 'GO ON FINISH IT.' 'GO ON.' 'GO ON.' The first punches landed with dull thuds. A boot made the same kind of dull noise on a groin. Blood was already appearing on the white fighter's face. The two bodies locked together and tumbled onto the ground. The brightly coloured pyjamas pushed and heaved and toiled their way to the top of the dusty heap. The crowd swarmed in. 'Don't touch them. Leave them to it. 'DON'T FUCKING TOUCH THEM.' A black fist was still free to work inside the hold. It smashed into the white guy's face. His teeth sank into his ear. 'He's going to bite his fucking ear right off.' The group of blacks opposite were going wild, sensing that their man was winning. 'Finish him off. Fucking do him proper. DO HIM', shouted one in dreadlocks. The blood poured out of the older white guy's face. The black guy standing over the pair of them took the initiative. 'He's had enough.' 'Do you want to call it over?', he asked of the battered and bloodied white fighter. No words were spoken, but then again perhaps none needed to be. It was obvious who had won. The black guy in the bright pyjamas got up slowly. Big Steve was trying to smile. The large contingent of blacks walked back through the park. The whole thing had only taken seconds from start to finish. The large gang supporting the white fighter looked crestfallen. 'He got too excited before it started', said Big Steve. 'He'd got nothing left when the fight itself started.'

Big Steve's brother got up off the ground slowly. His face was covered in blood. There was a deep bite wound by the base of his ear. It looked like the ear might have come off if the fight had been allowed to continue. 'How bad is my ear?' he asked his brother. 'Not too bad', his brother replied – 'it'll look better once it's been washed.' 'That was a load of bollocks', said the fighter. 'I never really got going. 'Never mind', said Big Steve. 'These things happen. Don't worry about it.'

The group made its way back slowly out of the park. Millsie was very disappointed. 'That was fucking crap. I've seen better fights than that in my local boozer.' This large gang seemed very disappointed with their man's performance. 'If I'd fought like that last night, I'd be in hospital today', said one with some teeth missing.

Suddenly a number of police cars screeched along the road. Police wagons and other vans with dogs hurtled across the park. Somebody had obviously rung the police. 'Don't run', said Big Steve. 'Just make your way out. Don't look up for fuck's sake. Just try and walk right past them. If they ask about his ear, just say that he was climbing a tree and fell off.'

We shuffled out of the park. 'Stop right there', shouted the senior officer on the scene 'What's been going on? What's happened to his ear?'. We were like the deaf and dumb. We just walked in a straight line. The police did not try physically to stop this group of large dangerous looking men. I kept my gaze focused on the ground in front of me, without glancing up I turned instinctively to the right of the gate. Unfortunately, my car was parked somewhere along the road on the left. I seemed to be out on my own. I had stuffed my camera up inside my bright-orange bomber jacket. I walked quickly, trying not to run. I got to the end of the road and turned right trying to double-back on myself to get to the car. A large van of police screeched to a halt beside me. My bright jacket must have stood out a mile. They asked me what I had been doing in the park, and what I had up inside my coat. 'You've been photographing the fight, haven't you?' they asked. I said that I had been photographing the ducks. They asked for my name. When I said 'Doctor Beattie', they said 'Go on Doctor, sorry for bothering you.'

I saw Big Steve that night in the same nightclub as the night before. He was in a foul mood. His brother had been beaten and his friend who had been given the video-camera to work had forgotten to turn it on. I wasn't sure which grieved him the most. The fact that his brother had taken a beating, or the fact that the gore had not been recorded for posterity. He told me that there was going to be a rematch, but his time it was going to be in a barn somewhere with no possibility of any interference from outside. He said that his brother had taken some tablets for a bad back and that these tablets had weakened him. 'That's why he lost. It was just because of these tablets, you see.' I didn't think that it was wise to dispute this. 'The next time though he'll be ready for it. I'll make sure that he is. The next time he'll win and win well.'

Before I left he asked me if I knew how to operate a video-camera.

October 1991

'It's like Chicago or New York or Belfast'

You feel safe living in the very heart of England. In the winter, a touch of snow on the Pennines, but well away from the sea and the storms that wreck the coastline. In the summer, the odd disturbance, but well away from the street violence of the South, or the North, that wrecks our complacency. Nice and safe – everybody knows their place, everybody knows how far they can go. Nice and ordered. Or so I thought.

But this last year seems to have been different. Things seemed to be changing. There's been a certain menace in the air. But don't take my word for it. Just eavesdrop on the casual conversations in the pubs and clubs in the nether regions of the night. Doubt has crept in. Doubt and fear, and, of course, that rather cursory glamour that goes with it. There has to be a positive side to everything. First there were the shootings, and then there were the bombings – or rather the suspect bomb. It seems that urban violence had finally arrived up here. And all in such a short space of time. 'It's like Chicago,' said one wine bar habitué trying to get used to the new ambience of the night – 'or

New York.' There was a very long pause as his companion tried to think of something topical and yet relevant to say. Eventually, he thought of it – never mind that it was five seconds too late. 'Or Belfast'. Voice number one ignored him, and turned his back. Voice number two went for new alliances – 'I'm John, by the way, and that's Gary – he used to be a footballer, once – a long time ago. He was famous then, now he's just a has-been. He's also a right shit-head. He went to the front of the queue tonight and left me standing in the rain. He probably went up to the bouncers at the door and said, "Remember me, the has-been?" That's the only way he gets anything. But not for much longer – things are changing around here – even for has-been superstars who've been getting their own way for far too long around here. You'd better keep your head down Gary, otherwise it'll be "boom, boom".'

Gary parried with a glancing smile, but he did look momentarily perturbed. He clearly believed that the rules were changing – the rules for survival in that dark hinterland where he had made his home, ever since his footballing skills had begun to slide, ever since the thrill of Saturday afternoon had given way to the greater thrill of Saturday night – with the hangers-on, and the parties and the girls.

John was clearly now enjoying himself. 'Gary's put it about just a little too much, you see. There will be a few husbands still looking for him somewhere out there – somewhere in the night. I don't think that he would have been quite so keen at the time giving the birds all that flannel and the rest if he'd known that he was going to be living in Chicago in the near future. Would you Gary, my old son?'

The has-been, and his one remaining hanger-on, went on contemplating their future in an uncertain world. For them now a very uncertain world. Clearly all this new activity was giving them something to talk about. And not just them.

I had heard the news the minute I stepped into the club. Big L had been shot, and it had all been done in such a cold, calculating way, as well. But Big L did have enemies – everybody knew that, and they had been saying that Big L had been getting his own way for far too long. No bouncer would tackle him. They just didn't fancy it somehow. On the nights at the top clubs, when jackets still had to be worn, Big L would turn up with just a shirt and a life jacket of gold chains glinting off his huge black chest. He seemed to like just wearing shirts, they showed off his muscles better. Some big men in jackets look a little strange – awkward, uncomfortable, compressed. Big L didn't like to feel compressed. He liked the freedom of movement – he liked to strut and swagger, and bend all the rules.

I'd talked to him a fortnight before. He'd confessed to me that he had now made it – he had a one hundred grand house and a ten grand car, and that for the first time in his life he was worried, worried that girls might go after him just for his money. 'How can I be sure now what they really want? I'm scared,' he had said. He may have been scared, but he wasn't expecting this. Shot in some city centre car park some months ago. The local papers had made the most of it – MAN GUNNED DOWN ON STREET, in great eye-catching capitals, before adding that 'his injuries were not serious'. But nevertheless he was 'blasted on the left side of his abdomen,' and the paper added for good measure that 'Last month a 21-year-old West Indian was blasted in the hand by a .22 bullet as he left Pinky's on Spital Hill,' lest anyone be in any doubt that there had been an epidemic of shootings, at least among certain sections of Sheffield's population. It was Chicago alright. No-one was being merely shot in this town anymore, everyone was being blasted out of existence. Or at least out of doors.

But we didn't even have a chance to recover from all this blasting that was going on, before the next thing we knew there were suspect car bombs in the street. A few weeks after the blasting, a punter was leaving the local casino at 4.00 am only to find his Audi Quattro some distance from where he had parked it. Now, if this had been me, I might have thought faulty hand brake. I might have even have thought 'bloody delinquents'. With a few seconds hindsight, I might even have concluded that Napoleon brandy is a little too strong for me after all. But not this punter. He immediately thought 'Gaddafi'. Gaddafi?

The police took the threat seriously after checking his identity with Scotland Yard's Special Branch files. The rich Libyan businessman concerned, who had recently moved to Sheffield from London, somehow registered on Special Branch files as being potentially at risk. Here in the very heart of England he had set up a very up-market fashion shop in a converted terraced house. Here in the very heart of England, he now found himself with a suspect bomb in his car at 4.00 in the morning. Everything about the man was improbable to say the least. A wide area around his vehicle on the Ecclesall Road in Sheffield was immediately cordoned off. The Royal Army Ordnance Corps bomb disposal team then arrived with its remote-controlled 'robot' equipped with a TV search monitor. Now, we've seen these robots on the streets of Belfast, we've even seen these robots on the streets of London, but not on the streets of Sheffield, not in the very heart of England. Three rounds were fired into the car in the search for a bomb, and everyone held their breath in anticipation of the big bang. The big one that never came.

That anyway was the excitement of Friday morning, now it was Saturday night, and here was the hunted man in person. Hunted men have a certain look, and here was the expression for all to see. Even uninterested by-standers were attracted by that look. He had apparently spent the weekend ringing round for some bodyguards, but they just didn't fancy it somehow. So here he was sidling up to the nightclub on his own at 1.00 am, complete with shades. 'Who the fucking hell is that old guy with the shades?' said Gary. 'Is he blind or what?' But his question was immediately answered as the fugitive removed the shades, as he took cover in the fluorescent gloom of the club.

All eyes were now on the blind man who had so miraculously shrugged off his disability. He took up a position that had everyone gasping. It was Big L's corner. What strange quirks of fate were linking their destinies? What was happening? What would Big L do when he heard about this in his hospital bed? The Libyan businessman did not look relaxed. Afterwards he tried to put us all at our ease by saying, 'I want to say sorry to the people of Ecclesall and anyone else who was inconvenienced. The authorities took steps to prevent any possibility of injury to people or their property. But I will not comment on why I think a bomb might have been put in my car. I was not in the casino to gamble or drink, that is against my religion. I am organising a fashion display there and was discussing business. The police have been fine about what happened and I do not think it will affect my business. This sort of thing could happen to anyone.'

Anyone? Our collective pulses were racing. Despite the deadening effects of all that alcohol, Gary's pulse was sprinting away from him. It was as if his whole life was flashing before him rather like a drowning man, which I suppose he was in a way – drowning in a sea of lager and brandy and maudlin reminiscences. His hanger-on was clearly enjoying himself. 'Just imagine if someone slipped a device under your beautiful white XR3. That's the last thing you'd ever know, Gary. No chance to play at Anfield, now, old son. It would be good-night world, and hello Bill Shankly.'

Gary's face descended into his brandy. 'Mindless bloody violence,' he said, and it echoed in a strange way around the cavernous glass. Even John looked depressed, as he realised that he had gone just a little too far. It's important to recognise change, it's quite another thing to use it for your own ends. Even he felt a little sorry and a little gloomy as he overheard ex-boyfriends and ex-girlfriends trying to patch up their differences 'because you only live once,' and 'you never know what might happen' and exhorting each other 'to live every day as if it's your last, because one day you'll be right'. Everybody was using the unexpected violence of the past year. Thugs were glorifying in it. Relationships were being repaired or ended because of it. The meek stayed at home and worried, or went to nightclubs to huddle together, as a result of it.

Gary's face sank lower and lower into his glass. But just at that moment a huge black hand descended on his shoulder. A hand of greeting. A hand to steady and calm. The hand passed through Big L's vacant territory and brought momentary peace and tranquillity to that unhappy space. The same hand reached across the throng and touched the rich Libyan businessman on the shoulder and comforted him in passing. The hand seemed to be saying that 'others might not fancy it somehow, but here we do. Here, you're safe in this haven away from the terrors of the street, and the hidden menace of municipal car parks.' It was the hand of friendship, it was the hand of comfort, it was the hand of a huge black bodybuilder who just happens to be a doorman at this particular club.

Gary pulled his face back out of the glass, and felt his old self starting to return. 'I feel like a right good drink tonight,' he said. His friend John had learned his lesson, and he went back to trying to persuade Gary to stop off at a sauna on the way home. 'You can sit at the reception, if you like. I'll not be long. It's alright for you superstar footballers. The rest of us have to get what we can.' Things were definitely looking up – even Gary's stolen status had somehow been returned to him, intact.

Perhaps it was all just a passing fancy – a gloom that had momentarily descended from the bleak Pennine Moors. A chill blowing in on a cold winter's night. But in a quiet moment I slipped across to the man whose job it was to comfort the world with those huge hands, to ask what he thought about all these new threats. His head gave an involuntary twitch backwards – it was more than a shrug, but not quite a guffaw, but it was a sharp enough movement to allow me to see right up his nostrils. 'Sometimes people want to believe that their lives are at risk. It helps them appreciate what they've got. But a couple of shootings and one non-existent bomb – what does that amount to?'

I nodded in agreement as the chill dispersed in the air-conditioned ambience of the club. 'But isn't there anything to be really scared of around here then?' I asked. His head shrugged again. 'Well, I'll tell you what I'm frightened of – do you know that I have to eat twenty-four raw eggs a day to keep my body in shape? Two dozen raw eggs a day, full of God knows what. Now that, believe me, is living with fear.'

I appreciated then that it really had been a very menacing year, it's just that I hadn't realised why.

January 1990

Knowing the score

Rod has always liked the old boxing adage – 'You can run, but you can't hide.' The ring is a very small place after all, not unlike many of the places where Rod himself has worked. 'The only difference is that the "ring" in which I work can be a little bit more violent,' said Rod. 'I do count some fairly famous boxers – both past and present – among my friends, by the way. I appreciate what they are called upon to do, and vice versa. Most ordinary people would have trouble imagining what it's like to square up to somebody and not be able to hide. The difference between me and other fifty-year-old men, I suppose, is that I've found myself in a succession of jobs where I couldn't hide. When trouble erupted, I had to be there. After all somebody has to sort it. When trouble occurs, Joe Public disappears into the crowd, even bobbies can mysteriously disappear, but I stand out in my bow tie. Violence is something I've had to face, and I was going to say "get used to" over the years, but you never really get used to it. You daren't let yourself get used to it, as if it's some old familiar friend.'

We were talking in Rod's club in Sheffield. It was 2.00 am. This is Rod's kingdom. All the punters, who are worth knowing, know Rod. They all greeted him. He can't remember all their names, so he greeted them generically and politely – 'Hello, Sir'. There was a certain rigidness and formality in the greeting, which harked back to a time when greetings were indeed rigid and formal – when everybody knew their place in the social order. In this club they still do. Rod belongs to that generation, where position and politeness reigned. I noticed that his shirt cuffs, just visible beyond the end of his jacket, were immaculate. There was something about his bearing – others have noticed it was well. 'Some police officers said to me recently that they could tell that I had been in the Forces, they could tell that I had been an Officer, but I was only a Private in the Air Force, during National Service. I was obviously flattered though,' explained Rod.

Brendan Ingle's Gym, Wincobank, Sheffield, 1992

Rod turned to greet some more couples entering the club. The greeting almost never varied – all men were 'Sir', all women 'Madam', except on occasions a 'Sir' could become a 'young Sir'. Punters who knew Rod well sometimes reciprocated, and he got 'hello, young Sir' back again. To an outsider it all sounded rather strange, as if some elaborate game was being played, perhaps even a slightly tongue-in-cheek game. Rod, after all, is hardly a 'young Sir', without stretching the imagination just a little. But it was no game. Herol Graham came in. He was accompanied by Johnny Nelson who was clowning about a little in the foyer of the club. Both their faces lit up when they spotted Rod. They looked genuinely pleased to see him. 'Hello, young Sir,' said Herol. For the first time that night Rod used the person's Christian name in greeting, but 'young Sir' was still reserved for Johnny.

'I always give them both the same advice before a big fight,' explained Rod, as they passed. 'I tell them that they have to imagine that their opponent has just done something really nasty to their five-year-old daughter, and that they've been given the chance to deal with him alone. I use the same technique myself when it comes to dealing with trouble. It's the best way of getting yourself all fired up inside, and you have to be fired up inside.'

Rod has worked on the door of a variety of nightclubs for over a quarter of a century. I asked him how violence had changed over that time.

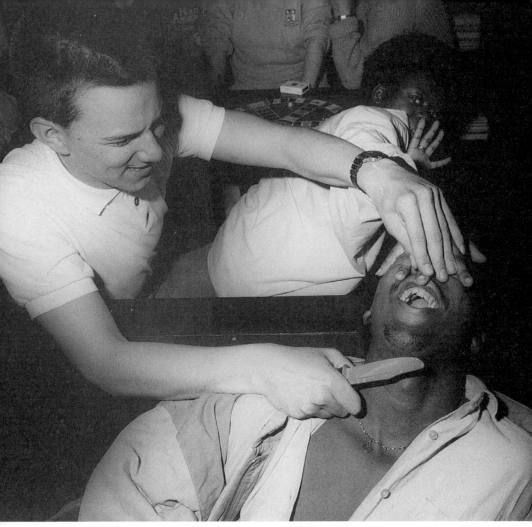

Boys play fighting, Hyde Park Flats Community Centre, Sheffield, 1986

   'The first thing you have to remember is that I've changed over that time as well, and not just the sorts of violence that you're confronted with,' he replied. 'When I was twenty-five, I thought that I was invulnerable. You do at that age. With time you start to feel a little bit more vulnerable. I started to feel very vulnerable a few years ago when my son, who was then eighteen, punched me in the ribs during some play fighting. I had to go into the kitchen to recover and pretend that he hadn't hurt me. Of course, in a real fight when the adrenalin is flowing, you don't actually feel anything. We were only messing about, there was no adrenalin, and that's presumably why it hurt so much. But it still worried me. I used to be a very strong person. I used to work out a lot, and run in weighted boots. I found them in my garage the other day. They're hard enough to life now, let alone run in. I was always testing myself in those days. I used to hit myself with a hammer during my lunch periods at work. I know it sounds ridiculous, but I needed to know where it hurt most – to see how hard I really was. And you've got to know where it's going to hurt others.'

'The way that I know that I'm not as strong as I used to be is that when I take hold of people these days I have to do it with more pre-planning. The main thing a bouncer has to do is to escort people off the premises. You have to take hold, and do whatever is necessary to remove them. In the old days I didn't give it much thought. I knew that I had the strength to hold them, but now I have to do it with considerable care. I always take hold of them from behind, and pull them backwards towards me. They're off balance and can't break free without strangling themselves – accidentally, of course. Everything you do is accidental in this business. As long as I keep walking they've had it. I could walk them for a mile, if I wanted to. They're falling backwards all the time, and it's one of those holds which really is easier with a bigger chap. The older I get the more I have to rely on safe methods like this one. So this feeling of vulnerability is bound to alter your views on violence.'

'There's nothing sadder, of course, than a bouncer getting past it. I remember working in this club, where there were these six right noisy lumps. I asked them to be quiet, but the leader of the group just called me over and said to me, "You don't know who you're dealing with here, mate." He then pulled out his driving licence and he showed it to me, and, believe it or not, his name was "James Bond". I think that he assumed that I was going to be impressed by this. But James Bond and his friends just had to go. I was very keen in those days. After we'd escorted them all out, I spotted this doorman, who I thought was really old at the time – he must have been about my age now. He was spitting on his hands and hitting the wall of the club. I asked him what he was doing and he said, "I'm lining them up boss." I told him that they'd gone about ten minutes ago. I saw him later that night with his hands above his head, asking blokes to punch him in the stomach. I thought to myself that I never wanted to end up like that.

'I didn't. I don't wait for ten minutes before I start getting busy. But I do recognise that I've changed. So, too, has the kinds of violence that you come across in clubs. Twenty-five years ago, it was extremely rare to see anyone being glassed. I remember very clearly the first time that I ever saw anyone hit with a glass. He was a foreman of this group of Irish labourers. One of his workers cut him from his eye right across his cheekbone to the side of his chin. It was a right mess. We got the guy who did it, and then got an ambulance for the foreman. I remember that we took the foreman down the backstairs so that no-one in the club would see him and become alarmed by this awful sight. The other thing I remember about this incident was that the following night the guy who had been glassed turned up at the club again, and tried to gain admission. He had got this huge bandage on his face, and it just looked like a giant white scarf. I just told him that he couldn't come into the club looking like that. It was rare in those days to see this kind of thing, nowadays you just pick up your local paper and everyone's doing it. They're glassing old men, women, anybody who's around, anybody who's in their way.

'Some things, though, aren't so new. Fairly recently there was all this fuss about football hooligans throwing darts at matches. I remember this happening in about 1963 in a mining village where I was working on the door.

Perhaps the guys who did it had been in the pub playing darts beforehand, maybe they didn't mean to bring the darts into the club with them. Sort of absent-minded like, but they used them all the same, and that was twenty-six years ago. These things go in fashions. I remember the fashion for flick knives, then the fashion for Stanley knives. Guys used to carry Stanley knives in their breast pockets – they just looked like pens. But they were lethal when they got them out. They're very inventive the people who carry weapons, of course. I know of one club where they've started using metal detectors on the door, so what do these characters do – they carry large splinters of glass with insulating tape wrapped around one end. These days too many people carry something on them. In my experience only about one third of these people will actually use the offensive weapon, the other two thirds are just bloody stupid. The problem, of course, is working out who belongs to that third.'

'Twenty-five years of working on the door has made me more wary of certain people. Out there are some people who are prepared to do whatever is necessary in a fight. Never mind who's hard, and who isn't, it all boils down to what you are prepared to do. I think that I've developed the ability to recognise such individuals. You have to when you work in this business long enough. Lower down the scale of seriousness, you also learn to recognise when someone is going to hit you, and when they're not. And, of course, the only way of dealing with this is to get in there first. But can you imagine trying to persuade a court of this? And as for the real hard men – the men that are prepared to do whatever is necessary – you can tell them by their eyes. There's this one little guy who sometimes comes in here – no-one would ever tackle him. He's got these cold, staring eyes. Of course he's got the reputation to go with it. He is heavy. My heart always stops when you see some kid bump into him, and you think, "Oh God, what's going off." Thankfully, most people who don't know him or his reputation, are put off by those eyes.

'You can always tell someone who knows what he's doing in a fight by where he hits another person. Somebody who doesn't know the score will punch another guy on the nose. What good is that? It just makes the other person angry. And it produces a lot of blood which makes it very difficult for the police to ignore. You can break the nose, of course, that's not difficult to do at all. But that just makes them even angrier. Somebody who knows what he's doing will always try to land a good punch in the stomach, particularly if the other person has been drinking. If they go and complain to the police, the police will just send them packing There's nothing to be seen, you see. Give them a bloody nose or knock them out and it's harder to ignore. I know of one case where a colleague of mine knocked a punter out and the police desperately tried to ignore it. They ended up going round the block four times, but every time they got back the guy was still lying there – flat out, with a crowd around him. They ended up having to arrest my friend. Now that's no good at all – it's just not very professional. I've knocked guys out – accidentally, of course, they usually just stay out for about five or six seconds. Whenever they've stayed out for longer than that I've always got a bit anxious. But that's often because they've been drinking. Imagine if you let guys into the boxing ring with alcohol in their bodies. It would make boxers a bit wary. We have to tread a very thin line.

'I think that one of the problems with violence today is that the police have their hands tied in dealing with some of these really violent punters. There's always a huge fuss if somebody gets a clip in police custody. But the police know what they're doing. It's not Joe Public that's getting the clip around the ear hole, it's probably some nasty bastard that's getting what's coming to him. The police can tell them apart. We're definitely living in more violent times, and in my view police leniency has got a lot to do with it. There are some right nasty bastards out there, and some of us have to deal with them.'

And as we talked, one man of diminutive stature made his way into the club accompanied by a much younger female who towered above him. 'And that's one there,' whispered Rod, as he started to adjust the immaculate cuffs on his shirt. 'Good evening, young Sir,' said Rod. 'Good evening Madam. It's nice to see you both again.'

The man of diminutive stature seemed to grunt back and tried to force his mouth into a smile. His eyes, however, which I couldn't help but notice were strikingly cold and staring, stayed exactly as they were. Rod just sighed.

October 1989

Hello, it's only the police

We had passed the 'For Sale' sign on the corner, seven maybe eight times. 'It's dead tonight', said PC Mayle almost apologetically. 'There may be some action later on. That's what I like about this job, you never know what's going to happen from one moment to the next.' The radio crackled away in the background. We began another circuit of Sheffield city centre on a warm Friday night in summer. Everybody was dressed up with somewhere to go. Everybody except us.

'We may just get some action later on from the BBC.' I stopped counting the recession's 'For Sale' signs for a moment and looked around in surprise. 'They're the real threat. The BBC, by the way, are the "Blades Business Crew". They are so-called supporters of Sheffield United, who still manage to keep active out of the football season.' At that very moment we swept down past the Sheffield United ground and onto the London Road. The warm air or the cramped conditions inside the pubs had drawn the clientele onto the pavement. Everybody was supping. Everybody except us. The PC scanned the faces on the pavement. They scanned ours. 'They've got a bit of a reputation for causing trouble at one particular nightclub in Sheffield. They let off some CS gas in there recently. They then went up to the City Hall, and let some more off. It wasn't directly at the police, but there was police in the vicinity.' The police had obviously taken this extremely personally.

'The BBC have got a bit of a reputation, but basically they're just a gang of daft lads who are all out associating with each other.' I loved this word 'associating'. It was prime police jargon. The PC scowled at one lad on the

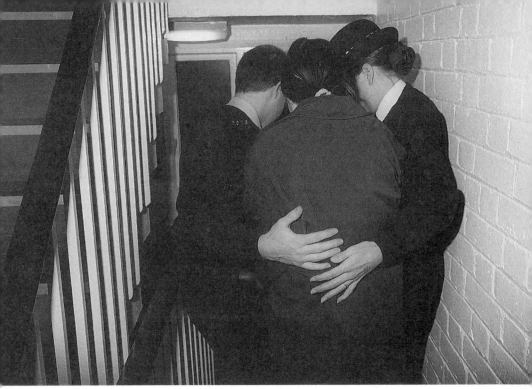

Police help a woman from her home, Sheffield, 1995

pavement. 'Their reputation far exceeds who they are, if the truth be known. They wander around in large groups causing small disturbances all over the city. That's why they're very difficult to deal with.' The big daft lad on the pavement scowled back even harder. 'We keep a couple of police horses in reserve to deal with them. Police horses seem to have a very soothing effect on them.'

The Panda car took a sharp left and drove up a very tight alleyway at the back of some pubs. Two young men in neat white shirts and fashionably cut trousers stood with their backs to us urinating against the low wall. The Panda crept silently behind them. The PC wound his window down. 'Can I have a word with you, *please*.' The young men looked around. There was a brief pause that stretched to eternity. 'SHIT!' shouted the one on the left. 'Now don't run off chaps, please.' There was then a moment's hesitation. They both looked at each other as they put their offending tackle away. Then bang! They were off. Sprinting down the alleyway. The PC quickly reversed the car. We were in hot pursuit. He was almost apologetic again. 'You see the problem is that I have to work out why they ran off. Have they run off because they think that I am going to do them for being drunk and disorderly? Or is it because they are wanted for something else. I have to chase them now to find out.' The Panda bumped and weaved down the narrow, rough alleyway. We didn't lose sight of them. At the bottom of the alleyway they turned and ran up a one-way street. We started off round the block, to try to cut them off. Suddenly a call came in that there was a fight in a pub near the bus station. We had to give up on our pursuit. Our Panda accelerated away, its blue light flashing.

'We'll keep an eye out for them later on when the pubs close. If our luck is in, we may spot them again.' A line of cars slowed our progress. PC Mayle sounded his horn. 'We do have flashing lights on the Panda cars, but we don't have any sirens. Probably because they're too expensive. But you'd think these motorists would notice the blue light.' Slowly, one by one, they pulled over to the side of the road to let us past.

'This could be it', said the PC. 'The big one of the night. It might be the BBC.' We pulled up at the far side of the bus station. The dog handler was there. So too was the public order van with a sergeant and five officers inside. Two other Panda cars had beaten us to the fight. A small male group were standing outside the pub looking towards the police. In the middle of the ring formed by the public order van, the Pandas and the dog handler's van stood one lone blonde female. She was in some distress, screaming across at the group in the doorway of the pub. There was no sign of any injury. 'If I lose this baby, you're dead. I'm pregnant, so why do it all.' Occasionally, the group by the pub shouted back. You couldn't really make out what they were saying, but it sounded conciliatory. It sounded like a vague explanation shouted across the carriageway separating the police and them. With the police at her back, the woman felt brave enough to approach the group from the pub. 'You started on me with a pool cue.' The warm summer's night had attracted some curious onlookers and they wandered into and out of the frame confusing the picture. The police dog was yelping in the background. 'Why did you pick on me? Eh? Well he's *dead* for a start', she shouted pointing at one large bearded fat man. The group from the pub did not budge. The bearded fat man came across to explain. The distraught woman was led away for a moment. Our Panda moved back towards the town centre. There were more than enough officers to try to sort the pub disturbance out. The bemused expressions on the face of the police suggested that this was not going to be an incident which took up too much of their time.

'You see that's the problem', explained PC Mayle. The call just said that there was a fight in the pub. It could have been very serious. It just turned out that it wasn't. Any incident can be totally innocuous or totally horrendous. I was called to a fight a little while back, and it was totally horrendous. There was this group fighting in the road, blocking this dual carriageway, blood everywhere. That was just called a "fight" as well.'

Back to the endless circling, to counting the 'For Sale' signs. One lone WPC seemed to be facing up to a group of five young men all dressed up for their night out in the very heart of the city. Reluctantly they moved off. But you could see from their facial expressions that there had been some aggravation. They sloped off slowly, frequently glancing back. 'What's been going off here', asked our sergeant. 'I caught them pissing in that shop doorway', answered the diminutive WPC. 'So I said to them "What would you do if you caught somebody pissing in your doorway?" So this big lad says "I'd kick the shit out of them." So I said to him "What's to prevent me from doing that to you?" And he said "Because you're in uniform." "Precisely." I said.' I didn't quite understand the logic of her last quip, but I didn't feel like querying it. She went back to her lonely sentinel at the corner of the street. We drove off.

PC Mayle shook his head. 'Some people have a real attitude problem when you stop them. You can tell that some will get violent. But a lot of officers are very good at talking people down. The only problem is if they've had so much beer that you can't reason with them.' There was a moment's pause. 'Or if they've got a certain kind of character. I believe that you can tell with ninety per cent certainty when someone is going to hit you. If people are shouting threats at you, then they're not going to do it. The ones that you have to watch out for are the quiet ones with a little smile on their face. They'll go along with you so far, and then bang. It's the ones who say or do nothing that are the real risk. The ones who are all mouth are getting rid of their aggression by mouthing off. That's my theory anyway.'

The radio was crackling again. The next call sounded foreign. I asked how he could possibly make out the message from something which sounded as if the people were speaking a different language. 'That's because it is a differ-ent language. We pick up Norwegian trawlers on our radios. It's something to do with the fact that Sheffield is built on a whole series of hills and valleys. The reception is poor. You can hear the men talking to their wives on shore. It's just a pity that we can't make out what they're saying.' The message from the Norwegian trawler was cut short by the report of an accident on Bridge Street. We got there before the ambulance. An elderly man lay half-on and half-off the pavement. He lay quite still. A policeman from another Panda car tried talking to him. He did not respond. An elderly woman leant into my ear. 'They'll get no sense from him. He's drunk as hell. He'll be alright in the morning, but I bet he'll have a hell of a sore head. My daughter works for the police, by the way, as a switchboard operator. And do you know some-thing she hates drunk men. She says that it's drunk men that cause all the problems in this town.' I wasn't sure whether 'man' was being used in its generic sense here, because the elderly woman herself appeared to be quite inebriated, as she leant right into my ear in the road. 'That's the thing about people when they've had quite a bit to drink', said PC Mayle when we had climbed back into the Panda car. 'They tend to bounce a bit when they've been struck by a vehicle. They're not hurt as half as bad as you would expect. The drink relaxes their body.'

Another call came on the radio. This time it was from an Indian restaurant on West Street. Somebody had threatened one of the waiters with a Rottweiler. It wasn't clear from the call whether the Rottweiler was actually on the premises or not. One Panda car had already got there. The waiter did not want to make a complaint. 'That's another of our problems', explained the PC. 'We get called to a lot of Indian restaurants. If somebody is being obstreperous or refuses to pay the waiters will threaten them by saying that they're going to call the police. But by the time we get there, it's all sorted out.'

The night was dragging. 'Nights like tonight, you have to make your own work. Running checks on cars, stopping cars, that sort of thing. Then you usually try to get back to the station from about 3.00 am to about 5.00 am to sort out some paper work, because the other thing about this job is that it generates a lot of paper.' Then the call came out – a domestic disturbance on the Wybourn Estate. 'Could be serious', said the PC. We went hurtling across

Sheffield City Centre, our blue light flashing, but still without the benefit of a siren. They were all already there – the public order van, two other Pandas. Only the dog handler hadn't made it, and the horses. 'You can tell it's quiet tonight', said the PC – 'everybody is present at every incident'. A woman in white leggings was directing the police cars up to her house. 'She's obviously the complainant', said the PC. Two men had been fighting over her. She had had enough. One man was having trouble controlling himself. He wanted to talk to the woman.

'Get the fuck in here now. Come here.' She stayed where she was.

'Get here now.'

The constable standing beside him told him repeatedly to calm down. It was having no effect.

'Get here, now.'

When it came, it came without warning. 'You're under arrest for causing a breach of the peace.'

'What's that?' The man looked confused and a little hurt.

'Alright!' said the officer taking him in a headlock. 'Just go my friend. You're not obliged to say anything unless you wish to do so. Anything you do say. . . .' The rest trailed off as the officer frog-marched the man to the public order van. The man looked more surprised that angry, more hurt than irate. Now. He sat in the back of the van with his head in his hands. Four local children still up well after midnight came to stare. We got back into our Panda. PC Mayle offered a gloss on this tiny fragment of life. 'You see the woman obviously rung up requesting the police to arrive. She obviously felt that she needed someone there, and that the situation was out of control. By removing that particular man when he's probably had a drink, you are re-moving the problem from the area.' There was obviously a script for this type of incident, but then again it probably happens so frequently that the script becomes indelibly etched on your brain. The man, however, was clearly sur-prised by the role written for him. The PC was ruminating on the incident. 'One of the biggest problems, of course, with domestic violence of whatever sort is that people are likely to withdraw their complaints after the situation has cooled off. You end up being the bad guys.'

Down in Bridge Street cells the man arrested for breach of the peace, sat on the low board, which functions as a bed. It could well have been his very first arrest. 'For nowt', he kept shouting. In the cell next to him sat a con-victed rapist brought to the station for an ID parade. The rapist had tried to kill himself the last time he was in a police station, with some electrical leads. So one officer was assigned to look after him throughout the long quiet night. He had to check his cell every ten minutes. The night was dragging down there as well. Pairs of trainers lay outside the cells that were occupied. There were only a couple of pairs that night. 'The breach of the peace will be let out when he cools off. He'll just get a verbal warning. It might make him control his temper a bit more', said PC Mayle. We hit the streets. A call came through that two youths were breaking into parking meters just off the Moor. The Panda sped across the pedestrianised part of the street. Two men stood at the bottom chatting. It was after 2.00 am. 'Excuse me, did you see two lads run off down here a few minutes ago?'

'Why?'

'Just asking.'

'Fuck off.'

'Okay, thanks.'

On that note, PC Mayle headed back to the station to catch up on his paperwork.

But the great thing about the British summer is its unpredictability. Last night might have been warm and balmy, tonight was like mid-winter. It was wet and misty. But the lads and lasses were still out in their summer clothes. 'Last night might have been quiet, but tonight there's a lot of action about', said Michael Hope (my nickname's 'Bob', by the way). 'We've had some pre-season football matches and we've got a crew in from Barnsley. A load of them have been locked up already.' It was only 10.00 pm. 'You can expect to see some violence.'

Nevertheless, our first call was a reported burglary on Park Hill flats, just behind the big roundabout as you drive into Sheffield from the M1. The lift stank of urine. 'Try not to breathe in', said Bob Hope helpfully. The burgled flat had no carpets. The floor was strewn with soiled clothes, cigarette butts, and bits of food. Holes had been punched in the door of the toilet and the door of the cupboard. A Treasure Trail map was hanging onto one wall. Just. 'God they've really made a mess in here', said the WPC. The complainant looked confused. 'Yeah, they smashed a bottle in the kitchen.' 'But what about all this', said the WPC pointing at the floor of the lounge. 'It's always like that. I'm not the tidiest of people.' Bob Hope took a statement. The flat looked empty, apart from the debris, but the only thing reported missing was the telly. The complainant knew who had taken in. In fact, he confessed that he had burgled a neighbour's flat to check that his telly was there. 'The problem here is that the flat is so dirty, you couldn't lift fingerprints from it', explained PC Hope. 'The other problem is that he got the telly from a friend of a friend in the first place. Therefore he hasn't got too many details about the telly.'

The WPC visited a flat a few doors away. An elderly woman had been complaining of harassment by local children. The WPC knocked the door. 'Hello, it's only the police.' There was no response. She turned to me. 'You see the elderly are scared stiff of opening the doors in these flats. They're terrified, in fact.' An age later an old woman made it to the door. She was housebound, she explained, and steep stairs led down to her living room. The contrast with the previous flat was stark. This flat was totally spotless. Children were tormenting the old woman by dropping lit matches through her letter box. 'It takes me ages to get up the stairs and my mother is bedridden. She's ninety five. What happens if one of the matches doesn't go out. How am I going to get her out of the flat. I wouldn't be able to carry her up the stairs. They pick on me because I speak differently to them. My father was a major in the British army. I was born in India. I speak proper English and they don't like it. They say that I'm not one of them. But it was my family who fought in the last war to keep them here in luxury.' The old woman went to attend to her mother. 'I can't blame the children', she said. 'Their mothers and fathers are in the pub all the time.'

Distressed woman, Sheffield, 1995

Her mother was shouting in the background. She was thirsty. Age had taken its terrible toll. The old woman was now shouting about her greenhouse. A greenhouse from some far off days. Perhaps a greenhouse back in India. You couldn't really tell. But certainly before all this. I noticed the calendar on the wall. It was from 1984. It read 'Bless this house/Oh Lord we pray/Make it safe by night and day.' The WPC, Vicky, said that she would sort out a smoke detector for the old lady, and told her that she would ask the community policeman to keep an eye out for her. It was the best she could do. It wasn't enough and she knew it. Her eyes were moist. 'But it's the best we can do with the available manpower.' When we got outside the flats, the WPC looked up to check that nobody was going to drop something down on us from above. Bob Hope noticed one fourteen year old with a brand new haircut.

'That's better than your last haircut, Brett.'

'Shut up you fucking twat', replied Brett before turning his back.

We stopped outside Bizzie Lizzie's fish and chip shop for Bob Hope to leave a note for the community policeman. A drunken woman insisted on getting into the car. 'Me mum died last Christmas day. Let me tell you this little tragedy. . . .' When Bob eventually got back she agreed to get out. 'I love you', she said to the WPC. She gave her a big wet kiss on the cheek. 'Jesus, she smells all of Persil. You smell lovely.' We left Bizzie Lizzie's for Sheffield's red-light area. A very thin white-faced girl stood on the corner, holding an umbrella. It was a miserable night for anybody to be out and about. Let alone to be out hanging about the streets. The Panda pulled in just by her.

Bob Hope wound his window down. 'Alright?'

'Yeah.'

'You're a braver girl than me on a night like that.'

The white-faced girl did not smile or respond.

'Take care.'

'Some of the girls have really tragic lives', said Bob, as we drove off. 'I heard from Vice that there's one girl who's got a boyfriend on crack who lets punters bugger her without a condom for a fiver.'

Suddenly another call came over the radio. A report of a stabbing in the Old Blue Bell pub. 'This is it', said Bob Hope. 'Could be the BBC.' The skid-start wouldn't have shamed the joyriders of Tyneside. Two minutes of adrenalin later, another call came over saying that it had been a false alarm. 'That's the thing', said Bob parking his Panda car – 'You never know when it's going to be the real thing.'

After the Panda, the public order van looked impressive. Surely no surly fourteen year old was going to call these officers fucking twats. The van moved slowly, almost stealthily through the town. He was spotted a mile off. 'He's watering!' came the cry from the front of the van. The van pulled to an abrupt halt. Two officers jumped out. The forty year old man in the cream trousers chomping at his doner kebab looked shocked. When the two officers got back into the van, they were both laughing. 'He said that he was standing there because he was lost. He'd got a big stain down his trousers. That's his fine for the night. He denied that he was having a slash, but it was still hanging out as we were talking to him.'

Heidi, an exotic dancer, Sheffield, 1982

We had just stopped laughing, when the van pulled in behind a Volkswagen driven by a large black guy. The car was wanted in connection with an assault reported earlier in the evening. The black guy was having none of it. He shouted about police harassment, before disappearing into a nightclub. The public order van parked just opposite, waiting for him to return to his vehicle. Ten minutes later, his friend emerged from the club and tried to move the car for him. The police stopped him so he went back into the neon shadows of the club. 'This one might take a while to sort out', said the sergeant in charge of the van, as he slumped down on the front seat. 'It could be a very long night.'

I left them to it.

As I walked back through Sheffield city centre strewn with dead litter bins, all I could think of was that others up in Park Hill flats were also going to have a very long night.

July 1993

'One of my clients tells me that I'm a very complex person'

Anita was a woman with a lot of 'oomph', a real go-getter. In Thatcher's Britain with unemployment at nearly 4 million Anita had managed to hold down not just one job – but three. She was simultaneously a part-time beauty consultant and a part-time secretary and she worked in a massage parlour. The last job was the most lucrative. 'You can earn up to £600 a week,' she said. 'Well, most girls earn a bit less but you can if you want to. It depends of course on what you are prepared to do. In this line of business hard work is rewarded.' Living proof that effort will get you somewhere in these times of recession.

Anita was twenty-three, blonde and pretty, but she had bad teeth. 'I could have been a photographic model,' she said, and she pulled out a wad of black and white contact prints. In them she looked very pretty indeed, she pouted and teased. You couldn't see her bad teeth. She would have liked to have been a model but the massage-parlour job came along. 'It probably pays better anyway,' she added. But what did her family think of the job? 'Oh, they don't know anything about it, they think I'm just a secretary. They're not my real parents anyway, they're my foster parents. They're in their seventies – very prim and proper, very strait-laced. They'd die if they knew. I had a very strict upbringing. Some of the girls are a bit rough. One of my friends worked on the streets in London before she came here. But I had a very proper upbringing. I hardly ever went out. I was very shy with boys. They'd just die.' But what about her friends? 'Well, most of my girlfriends know because they're in the business too, but I never tell my boyfriends. Well, how do you think they'd react? They wouldn't respect me for a start. They'd think I was an easy lay, and the funny thing is I'm not.'

Anita worked in a sauna/massage/adult-movie emporium, open twenty-four hours a day. Hers was a 'bent' sauna. Massage plus extras. They're always very busy. 'A lot of men call in on the way home from work and a lot on the way to work. Well, you know what men are like in the morning. Then we're busy at two o'clock in the morning when the nightclubs empty and even at five o'clock in the morning when the punters come from the casinos.' Anita's best friend was the receptionist in the massage parlour. Anita had been doing it for three years.

'Two of my best friends were in the business at the time. This was in Leeds. They brought me along. When the first customer came in I wouldn't go anywhere near him. He had picked me for the massage but I just couldn't do it. One of my friends had to do it for me. They were both mad at me, my friend and the punter. He thought it was something to do with him. My friend said, "How are you going to earn any money like this?" The first customer I did massage was a gentleman about fifty – very toffee-nosed, very prim and proper. He really put me off with his manner. The massage lasted about two hours – it's only supposed to take about fifteen minutes. He was lying on his stomach all that time. I didn't want him to turn over. But as soon as he did, he came out with the line I was dreading. "Any extras?" I could have died. I told him it was £15. I hoped he'd say he couldn't afford it. But he didn't. I had to go through with it. He said he knew it was my first time. I did it without looking at him.

'Most of my regular customers are between about thirty-five and seventy. I hate doing younger ones. Especially ones I fancy. I find it really embarrassing. Loads have asked me out. I've even been out with a few although I make it a rule never to go out with clients. I can't respect them. One of my older clients – he's sixty-three and called John – says he's in love with me. He comes twice a week – that's £7 to get in and £15 for the massage with extras – twice a week. That's £44 per week and he's retired. He's not that well off. He sends me letters nearly every week and keeps saying he'd like me to marry his son. But he never brings his son with him! He says I'm different from the other girls and should be doing something else for a living. He says I'm a very complex person. On one occasion he even asked me to kiss him. But that's something I would never do. Kissing is an emotional thing, it's not a sexual act. I hardly ever even kiss boyfriends! If I go out with a boy a couple of times I'll let him feel my tits – that's because he fancies me – but I won't let him kiss me. When you kiss someone you show your emotion. When John asked me I told him to get stuffed.

'I sometimes see clients when I'm out – well, you can't avoid it in a small place like Sheffield – but I never say hello unless they say hello first. It might make explaining who I am a bit difficult. It's amazing the number of girls who'd like my job. See the girl there – that barmaid [we were talking in a pub] – she was asking about a job last weekend. The money is so good. I did it first when I split up from my boyfriend. He was a Jewish wheeler-dealer, whizz kid making a bundle, some of it illegally. We lived together and he supported me completely. We lived on a kibbutz in Israel for a while. When we split up, I wanted to be independent – my own flat, nice clothes, a car. It was the only way I could achieve independence. I thought I'd just do it for a little while – all the girls do – but it's addictive. It's not the sex, it's the money. You get used to having it.

'But there's something else about the job which I really like. It's the status. In the massage parlour the girls are right high up in status and the men are so low. They know it and we know it. You get respect from the men. It's a good service and we have to be professional – cool, calm and collected. The men respect our professionalism. I've been offered a number of jobs through my work – selling, modelling, one client even offered to make me a director of his company. He said that I was good enough to be able to handle any-thing. But he also said that he wanted me to fall in love with him first. I told him I couldn't do that.

'Working in a massage parlour has done a lot for my self-confidence. I used to hate my body and be really shy with boys. But all the clients say that I've got a lovely pair of tits. I love compliments. I've also become a bit of an actress – I can act dead sexy, watch.' She narrowed her eyes and pouted her lips and Bardot circa 1960 shone through. 'You have to be an actress. I do a two-girl massage with my friend Debbie. I've learned a lot from her. She's been doing it for much longer than me. She can act dead sexy and she really turns the punters on. It's great to watch. The first couple of times I nearly burst out laughing, though. But Debbie's a real professional, she never laughs.

'I really respect the girls at work. The ones I don't respect are those that hand their money over to a pimp. They're as bad as the prostitutes on the street. But the other girls are real professionals. They're making a bomb. One or two have even opened their own businesses.

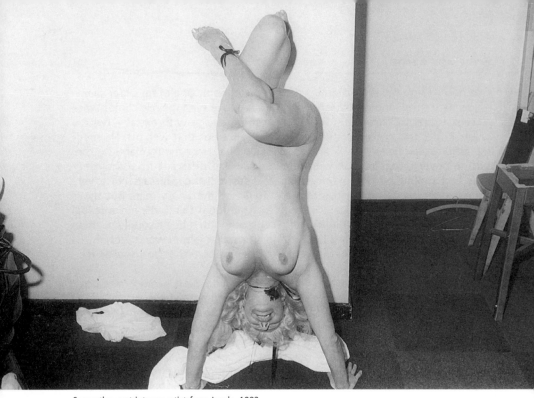

Samantha, a striptease artist from Leeds, 1982

'All the men want to chat to you while you're giving them a massage. They tell you about their wives and their businesses. They always say the same thing. "What's a nice girl like you doing in a massage parlour?" I tell them I'm just saving up enough money to go to university, which is true in a way. I used to want to do psychology in order to sort myself out, but now I want to do law. We get a lot of lawyers as clients and they're all very nice. I moved flat recently and John sent me a card with a little note inside telling me about visiting Bristol with his wife and how he missed seeing me. Wouldn't it be a laugh if I bumped into him one day with his wife and son? I wonder who he'd say I was. He says I'm a complex person and he'd like to sort me out. Perhaps if I study psychology I'll be able to sort him out.

'Working in a massage parlour hasn't put me off men. I've got lots of boyfriends but they don't know what I do for a living. God knows where they think I get my money from. I'm very clean. I don't do sexual intercourse. I have about three showers and one bath a day. When I get home from work I always have to have a bath to wash the dirt off. Sometimes I feel really filthy. I always like talking, as you can see. I never stop. I chat the whole time I'm giving a massage. Some of my clients can't get a word in. Just as well, some of them are a bit quiet.'

April 1985

'He's alright and he can even fix you up with a bird if you want'

Bill originally worked as a night porter in a hotel outside Sheffield. Life wasn't easy. 'Long hours for fuck-all pay. I was fighting a lot and getting all my exercise that way. But when I moved to a hotel in Sheffield, I wasn't getting enough exercise, I was getting fat. So after I finished work in the early morning me and a friend would take some weights and a punchbag out to the country. We'd tie it up to a tree and work out every morning. Oh, it were beautiful. Fantastic. My friend had a bit of a bad back but I knew enough about weights to help him out with different things. We'd wash in the cold stream afterwards. Oh, it were beautiful. Then I'd take my friend back down to the station to get the train home. But then the weather got bad so we were missing a few mornings. So we mentioned this to a guy called Bob we vaguely knew, who's very interested in boxing. We were telling him about our training and how it was disrupted by the weather. He told us that a friend of his had got a sauna with a gym so why don't we go down there. So we went down to see the bloke who owned it, and he said we could put our punchbag up, use the weights, the sauna and the Jacuzzi. Fantastic. All free. He also said if there were any trouble could we help out. We said of course we can. That's how I got involved and got to meet the girls. I knew most of them from around town anyway.

'I started looking after four girls, finding them customers and all the rest of it. I used to take one of the girls out. I told her she had to get herself smartened up though. I've got a big car, you see, a bit flash. I used to go round the clubs finding her good punters, you see. Earned a bit of money for myself and them as well. I used to go to a lot of blues as well – you know, the all-nighters for blacks. I started mixing with these black guys and their girls. You should see them up Spital Hill in Sheffield on Tuesdays.'

Bill was critical of women with black pimps. 'They're the low-life girls; they've got a way of talking. They imitate the black men's patois, they develop a sort of accent. It sounds so cheap. You can always tell them, they always say "You know", "You know what I mean, right". They slur on the "right". It's just me that notices these things, I think. "Do you want a cup of coffee, you know?" slurring all the time. Or "He's my man, you know, you've got to leave him". They slur all over the bloody place. They try to talk like black men.'

Bill had his own views on how women get into this line of work. 'Well, a lot of them have a rough background and leave home. And often, a lot of black men are out looking for these young girls that leave home. The blacks have got the run of it, for some reason. I wish I knew why! They take half their money, or even two-thirds of it. He then protects them against other pimps. But it's all a bit of a joke. The pimps get their mates to harass the girls and the pimp will come up and say "You leave my woman alone" and she's thinking "Oh, thank God for that", and it's just a game the pimps play for each other. It's psychological, I suppose. And these guys will be dealing in hash as well.

'In the saunas the atmosphere is more relaxed but quite a few of them have pimps anyway. I look after some of the girls there. In the saunas, they only let in the people they want. They've more control; but to be honest, they let anybody in. They don't really know what they're like until they get in. Some get a bit violent and slap the girls about.'

Bill had had to step in on a number of occasions to help the woman he was going out with. 'There was this guy, he was a bit mucky and my girlfriend didn't want to do anything, you see. He smelled; she wanted him to go and have a shower and all that, and that's what started the argument. So I went up and he was standing at the back with a wine bottle in his hand. He wanted to have a go, you see. So I took it off him, but he got that violent, I had to let him have it. When I say let him have it, I don't mean I brutally made a mess of him, I just sort of knocked him semiconscious.'

'But,' I said, 'weren't you a little worried for your girlfriend's safety?'

'Not really, I wasn't thinking of her as a steady girlfriend. She was just a steady fuck.'

'But weren't you a little worried for your steady whatever's safety?'

'It's part of the game,' said Bill, 'the same as what bouncers do or anybody else. You can't worry about things like that. The only difference was I was getting a tenner a night when I was a bouncer, she was picking up a hundred a night.

'Our relationship was quite simple. We both knew the crack. There was none of this "I'll take you out for a meal because I might be able to give you one afterwards". You know what I mean. I could give her one any time I wanted. It was nice to go out for a meal. It was nice for her to take me out for a meal. We could talk plainly to each other. I just lined up some punters for her. In the sauna she pays the owner £20 a week to work there, anything else she makes is entirely on her own back, to coin a phrase. It's £10 for a gobble, £15 for a fuck. But I've arranged for girls to go to punters' houses. Then they get up to £100 from one punter. The majority of girls who work on the streets are the girls who don't know what they're doing. They've got young pimps who think they're a bit clever, who are trying to work their way up the pimp scale, shall we say. They've got a few girls working for them who are often under age, who don't know anything else. Some of these girls in winter try to get into the saunas. The only way to categorise girls really is those who are working for blacks and those that aren't. Those that work for the blacks might go to the blues with them but they've no real social life. The girls who do it for themselves and any girls I know do have a social life. They're nice clean-living girls that you wouldn't think were on the game. They know the crack, they're very wide. They know what all the chat's about.'

Bill was especially useful for fixing women up with punters from out of town, through his other work in the hotel. 'When the snooker's on at the Crucible or when there's businessmen's conferences there's a lot of visitors to the town. It's entirely on your own back – it's nothing to do with any place you work for, it's entirely as a bloke to a bloke. They don't want ripping off and it's got to be a decent-looking girl, otherwise they'll think, who the fuck's he? What's he doing to me? So rather than send him to a sauna, I'll fix him up with some nice-looking girl I know that he can take out. And nobody will be saying "Look who's out with brass". They can go out with some nice company who can talk, present herself well and even associate with his friends if necessary. She'll get £100 and I'll get a drink from the businessman. The last bloke gave me forty-five quid for looking after him. He was worried, you see, that he'd end up with a right dog.

'The art is not to be known as someone who is always mixing with prostitutes. The art is to get people to say "He's all right and he can even fix you up with a bird if you want". That's the difference. Do you understand? I want to keep myself on that middle line. I'd hate to have a bad name for anything.'

August 1985

Being somebody

The vast majority of the workers are clad in rags. The material from which the workers' clothes are made is by no means ideal for its purpose. Linen and wool have practically disappeared from the wardrobes of both men and women, and have been replaced by cotton . . . All workers in England wear hats and they are of the most varied shapes – round, cone-shaped, cylindrical, broad-brimmed, narrow-brimmed, or without a brim. Only the younger men in the factory towns wear caps. Anyone who does not possess a hat makes himself a low, four-cornered cap out of paper . . . Their heavy cotton clothes, though thicker, stiffer and heavier than woollen cloth, do not keep out the cold and wet to anything like the same extent as woollens. (Friedrich Engels, *The Condition of the Working Class in England*, 1845)

'The most beautiful man in the world'

Christine was twenty and unemployed. She had been unemployed for almost exactly one year, having dropped out of university. One of the first things she did with her new-found leisure time was to change her appearance. Not in any slow subtle way but quickly, suddenly and dramatically. Her hair was swept up into a spiky bob above the ears and down to the neck on each side. She had a ritual to keep her hair like this, a painful but necessary daily ritual:

'When I get up, I scrape out the remains of the previous day's can of hair spray. I do this in my room so there's usually bits of flaky white stuff all over the cassette recorder. It takes about five minutes, depending on my pain threshold that day, because combing out hair spray is incredibly painful. Then I stick a load of gel or setting lotion on it. I only wash my hair about once a fortnight, because the gungier it is, the better it sticks up. Sometimes it gets so gungy that there are little white flakes in my hair, but when this happens, I just stick my head under the tap to remove the bits – that way I can wash them out without getting rid of the gunge. Then I get a piece of hair and pull it up as hard and straight as I can and dry it so that it stands up stiff. When all the hair is standing up, I get a jumbo-sized can of hair spray and spray the roots, and then I pull the hair up at the roots while aiming a hot blast from the hair dryer at them. Then I spray the whole thing all over and blow it with the hair dryer so that it sets – like concrete! If I think it still needs a bit more support, I spray over the sides and roots again. Then another quick spray all over and a bit of gel on the back to smooth it down. It takes about one hour a day – I have to do it every day. And I get through about three jumbo cans of hair spray a week.

'I've had my hair like this for about six months, I thought it was really me. I hate the attention I get, though, because most of it is really abusive. People come up to me in the street and say really nasty things. I never thought people could be like that. It's nearly always men – men that pass you in the street. One bloke came up to me and said, "I think you put it in the wrong socket, luv" – but he didn't say it in a jokey way, he was really threatening. Also, a bus conductor picked on me – tried to make out I'd paid the wrong fare, and started shouting at me – and I knew I hadn't. Then one time I was walking up the street and a bunch of policemen came out of a building. They started shouting at me across the street, saying things like, "Do you think we could fit a helmet on it? Can I have a feel?" I don't know why they do it, though, because I wear the same clothes as I've always worn, and it never happened to me then. I think men feel threatened by my hair. It's as if they think I'm trying to make some kind of statement, and they're saying, "Who the hell do you think you are, trying to be different?"'

Style maketh the person. You can look like a Mohican, you can be treated like a Mohican (i.e. uncivilised), you can even feel like a Mohican (threatened, virtually extinct). At least you are something. It may even get you noticed – and not just by the sneering public. UB40 (the band) have often been described as the voice of recession-bitten Britain – songs about the unemployed

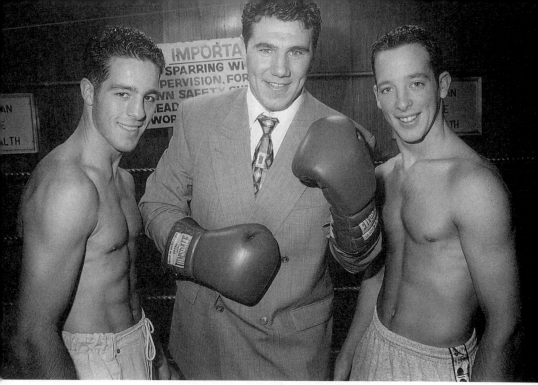

Nigel and Thomas Bradley with their sponsor, Brendan Ingle's Gym, Wincobank, Sheffield, 1994

joining the army to escape the dole queue. Songs about hard reality. But one of the most popular bands of the 1980s so far has been the Human League. Songs about girls plucked from nowhere because of their looks to become a member of a successful rock band. Songs about soft fantasy.

Sheffield is the home of the Human League. Hard Steel City, home of soft plastic fantasy. The fact that one of the female members of the group really was plucked from nowhere just adds to the fantasy. You can see the girls with their distinctive, elegant, individually styled gowns and long black elegant gloves dancing and waiting. Dancing in that exaggerated practised style which that type of girl does to that type of Human League song. Dancing and waiting – to be picked out and turned into someone new. A life away from the rain and wet and drabness of Sheffield's streets. A life away from the dole. A life in the sun. Most of them will have a long wait.

Trevor, however, felt that it was imminent. When Trevor walked down the street, people stopped and stared. Tall and dark – but with a shower of ringlets and a peroxide kiss curl in the middle of his forehead. His outrageously effeminate hairstyle triggered the initial head-turn but my attention was drawn principally to the clothes. He made them himself – out of curtains.

He was swathed in a voluminous black cape with matching vest, boots and trousers. Without the ringlets and a strategically placed Dexy's hat he might have been mistaken for a sartorially elegant Hammer version of a vampire – except that no self-respecting mid-European nobleman (even a Hammer films' one) would wear a cloak made out of blackout curtains.

When the weather was brighter, he would wear reversible outfits fashioned from strikingly patterned curtain material, enhancing the look with plenty of make-up. When we met he wore just a touch of mascara, because he was working for the Manpower Services Commission, which didn't leave much time in the mornings for getting his 'look' together. Before this job he was unemployed for a number of years.

'When I was on the dole I used to spend all my money on travelling around the country to different nightclubs, which meant I didn't have anything left to spend on clothes. I used to rifle my mum's drawers to see if I could find anything, and I came across all this curtain material, which I realised I could make into clothes really cheaply. I sometimes got the basic ideas in various clubs – but from clubs down in London – in London they've got all the resources, but they don't seem to know how to use them. It was in Manchester that I saw really different looks – I think they make more of an effort up north because they're kind of striving against ignorance. Once you start making the clothes, you sort of develop into making other things too. Like I've got a friend who's making his own shoes now – sort of ballet-type shoes; and I used to make hats – all you need is a bit of net and a few feathers. Oh, and then I found some toothpicks in one of the drawers when I was hunting for curtain material, so I painted them black and other colours and stuck diamanté and bits of broken glass onto them and made them into earrings. I'm making them for a lot of my friends now. I don't really notice other people's reactions until people start throwing things or spitting at me. Girls are too shocked to be abusive. The thing is, when I've got a lot of make-up on, I get less aggro, because people just assume I'm a woman.'

The creations sported by Trevor's friends were all originals – or so they liked to think. Rather than praising them for their individuality, however, Trevor bemoaned their anti-intellectualism.

'You see some in the street wearing something really striking and you think they must be really interesting – but when you get to meet them, all they want to talk about is the way they look. I had all my best discussions when I was still at school.'

And Trevor did make it – in the summer of 1984 he was famous – for a while. He was hailed as 'The Most Beautiful Man in the World' by all the tabloids. He was plucked from obscurity in 1984 from his native Sheffield by Mickie Most, record producer and entrepreneur, to become the next pop superstar. The gauntlet was thrown down to Boy George and Marilyn – they were warned, they had a new rival – six foot two inches, cavalier tresses, hairless chest, long fingernails, mascara, stubble – a real gender bender if ever there was one. He was hyped to the hilt. Spread out in the tabloids for public consumption, elevated to huge posters. A record was released but 'Cold As The Coldest Sea' got a rather icy reception from the record-buying public, despite all the hyperbole.

But one year later the tabloids had tired of him. Howcher was last year's big deal, last year's boy wonder. He's now back in Sheffield – his fame nevertheless guaranteed. There goes Trevor, they say, as he parades down the street, hair and cloak billowing. The most beautiful man in the world. Once.

He greets his friends – there they all sit, the style boys (and the occasional female hanger-on, usually very plump). The boys who are going to make it to the top using style, panache, individualism as their hand grips.

Air guitar contest, Rebels Nightclub, Sheffield, 1994

A boy with cropped blond hair bleached oh-so-white, harem pants and vest (on a cold summer's afternoon in Sheffield), a boy with baggy cotton pants (not quite harem pants these, but nearly), and cavalier tresses (again). A black boy with Grace Jones cut, dark suit; his modest sartorial style compensated by a camp manner so grossly overplayed that it needs a cigarette to get the performance right. All in a Sheffield coffee bar, for God's sake. But they have been validated and the huge validation stamp towers over them. Howcher showed it was possible. The Human League used to sing about it.

In Trevor's case, it was the Manpower Services Commission he was plucked from, but after a year he was put back down. But no matter. He was still a shining star that was far from extinguished, back in Sheffield at least. A group of teenagers passed by and gawped at Trevor and his mates. 'He made a quarter of a million,' said one star-struck teenage.

I did my cynical turn.

'He did, he really did, a quarter of a million quid.'

'For one record?'

'Well, he had to do a bit of posing as well, for photos and things. He's famous – there's a lot of money in modelling, you know.'

'So if he's famous, why hasn't my mum heard of him then? When she can tell you with some authority that Boy George hasn't been to bed with Marilyn yet and that he's in love with an American film star. She can even make a fair stab at Boy George's real name.'

'Who the fuck's your mum anyway?'

Well, quite. I went back to studying the group who'd shown that anything was possible. Trevor, who for years had been hounded around Sheffield as a

Mr Wimp contestants, Sheffield, 1983

queer and a fairy, had suddenly found himself not just famous but proclaimed as the most beautiful man in the world – note 'man'. That's why he acquired the stubble, to act as a sign vehicle of masculine gender, to compensate for the steady stream of sign vehicles hurtling in the opposite direction. So there they were – the style merchants with the world at their elegantly sandalled feet, discussing tonight's big event – the opening of the new club to be fronted by Trevor – Le Bon-Bon – 'a melting pot of style', as it said on the ticket.

Le Bon-Bon was to open in Turn-Ups – a club owned by Les Vickers, one of the biggest scrap dealers in Sheffield and famous (once) for scrapping the *Ark Royal*. To attract custom on every night of the week, it's necessary for most nightclubs to vary their theme a little bit. So on Monday nights at Turn-Ups they had drinks at half-price and denims allowed, on Tuesday nights it was reggae night for a mainly black clientele. On Wednesday nights it was, as one bouncer put it, 'weirdo night' for Trevor and his likes, and then it was back to the more ordinary clientele for Thursdays, Fridays and Saturdays. The precursor of the current club was the Sin-Bin but Le Bon-Bon was an attempt to attract the up-market weirdo and to deny access to the rougher element of the Sin-Bin – the punks and the skins.

Trevor was to select and play the records. 'It's going to be seventies funk' said one of the *cognoscenti* – ' "Supernature", "I Lost My Heart To A Starship Trooper", that kind of thing.'

'Why?' I asked naively.

'Trevor likes it,' he replied.

'Oh,' I said, if it was good enough for him, and all that.

Ernest 'Butcher' Gasgoigne, ex-professional boxer, and still a big name locally, City Road Working Men's Club, Sheffield, 1995

And play the records he did. And that's not all – he got dressed up and winked at some of the lucky boys. No speaking, mind, none of the usual DJ patter. Trev's singular style said it all, he thought. The cavalier tresses were gathered up inside a little sailor's hat, complemented with extremely large gold earrings and a little white sailor's top. He was smiling a lot and clearly enjoying playing his record collection to us. The *cognoscenti* had informed me that the Human League and ABC were sure to turn up to pay homage to Trev, but it was not to be. There were, however, lots of Boy George clones, invariably little plump blokes who had discovered (perhaps like Boy George himself) that they could disguise their mature puppy fat with a shapeless dress. And there were lots of Trevor clones – cavalier tresses, harem pants, bare midriff a must (now we know why Trevor went as a sailor). One female also sported the look – she wasn't going to let the boys have all the fun.

Now seventies funk does provide some problem for weirdo dancing because it is good, solid disco music. It's difficult not to do good, solid disco dancing to it. But the boys did their best. They expressed their individuality all right – they waved their arms about wildly (but, as it turned out, almost in unison) and they punctuated their dancing with the occasional roll on the dirty floor. But again, they nearly all did it – like orchestrated steps from a fixed routine. Not so much gay abandon as abandoned imagination. A desperate attempt to do something outrageous, to be original.

Now, if a new nightclub is to make it, the disc jockey has to have a host of skills. He must be able to get the punters on to the dance floor and keep them there, and I've even talked to club DJs who say they can lose an exact proportion of the punters back to the bar when the bar sales are flagging.

But Trevor didn't seem to want to be bothered by these mundane skills, and eventually he paid the price – one unfortunate choice of record emptied the dance floor. Now this was original; the party people had stopped partying. One lone male fan-dancer then took the floor (I suspect he'd been held in reserve for just such a contingency) and started his routine. Trev's moment had come. The hat came off, the tresses were shaken out, and Trevor got down to it with the fan-dancer. For a moment the audience, for that is what the style merchants had become, gaped (in unison) and then they too got down to it. The record wasn't so bad after all. Just look at Trevor. Oh, how could we doubt you, Trevor? Isn't this just divine?

I sidled off to one of the bars. They weren't doing much business. The bouncer was standing there looking morose. So what did he make of Wednesday nights and the melting pot of style?

'Oh, I don't mind the weirdos,' he said. 'They never cause any trouble. They're always very quiet and leave right when you tell them.'

'But what about all the camping about?'

'Oh, I just ignore it and leave them to it as long as they don't try to touch me. They don't buy much drink though, they don't seem to need it.'

And another Trevor clone walked past, high on narcissism, intoxicated by his looks, drunk on the attention he was being paid by the Boy George clones – plump and passé.

'At least they've got their dreams, I suppose,' said the bouncer.

September 1985

The most famous man in Sheffield

I first saw 'Cockney', no, let's start again, I first heard 'Cockney' in Josephine's in the section reserved for VIPs. He was loud, brash and very verbal. He was introducing someone to his 'very best pal', Terry Curran, the ex-Everton and ex-Sheffield Wednesday and ex-Sheffield United footballer (and arguably one of the best-known footballers in Sheffield). Cockney was drinking 'a little shampoo'. Cockney had a silk suit and a Cartier watch, a diamond earring and a pair of handcrafted shoes. Terry had some of these things as well, but not all. They made a formidable couple, with Terry's fame and Cockney's loud voice. Someone asked Terry for his autograph. Terry signed.

'That's the thing about Terry Curran,' said one watchful bystander. 'He may be the Sheffield George Best, but he's always a gentleman, even on his night out.' Terry passed the signed napkin back and the eager autograph hunter passed it to Cockney. He smiled and signed 'Cockney Richard'. The eager autograph hunter wasn't quite sure whose signature she'd managed to acquire – she knew he was definitely a somebody, she just wasn't sure exactly which one. Cockney went back to the 'shampoo'.

'I think I'll get another bottle,' said Cockney, 'or what about another two? I feel like a right good drink.' He turned to a hanger-on. 'This is nothing, what I'm getting through tonight. Last week me and a few mates got through nine bottles of champagne, and a while ago I was in Stringfellows with some lads and one of them ordered eight butterfly cocktails – they're one hundred

Bar girls and manager, Josephine's nightclub, Sheffield, 1993

guineas each – there are two bottles of champagne in each one, and they're meant to be for eight people. But my mate ordered one for everyone in his company. The barmaid said, "Excuse me, sir, are you sure you haven't made a mistake here?" And he said, "You're quite right, luv – I have made a mistake – I forgot you – make it nine." Nine hundred guineas for a round of drinks – that's style. Mind you, he got barred a week later for running up and down the bar with his trousers down. He was a scrap dealer, by the way, and he looked a bit ridiculous when he dropped them. Even though you buy all that drink you can still get barred. You have to have genuine style as well. It's not enough to be a big spender, you've got to have class.'

Some of the younger Sheffield Wednesday players arrived. One had just been given a transfer. His large doleful eyes were like basins full of dish-water, slightly discoloured. He looked a bit like a Disneyfied fawn gone a bit wrong. It was obviously an emotional moment and he certainly wasn't over the moon about the whole thing.

'How much are you getting again? . . . Bloody hell, is that all? . . . What about a car? I don't care whether you've got one or not, ask for a car. You never get anything unless you ask . . . Do you know how much Terry got when he went from Wednesday to United? . . . and all you're getting is that . . . I was down at the PFA dinner last week as a guest of the Everton lads and Andy Gray was telling me . . . You don't want to be taken for a mug, do you? . . .'

The fawn was beginning to resemble a parrot. He had gone a bit green and he was only able to repeat back the odd word that Cockney was firing at him.

The slightly surprising thing about all this is that this particular fawn was a well-known footballer, difficult to imagine in his role as victim. But in the concrete jungle, Cockney was the ultimate survivor and he'd got proof. He pulled out a wad of photographs. 'Here's a photo of me and Freddie Laker on his yacht in Palma and here's a picture of me and the Everton lads at the PFA dinner in London.' He was keen on Everton (after all they did win the First Division) and Fred, before the collapse. His verbals started again.

'See, Everton and Liverpool, they're in a different class from other football clubs. They don't even bother training – they run around the pitch five times and that's their lot. Sheffield Wednesday have to run ten miles on a Monday, never mind the rest of the week. And Wednesday have to stay in nearly all week – the only time an Everton or Liverpool player doesn't drink is the day before the game. But I'll always support Wednesday. Wednesday and I go back a long way. When I was eleven I broke my arm playing football and I wrote to three England players, and only one wrote back to me – Ron Springer from Wednesday. He sent me a load of autographs so I started supporting them. I only moved to Sheffield because it was cheaper to get to the games. It caused the break-up of my first marriage, though. My wife said to me, "You prefer Sheffield Wednesday to me," and I said, "I prefer bloody Sheffield United to you." She was a millionaire's daughter, you know. I met her on 11 July, we got married on 11 August – Sheffield Wednesday played Swindon away and got beaten 4–0. She first left me on 11 January, Sheffield Wednesday were playing Portsmouth away. The second time she left me – when she gave me the ultimatum, Sheffield Wednesday or her – it was the 11th again –

they were playing Portsmouth again – at home – this time Wednesday won. I love this club, I'll always support them.' Cockney's magnanimity was clearly impressing his audience.

Cockney picked up on my Irish accent. 'What poets the Irish are,' Cockney said, and launched into Oscar Wilde's *The Ballad of Reading Gaol*:

> He did not wear his scarlet coat,
> For blood and wine are red . . .

He got to the fifth verse before he was stopped. The audience was clearly impressed by his literary knowledge. His offer to recite 'the first three verses' from any Shakespeare play was, however, graciously refused. What scholarship! What adaptability! What verbals! From extravagant consumerism to football mastermind to English scholar – all in the space of one large swig of 'shampoo'. A lord of the concrete jungle who could change his spots.

In a city of moderate public behaviour and moderate, if not downright dour, talk, Cockney's colourful and adaptable hyperbole, like a well-known brand of toothpaste, got him noticed. 'I'm the most famous man in Sheffield,' he said.

But what exactly did Cockney do? My question met with a stony silence, then evasiveness. 'Let's just say I'm a man with no visible means of support. I get by but don't worry, when I'm out with the lads, I buy more champagne than they do.' How did he get promotion into the first division of champagne cocktails, famous personages and public recognition? 'Let's just say I know everybody who's worth knowing. I've introduced Terry to quite a few of my famous mates. Sheffield's just small-time. As to what the celebrities round here think of me – maybe they just wonder how I can get out every night of the week drinking champagne.' How did he get to know Freddie Laker? 'I saw Freddie in Palma – I'd never met him before – I just went up to him and said, "Hello Fred, long time no see." He said, "It is a long time, please forgive me but I seem to have forgotten your name." A friend and I were with a couple of birds he wanted to meet so we got invited out to his yacht that way. I've been out with loads of famous people. What's that guy from the Who called? I'd go up to anybody. I've been out with some right upper-class birds but I haven't met old Prince Charles yet.'

But who financed the old shampoo? What were the invisible means of support? He agreed to explain. We met back at his small flat – 'my little palace', bursting with all the expensive ephemera of the consumer age. A video with a screen that wouldn't shame a cinema, silver cutlery, expensive carpet.

'It's handy living here,' he said, 'right in the centre of town, since I got done for drinking and driving in my XJS.' He'd been on the dole for the past two years. 'I get £60 a fortnight, but I can spend that on a Friday night. Who could live on that?' And he showed me his wardrobe with its seven silk suits and twenty-odd pairs of expensive shoes. He looked at my clothes. 'You're a right scruff bag, you know. You can always tell a man by his shoes, and look at yours – they're a bloody disgrace.' I had to agree. His weren't. So how come, in the style wars, he was a fighter ace and I was trudging around like a refugee?

'Well, the first thing to know is that I've been in trouble a few times. But who hasn't? Scratch any rich man and you'll find a thief. I was a thief since I was fourteen until last year when I was thirty-two, but I've come to the conclusion that it's just not worth it. I've had six custodial sentences but I've been nicked thirty-seven times in all. I've been out of prison for nearly a year. Nothing heavy, mind. I got into trouble for the first time when I was at school for stealing by finding a motorbike. But the first time I got sent away was for stealing from a dwelling house (they didn't call it burglary). I nicked some cufflinks from a house in which my girlfriend was baby-sitting. I got five quid for them and then ten weeks in a detention centre. Ten weeks of marching up and down. When I got out I started hanging about with some lads who had never worked. We used to buy something small in a Marks and Spencer's and as the girl opened the till we'd grab some money out and run. I don't mind talking about these things – I've been done for them all. The lads I knocked about with then got into armed robbery but I never got into anything too heavy. I got into deception, you know, buying stolen cheque-books for four quid a page and passing the cheque.

'The person who nicks the chequebook never tries to pass the cheques off himself. He sells it. People always wonder how you copy the name so well – you don't. You take the original name off in a solution of warm water, brake fluid, washing-up liquid with a little bleach and you just sign the name yourself. I've had Sheffield police puzzled as to how I did it. In fact I even explained it to them. They're making it more difficult now by having a patterned strip where you sign the name. My wife and I got done for passing off these cheques. We used to go to DIY shops because they cash cheques there so you don't have to queue at the till. They were easier than banks. I used to do a lot of this in London as well – at one time I was making ten grand a month. I got my wife involved – I think she was just doing it to impress me.'

His wife interrupted. 'Tell him where you got your Cartier watch, though.' He declined. 'I came back one day and he'd sold my Mini. I paid 600 quid for it,' she said. 'He bought himself a Cartier watch.'

'What are you complaining about?' he said. 'I bought you a gold sovereign from the sale.' Cockney clearly brought his worldly ways home with him.

'Look, I admit I've been a thief and a con man but who isn't bent? I'm making a bit of cash at the moment through some people I know who work for the council. You can get anything fixed, you know, if you know the right people. Housing lists, anything.' He winked. 'I hate this bloody council as well, by the way – talk about the blind leading the blind. I'm Margaret Thatcher's biggest supporter. Anybody who wants to earn a living can earn a living. I'm on the dole through choice. I'm taking a break from work, that's all. I do keep myself busy – I use my contacts. I know all the big jewellers in Sheffield and I'll sell things for them. See this gold chain – it's worth nearly 500. I paid one and a half for it and I'll get two and a half. I know the kinds of people who would want a chain like this. I also sell tickets – I know all the famous ticket touts down in London – Stan Flashman, David Brown. I was selling £15 Bruce Springsteen tickets recently for £30 and £25. Live Aid tickets for £50.'

Didn't he have any reservation about making money out of the latter venture? He looked at me as if I was some kind of idiot. 'Nobody, nobody does anything for nothing. Those bloody groups got an audience of millions – a good free plug. Do you think they'd have done it if it wasn't for that?' Cockney was proselytising now – the doctrine of the free market economy and the sanctity of the entrepreneurial spirit, unhampered by common morality or civic law.

'I also do a lot of Cup Final tickets. I give the players who get them five times their market value – that's thirty quid. I get fifty quid for them. Just a bit of bobbing and weaving, that's all I do now. But, as you know, I'm well in with the footballers – I also sell them clothes, for example snide [false] Lacoste shirts, even suits. I once sold a load of suits at fifty quid each to the Hillsborough players. It's all right, they weren't nicked or anything. It's all down to who you know and what you know. I'm not ashamed of what I've done. Why should I be? The world's full of bent people – in any section of society, just look at the judges and the police. How come the police can afford to go out to nightclubs every night? You just have to have the cheek to get by. I had my eyes done recently by one of the top cosmetic surgeons in Britain – the bill was 600 quid but I didn't pay – they weren't quite right. So why should I?' And then he returns to his second favourite subject (his first is naturally himself). 'I learned Wilde's *The Ballad of Reading Gaol* when I was in prison. It was Oscar Wilde who said "There's only one thing in the world worse than being talked about, and that is not being talked about." That man had real style; he didn't have any money, just plenty of style. If I don't have any money I'll just get things on account – meals, champagne, anything. I've even had bets on account at a racecourse, believe it or not.

'They made a scapegoat of Wilde, he wasn't really a queer – he just had syphilis and he didn't want to give it to his wife. Half the bloody aristocrats and half the judges in this country are bent anyway. They just wanted to victimise him. All great Irishmen are sent to prison – look at George Best. Only Barry McGuigan has got to go. God help him if he gets into trouble. When you're in the public eye you have to expect trouble of this sort, especially if you're Irish. My grandmother's Irish so I'm watching out.'

And as I left, Cockney was just fixing up the use of a friend's apartment in Marbella for his holidays. He then requested a fee for the interview. 'Five hundred pounds will do nicely,' he said. 'Well, you don't do it for nothing, do you?' But, as I left, he looked at my shoes once again with the look that said, they can't be paying you very much anyway.

September 1985

Me and my Silver Shadow

It was 12.15 am, the nightclub was already full. He made his entrance. A vision in black and gold – black silk shirt unbuttoned almost to the waist, black trousers, black shoes and gold – everywhere. Three gold medallions dangling on his chest, two gold rings on the same hand. He was about forty, his hair was cropped short, he was smoking a cigar. He walked slowly in a cool, confident manner, scanning the faces. He greeted the bouncers, they greeted him. Don Corleone was back. He walked to the wine bar and greeted the owner of the club. The owner ordered champagne. Don Corleone kept watching, he kept scanning the faces. Strangers to the club stared back at this small dark man. But Don Corleone was not what he seemed. He was just an Italian waiter from a restaurant in a Sheffield. He hadn't any money, he hadn't even got a car. He got the bus into town with all that jewellery hanging around him. He knew the nightclub owner from way back and he'd got a free pass to the club. If he hadn't, he couldn't afford to go. But there he was – six nights a week, laden with gold, almost certainly fake. But in the dim light of the club, all that glistened was surely gold and people assumed that he was somebody. When he was standing at the bus stop during the day, with a bag of washing for the launderette, he would jump into hiding if he spotted anybody he recognised. He lived alone in a bedsitter. Luigi, the waiter, by day – Don Corleone, the somebody, by night.

Another character strode in. He was also small but he'd gone for the sailing look. Blue double-breasted jacket with a silk handkerchief in the pocket, his tie had a crest on it. He was getting on a bit and was balding. His hair was in the Bobby Charlton style and the long strands were woven around his bald patch. But in here there were no cruel winds to give the game away; he could relax. He walked about as if his Rolls-Royce was ready and waiting to take some lucky lady off to this yacht on a moonlit bay. But there was no yacht and no Roller, just drizzle and a J-registration Hillman Minx. There was a flat of sorts – a little terraced house full of unwashed pots and pans (he lived alone and hadn't time to do them before he went out) and aftershave. By day he was a bus conductor, by night, well, he was a randy, old, rich seadog, four hours a night, six nights a week. He'd also got a free pass. He knew the club owner from the time when the club owner still used the bus service.

Anyone who had seen Don Corleone on a bus or Lone Yachtsman in his Hillman Minx could not take them too seriously, but Alan was different. He was thirty-six, tanned, fit, his hair streaked blond. He looked the part in a way that Don Corleone or Lone Yachtsman didn't. They had become submerged in images from the past; his was more contemporary. Alan got to the club about 11.30 pm in his brown Silver Shadow. He parked it in the underground car park just by the club. The car park is used by many of the club's customers. As he was parking it, he noticed that he was being watched by a gaggle of girls emerging from a white Mini.

'Did you see that car?' a tall blonde girl with buck teeth said to her friends. Alan pretended not to hear and turned round and walked to the exit. He walked slowly to give them a chance to identify his features. When he had left, the girls went over and looked at the car. They peered inside; one touched the paintwork, her sweaty palm leaving a thumb print on the door. 'He must be bloody well loaded. Imagine going home in that tonight.'

Alan went into the club and ordered a gin and tonic. He stood by the bar. The four girls, now arranged in two sets of two (a strategic configuration for picking up men), passed him at the bar. The girl with buck teeth gave him a quick smile, as did her friend (the one who had been admiring the paintwork).

They thought he might buy them a drink, but he just smiled back. They ordered four Bacardi and Cokes. It came to £4.80. Alan looked nonchalant. A male acquaintance came over. 'Not much in tonight,' he said. 'No, not much talent tonight,' Alan replied.

It was Buck Teeth's round. She glanced over at Alan again. He was still sipping his gin and tonic. Buck Teeth forked out another £4.80. Alan was making his gin and tonic last. He went to the toilet; he took his drink with him and filled it up from a quarter bottle of gin he'd been keeping in his inside jacket pocket. He came back to the bar with his glass full. Buck Teeth assumed he'd been to the other bar. He quite fancied Buck Teeth's friend and he started chatting her up. Buck Teeth hung about until her friend started touching Alan's arm. At this point she felt really excluded and went in search of her other two friends. 'Joanne's got off with that filthy rich man in the Rolls,' she said. 'Lucky bastard,' they replied in unison.

Joanne had finished her Bacardi. 'Would you like a drink?' she said to Alan and they both laughed at the suggestion and the situation. Joanne had just told Alan that she was unemployed (she borrowed a tenner from her mother for the evening). Alan had just told her that he owned a company. One of them was telling fibs. Alan said, 'Oh, go on then.' Joanne didn't think he was mean, she just wanted to show him that she was not after his money, which she was. Alan accepted the drink and made this one last as well. The manager went past and said to one of the bouncers, 'I see Alan got one on.'

The evening progressed. Alan went to the toilet and met a friend who bought him a drink. Joanne bought herself a double while he was away. Alan had told her that there might be a job in his company for her. Joanne had been unemployed for three months – she was over the moon and nearly under the table. They danced to the slow music at the end. Alan asked her if she'd like a lift home. 'Oh, have you got a car then?' she said innocently. 'Yes, a Rolls-Royce,' he said. 'You're kidding.' 'No, I'm not. Come and see.' They left together. The manager said, 'Goodnight, sir; goodnight, madam.'

The Rolls gleamed in the artificial light. The thumb print was still there. Alan let her play with the electric windows. 'Can we drive round past the front of the club so that my friends can see me?' she said. They did, but her friends had gone. 'Oh, it's a real pity,' she said. Alan asked her where she lived. 'Upperthorpe,' she said. Alan knew it was five miles out and not in his direction. He gulped but didn't say anything. All the way there, at every set of traffic lights, she looked around into all the taxis, hoping to see someone she knew.

They got home about a quarter to three. She insisted on waking her mother up to show her the car. Her mother came downstairs in curlers and stared out through the curtains. 'It's a real beauty,' she said. 'Yes,' said Alan. The mother made tea. It wasn't exactly what Alan had had in mind. After he'd gone, the mother said, 'What a nice lad, success hasn't spoiled him at all. He's very down-to-earth.'

He had promised Joanne he'd ring the following Tuesday but he didn't. Joanne went round to Buck Teeth's house. 'I'm not going back to that club, it's full of rich flash bastards who treat you like shit.'

But Alan hadn't meant to let her down or hurt her. It was just that she lived too far out. He simply couldn't afford the petrol to Upperthorpe. If she'd lived closer, he would have taken her out. Alan didn't own a company; he was a van driver, married with two adolescent boys. Most of his salary went on running the car. His wife worked – she paid reluctantly for the running of their council house. He had friends in the motor trade and he had got the car at a good price about four years earlier when he'd made some money selling another car. He only used the car at night. He couldn't afford the petrol to take it to work. He ran instead – five miles there and five back. One of the new set of marathon men, but out of necessity rather than choice. And it saved him going to a trendy and expensive fitness club.

But sometimes he did score. He had a two-year relationship with a girl called Debbie who worked in the make-up section of a large department store. Her make-up was always immaculate – a perfect mask. Alan's mask was more subtle. She was blonde and always wore white – tight white jeans or white dresses. Men always gawped at her and Alan loved the attention. They would drive out to pubs in the country and leave the car in the front car park. The customers would stare. 'It's all right for bloody some,' they would say. Alan saw Debbie every night from 10 pm to 2 am. They were a lovely couple. People in the club would enquire when they were going to get married. At weekends, Debbie said, they would go and look at £80,000 houses. 'We'd drive up in the car, and I'd get really made up. I used to have to loan Alan the money for petrol.' During this time, Alan had his electricity cut off for nonpayment of bills. Alan used one set of pubs for his wife and one set for Debbie. Everyone thought that Debbie and he were the perfect couple. 'We even went looking for an engagement ring,' said Debbie, 'a £500 job, but he hadn't a bean; it was all a bit stupid. I didn't even see his wife until after we'd split up. She was all right, a bit rough but even she's too good for him. She looked at me as if I was a real tart but he always told me the marriage was finished anyway.'

Alan was on his own now. He still missed Debbie but her absence didn't prompt him to take his wife out instead. 'People would wonder who she was,' he said. 'And I couldn't afford it anyway.' Instead he had one or two male friends. One of his friends had got a yellow Rolls-Royce with a TV in it. 'He's really cracked it,' said Alan. 'He'll pick up a girl on Saturday night and instead of taking her to the pictures on Sunday – that would be four quid at least – or for a drink – nearer eight quid – they just sit in the Roller and watch TV. All he has to pay for is the petrol and sometimes he can get the girl to pay for that.'

Alan only ever went to one club and one might imagine that after a short period, everyone would know that he was a van driver rather than a company director. But no, that kind of news seems to travel slow. It was almost as if people wanted to believe his story, despite evidence to the contrary. For, after all, the club was founded on fantasy for the Martini set and Alan came as close to the image (at least in terms of appearance) in this northern town as anyone. If he wasn't what he seemed, then who was? And he could always update his story to keep just ahead of the news hounds and the blood-hounds of gossip. 'Oh yes, I used to be a van driver when I went out with Debbie, but that was before I opened my own company, and have you seen my Rolls-Royce, by the way?'

October 1983

Wee Georgie Wheezer, club comedian, Sheffield, 1982

The country club

I've always wanted to be upwardly mobile, even before it was fashionable, even before there was a name for it. Well, when you start pretty near the bottom of the social heap, you do, don't you? I always wanted to get on, to socially climb, to become a bit of a nob. Now being a nob in my book was always fairly straightforward – big house, big car, good club. The car was easy, my father swore by Jags and he should know. He was a motor mechanic and he used to buy cars from scrap yards, and do them up. I spent my early childhood sharing the backroom with assorted car engines. The backroom was the room that functioned as the kitchen, the dining room and the 'bathroom' (the room containing the basin to balance in while you washed yourself from the geyser) all rolled into one. The engines, always in the process of being 'done up', took pride of place in that room. My father was never really happy when he was driving. He would listen out in a compulsive fashion for any sounds in the car, any slight vibration, any rattle, any unprogrammed noise, and that would be it. The engine would have to be stripped down yet again. Indeed, whilst driving he would insist on travelling at speeds which would maximise vibration. My older brother would ask him if he was stopping. But at those speeds any slight mechanical defect could be detected. 'That's it,' he would say, 'the engine will have to come out again,' and for the next month you would have to thread your way rather carefully past the engine on the way to the toilet in the yard.

Hen night, Sheffield, 1994

But when the car was on the road, and wasn't vibrating – then bliss. Trips down to Bangor to view those grand houses in Holywood. My father would drive even slower to give us a better view. 'Imagine living in one of those, Eileen,' my father would say to my mother. 'I can't,' she would reply. 'Look at those gardens, those rooms, those curtains, imagine sitting there looking out. You'd feel like the queen. Look there's some woman there now. Money people, real money people, they're not like you and me.' 'No, they're not,' my mother would add.

Well times pass, and we live in different times now, or so they tell us. Mrs Thatcher says there's no such thing as class anymore. She's working class, she tells us, because she works. My mother disagrees, she's still not seen any of those big houses from the inside, and she still talks about membership of golf clubs as if it was a sign of nobility. You should hear the way she says that 'so-and-so plays golf'. It's the way she enunciates the word 'golf'. I don't quite aspire to 'golf', it's too value-laden, it's much too loaded a concept for the likes of me. I thought that I'd settle for a good country club instead, especially when an advert for a local country club in Sheffield, called Pinegrove, popped through my letterbox. 'It's a bit like a drinking club, but where they play bridge,' my mother explained when I told her that I was thinking of joining a country club. She didn't disapprove. 'That's where all the money people hang out, not like the snobs that you find in golf clubs, just the real money people, the nobs.' My mother, you see, draws some very fine distinctions in her lexicon of class-related terms.

So I went off to meet the nobs. It was about 9.00 pm, and the car park was full. I had to thread my way across the car park from some distance away. An old Capri just missed me, and I jumped towards a Y-reg Vauxhall cavalier, the back seat of which was full of toilet rolls. Don't ask me why. And don't ask me why I notice the year of registration of the cars, it's probably always been important to me. Six years equals sixty thousand miles, which in turn equals perceptible vibration which equals the engine being taken out, which equals a stubbed toe when you go to the toilet in the middle of the night. Some associations are stamped into you early on. I walked past the cloistered walls of the country club, but when I looked closely I could see the columns of the cloisters were just piles of bricks cemented together and the roof was supported by a joist. I was not going to be discouraged, however, that easily. It turned out, by the way, that one of the owners of the club was in the building trade.

My expectations were still high. I had heard about Pinegrove's fabulous high-tech gym, its glass-backed squash courts, the magnificent snooker rooms, facilities second to none. I just wanted to meet the nobs, to see where they do their drinking. I was invited to wander around. There was the new badminton hall, but who was that nob resplendent in Fred Perry shirt and matching shorts. Why, it was none other than Honest Gerry, second-hand car dealer. The car dealer whose golden rule was that if you want to sell a car to a customer, go for the wife. I always expected that after hours, Honest Gerry would be found in some backstreet drinking club, playing cards, but no, here he was down at the country club playing badminton. 'My serve, Maurice, I think.' It was not what I had expected from Honest Gerry.

I hurried out, leaving Honest Gerry to his foot faulting. I made my way to the high-tech gym. Here indeed was the kind of weight-training facilities for the next century. The kinds of machines that exercise improbable muscles in even more improbable ways. The instructor spotted me trying to do bicep curls in the machine designed for exercising hamstrings. 'No, perhaps you should try it like this, Sir,' he said. The instructor turned out to be Chris, the bouncer, from the local casino. As he guided me around parts of my body which I had up to that point in time studiously ignored, he filled me in on the ethos of the place. 'A country club which appeals to the ordinary work-ing man, the working man who's come on a bit. We have one or two money people, but then again we've got quite a few unemployed as well. They can spend the whole day here, one way or another. The really big boys use the free weights in the other room, this room's really for girls and those getting started.' And sure enough the room was occupied by an assortment of lovelies in pink leotards, and a few not-so-lovelies in 'I drank the world' T-shirts, covering the kinds of stomachs which would indeed suggest that there was some truth in the proposition. 'There's rarely any trouble here,' said Chris continuing again – 'we haven't barred anyone yet.' 'Don't you mean ex-cluded from the club, Chris? Blackballed?' 'No, just barred,' said Chris.

'The biggest problem,' said Chris, 'is that it's now fashionable for ordinary working-class blokes and their wives or girlfriends to exercise, when it wasn't once upon a time. Some of these new fitness-conscious people aren't very fit to start off with. When a new client comes here, we take them on the exercise bike to warm them up. One guy in his forties came last week, he wanted to start training, but he was on the bike for just two minutes when his pulse rate climbed up to 180. There was no way we were going to let him loose on the weights, one of the instructors took him for a walk instead.'

After my hamstrings had been sufficiently 'worked', I limped off to the snooker room, decorated with huge portraits of those other working-class heroes – Jimmy White and Alex Higgins. A young Chinese couple were on one of the tables. They wore matching Mickey Mouse T-shirts. All of the balls were lined up against one of the side cushions in a way that I would have thought was technically impossible. 'There's a lot of money in chip shops,' said one regular when he noticed me watching the young couple play. 'They're the real money people about today – the ones with the Chinese chippies.' Diana Ross sang in the background. Two men in their late forties played on the table closest to me. They eyed me suspiciously, as if I was trying to pinch their table or their drinks. One was going for the brown. He missed. 'That were a double clanger,' said his friend. It was his turn, but the lights on the snooker table went out. He put another coin in the meter. He was talking to the balls – 'Get right up to that cushion, boy.' The ball might have heard, but did not seem to be listening. 'Fine hit,' said the wife sitting to the side. 'Did that go in?' said the other wife in the corner. 'Of course it did,' said wife number one. The pink had hit two side cushions and then had somehow miraculously dropped into the pocket. 'That were a good finish, well played, Arthur.' Arthur then took a long drink of his bitter, obviously very pleased with himself. The wife's conversation then returned to one of their daughters. '. . . all she spent on her holidays was what she brought with her. She only had twenty pounds left when she got back, no I mean twenty of them other things – Deutsche . . . marks, that's it. This German girl she met on holiday were a right nice lass.'

It was a night for name-dropping, and talk of foreign travel, for talk of all things foreign and exotic. A night for showing that you'd been 'abroad', and for looking the part. 'I got this leather belt in Spain, you know. I never take it off me. We went with Marjorie and her husband. You should see the tan she's got now, she's got one of them twelve-tube super-tanning machines. The one like the coffin that you have to climb inside. She keeps it in her front room.'

I even got a five-peseta coin in my change when I went to the bar, from the barmaid with the French knickers on under her tight, white cotton pants. I was joined there by Peter Hayman, one of the three owners of the club, and an ex-bookmaker. It was partly his vision to build a country club on the site of a rubbish tip in Sheffield. 'The basic idea was to attract the Rolls-Royce set to a new better-equipped club, but unfortunately the Rolls-Royce set stayed where they were, even though the facilities weren't as good. We tend to attract the local punter from Hillsborough. This is them going a bit upmarket. I don't think the council really liked us calling it a country club, it sounds a bit posh. Some people think that the working class should stick to flying pigeons. But this club is very successful. A lot of its members couldn't get in to some of the other clubs, which are a bit snobby. If you're in a golf club, if you get sent down, that's it. We wouldn't necessarily judge them that harshly. I even know of one bloke who had to resign from his golf club because every time he went in to the rough, he went in with a white ball and came out with a yellow one! Golf clubs can be a little strict. We're a different sort of club – here social status isn't a prerequisite. About 100 of our members are unemployed – it's hardly their fault after all, and they need the facilities more than most. We have an instalment plan for them of a tenner a month. It makes it a bit easier for them to pay. It's not like the council's "Passport to Leisure" scheme, here they're still paying their own way. They can hold their head up high. We treat everyone alike.'

'It a bit like the Thatcherite dream, here, I suppose,' said Peter – 'the dream come true – everyone who aspires to join a country club, now can. A bit of a classless society, if you ask me. Ordinary working people, who always wanted to mix with the nobs, can now join the executives for a quick game of squash and a drink in the bar. No social barriers exist any longer.'

'Just as long as they don't get blackballed,' I said.

'No, barred,' said Peter – 'just barred, we wouldn't ever go that far.'

June 1989

Mr Big

Up in Rotherham, when it comes to the fight game, Bernard is Mr Big. Big fan, big benefactor, one day maybe a promoter. 'There will be no dead bodies in the ring when Bernard promotes', Mick Mills had told me. 'They'll be going in there to scrap. Bernard will make sure that the ordinary punter gets value for money.' Bernard is the self-made man of legend. From Dalton in Rotherham to Dallas-style housing. 'You wanna see his house. It's only half done but you wanna see it. If he brings a bird back there, she'll be easing her knickers down as she goes up the drive.' Up in Dalton, there are few role models. You fight your way out one way or the other. Locally, they call it the Bronx. Bernard got out, now he wanted to put something back. The rumour was that Bernard wanted to transform the equestrian centre on his new estate into a training facility for local boxers. 'He wants to give the lads up here a chance. He wants to help others. He knows it's hard in Dalton, and harder now with all the pits closing.'

Bernard had come up the hard way. I was told that he had been shot when he was younger. But there was nothing glamorous about this shooting. He was shot by accident when he out rabbiting, in a strange old-fashioned place where rabbiting still meant hunting rabbits rather than shooting your mouth off. 'But he can still fight like fuck', I was told. Everyone was talking about Bernard, as if their future depended upon it. For some their future probably did.

I was to meet him in a dark, dreary bar at noon. I recognised a colleague in the corner. I described Bernard to him. 'There's a couple of likely looking lads here. Look at those two in the corner.' In a dark recess sat the two likely looking lads – Chris Woods and Danny Wilson, then of Sheffield Wednesday. This was a lesson not to jump to hasty conclusions. Bernard was waiting patiently. The first thing to say about Bernard is that he looks the part. You don't have to look too closely to see it. Everything is out in the open. Everything is big and chunky and out on display on his thickly set body.

Mr Big from Rotherham, Josephine's nightclub, Sheffield, 1993

It's useful to get these sort of credentials sorted out at the very beginning.
'Is that a real watch', I asked trying to break the ice.

'Oh yes, that's real', answered Bernard. It was a funny sort of opening. I
laughed about it afterwards. We were not discussing the veridical nature of
perception, or the philosophical problems posed by sense data. We were not
discussing whether the watch was real or merely an illusion. We both knew
what we were talking about.

'Of course, it's bloody real. Feel the weight off the thing. That didn't cost
me fourteen quid down in some shady club. That was about eleven thousand
nicker. If I was walking the streets of Las Vegas or New York I might take it
off because it is a little bit ostentatious, but if I'm walking the streets of
Sheffield or Rotherham, I leave it on. It's a Rolex Oyster. With a day date', he
added for effect. Exactly what this additional information conveyed was
unclear to me, except that the watch told you the date. However, if I knew
anything about Rolexes, which I don't, it probably would have told me a
great deal more.

'I bought it in Miami', he continued, 'and then I had the diamonds put all
around the face in Las Vegas. They're real diamonds. The watch were eight
thousand and the diamonds were three thousand. That's where I get my
eleven thousand from.' Bernard was counting every penny in that careful
Yorkshire fashion, making sure that it all added up.

I asked Bernard if could I feel it. I've held snide Rolexes so light that the
wind in the corner of a bar in a niteclub could carry them away. Paper thin,
like the veneer of their owners. This one was heavy, like a lump of lead. I
started apologising about leaving sticky marks on the face of it. Bernard sat

back and took a long hard puff on his cigarette. 'Don't worry, lad, examine it all you want.'

I began by asking Bernard to explain how he had made it in these hard times. But this was the kind of account that Bernard liked to avoid, not because there was anything dodgy or unseemly about it, rather it was because it was all about graft. In Dalton, you take graft for granted. You can safely assume that making anything let alone millions takes graft, you can safely assume that moving out of Dalton to any other part of Rotherham takes graft. You don't talk about graft. They graft in the mines and in the steel works. It's a fact of life.

'I made my money in fire protection for factories, you see, cladding steel work. I was a millionaire by the time I was thirty nine, that were three years ago. The business is really pretty obvious if you think about it. In the eighties everything was being built in a hurry, but you need to protect these structures against fire. I got in there at the right time, and worked hard at it. Now I like to live like a millionaire. I spent a third of a million quid on a villa in Spain. It's in La Manga Country Club on the Costa Blanca. I'm also having a Victorian House in Sheffield done up with about twenty eight acres attached. I've had it gutted and done it really nice. By the time it's done, there will be a million quid's worth of house there. It's nice to have the money to buy the things you like. I bought my daughter Kerry a gold sequinned suit worn by Marilyn Monroe for her fourteenth birthday. It cost me two grand and came with a letter of authenticity and photos of Marilyn wearing it on her honeymoon with Joe Di Maggio. But my big hobby is boxing. I've seen all the big fights. Buster Douglas v. Evander Holyfield at the Mirage, Bruno v. Tyson at the Hilton Hotel, Las Vegas. It's more than a hobby. If I'd had the talent, it would have been my way out of Dalton. I've got a lot in common with the boxing boys.'

Bernard reached inside his orange jacket and pulled out a large wad of photographs. 'Just in case you think I'm all talk. Here's a photograph of Eddie Murphy, which I took myself.' He passed me a photograph of the back of the head of some black man in a blue blazer. It could indeed have been the back of Eddie Murphy's head, but it could equally have been the back of anyone else's head. 'Here's a photo of Mr T from the "A" team, with a knife, a fork and a spoon round his neck. Do you watch the "A Team", it's on TV on a Saturday morning. When I bumped into Mr T, he turned round to me and said "from the ghetto to this" and he had a gold knife, fork and spoon round his neck. Here's a photo of Thomas Hearns and his henchmen, and here's one of Frank Bruno at the weigh-in for his fight with Mike Tyson. You can see that Frank is shitting himself there. Here's one of Frank where he seems to be hiding behind the curtains. In my view Frank lost it right then. My dad was a big boxing fan. He always wanted to see Muhammad Ali in action, but he could never have afforded anything like that. He was a miner all his days. He ended up as a cripple walking on two sticks. He's dead now. So are the mines', Bernard added after a moment's pause.

Bernard was making up for all that his father had missed. 'I'm a big fan of world championship boxing. It cost me five grand to take me and two of my boxing pals to one of these fights. I offered to take Mick Mills with me because of his involvement in his early days with boxing. He's a pal of mine from Dalton. One of the roughest little fuckers ever to come out of the place. He's broken six jaws – only one of them in the ring. Mind you, he's had his own jaw broken, but that was in a professional fight. He's known as Mick "The Bomb" Mills. Well, every great boxer has a nickname. Thomas "The Hit Man" Hearns, "Iron" Mike Tyson, Mick "The Bomb" Mills. Or "Millsie", as I sometimes call him. The only trouble with Mick is that he had a raw deal. It's not the boxers that get the cash unless they're right at the top of the tree. I saw the trip as a reward for his efforts. I brought Gary as a travelling companion for Mick. I went first class, so Mick would have been on his own. I stayed in the Mirage, Mick and Gary stayed in one of the smaller hotels. So Mick really needed a travelling companion. Gary is a bouncer, he's never really done any boxing, but he loves the sport and all the trimmings that go with it.'

So what was in it for Bernard? Was he as magnanimous as everyone was suggesting, or desperately needing to believe? Was he trying to do his bit for the boys who did not have his breaks? 'To be honest it's a bit of a nobble to travel with two tough guys in tow. They look like my bodyguards. I've seen Arnold Schwarzenegger with his body guards, and Mike Tyson with his. When I walk into the Mirage with Gary and Mick beside me, I look like a VIP. I've spoken to Arnie and Iron Mike. I just walked up to Arnie and said to him – 'Hi, Arnie, I've come all the way from Sheffield, England. Well it's actually Rotherham, England, but I guess he wouldn't have heard of Rotherham, so that's why I said "Sheffield". "Knives and forks", Arnie, "knives and forks". He got my drift. "Do you mind if I get my photograph taken with you?" The Terminator and Bernard Atkinson from Rotherham, England. Something to show the lads back in Yorkshire. Iron Mike talked to me. I was sitting a few seats away from him. Only the best. Iron Mike came up to me and said "shift!" At least, I can say that I've spoken to one of the greatest scrappers this century.'

'I like to be around boxers, I always have done. Do you know Big Clifton – the big black guy, the big heavyweight, I've bought him four or five hundred's quid worth of training tackle. It's because I like to be with them. I like the company. I like to talk to 'em. I just like to be around boxers. It's a tough sport. It's different to your ordinary everyday football matches. I definitely like the heavyweights. I will watch the other weights fighting, but I prefer the heavy boys.

'When I told Mick that he was going to Las Vegas with me, he couldn't believe it. I told him a good three months before the trip actually happened. He told a lot of his friends who all live in the back of beyond. I wouldn't say that they live in the slums, but near enough. They all told him that I wouldn't take him, that I was just making it all up. Mick asked me two or three times 'Is it right, Bernard, are you really going to take me?' I said to him 'You just wait. You'll have the tickets in your pocket within a couple of weeks.' He still couldn't believe it, until I handed him his tickets. He was over the moon when he got them. He just couldn't thank me enough. I think that he thought it was the drink talking, and then it all became realism when he got the tickets in his fist.'

'We flew from Manchester to Chicago, and from Chicago to Las Vegas. It was lucky that Mick had flown before. He had flown in his amateur days. He'd been out to New Zealand or wherever. I was in first class. Mick and Gary were in economy. I think that one of the things about Mick is that he is a very good talker. He had this oldish lady at the side of him, and I think that her ear hole must have fell off by the time she got to Chicago. He talks like he's in the bloody launderette, like a bloody woman talking about what's gone off the day before. Mick is the type of person who can talk with almost anyone. We had a few drinks on the plane, and talked to people mainly about the boxing. People were asking us why there were three chaps travelling together. I mean I don't think that they could weigh it up. They were asking us why we were going to America and we were telling them that we were going on to Las Vegas, to the Buster Douglas – Evander Holyfield fight. I think that it excited them as well. I mean one or two people on board the plane were interested in boxing, so it was of interest to them.

'By the time we got to Las Vegas, we were absolutely knackered. And I must admit that I went to bed me, because I had been to Las Vegas before, but I'm told that Mick and Gary just chucked their bags down, and they were out. I don't think that they went to bed for twenty four hours, because they were that taken in by all the bright lights and the casinos and the slot machines and everything else. And also Mick and Gary like their food. In Las Vegas the food is really cheap. You can get a steak for a couple of quid. If you sit near the slots, you can order a steak and they'll give it to you for nothing, and the drinks as well. I think that the size of the meals amazed them. So the cost of things were far cheaper in Las Vegas. You could eat as much as you like in the casinos. Their revenue comes from the gambling. Mick and Gary had their own spending money. The only thing I paid for except for the flight was the hotel and the fight tickets.

'I stayed in the Mirage. I don't know what they were up to. They were out and about as soon as they arrived. I was very much the same on my first trip to Las Vegas. This was my third trip. I'd been previously to see the Bruno–Tyson fight, then the Tyson–Razor Ruddock match. I'd pretty much seen an awful lot of Las Vegas. The first time I stayed for four days, the second time for a week. I had time to adjust, to see the sights. I went into Johnny Tokos's gym, where Tyson trained, I called in to see old Johnny Tokos. Johnny Tokos is a real old guy, about eighty, a typical trainer. We just shouted through the doors 'Can we come in, Johnny?' We've come all the way from Rotherham, England.' He just invited us in and showed us all around. Tyson wasn't in at that time. He had been training previously. We had a chat to old Johnny, and got to know a bit about him. Johnny were white, he was a white guy. He had been in Las Vegas for many, many years. To be honest he didn't say a lot. He were quite an interesting guy, but he wouldn't give a lot away, when we asked him what shape Tyson was in, or how did he think that he'd fare against Bruno. He just told us that Tyson would probably knock him out, and that Tyson was training very hard. Tyson had gone through at least half a dozen sparring partners by the time I was there. Johnny didn't say a lot. Basically, you couldn't get a lot out of him. I thought that he'd be a lot more forthcoming with the questions that we were asking him. He'd obviously been told not to talk to anybody. At that time, Tyson was in the news a lot with Robin Givens, and his divorce and all this business. The press were saying that he were in bad shape. I think Johnny Tokos had been told not to talk to anybody.

'On the trip with Mick and Gary, I didn't see an awful lot of them. In the Mirage where I stayed, it's sort of out of bounds, unless you're staying in that hotel. But as Mick generally does, he got in there. He got in by the pool. Mick has got the gift of the gab and the cheek of the devil. He got past the security guards no problem. I'm laying in the pool with a gin and tonic beside me. All of a sudden I get chucked in the pool, and there's Mick and Gary stood there. Mick is in his union jack shorts, crew cut and dark glasses. He looked like one of the Blues Brothers. He says to me "Bernard, I've met this dark, coloured guy down the road, and he's selling diamond rings." I said to him "Mick, they'll not be genuine. These coloured guys are pretty fierce in what they do, and I don't think that we should mess with them. The rings won't be genuine." But Mick says "No, I've spoken to him, I've had a word with him. I've spent at least an hour talking to him. The rings have even got the tabs on. They're stamped. They're knocked off like, but they're genuine." Mick had come to get me to go down there with him, and to lend him some money. So we goes down to this car park, just down from the hotel in Las Vegas, and there's two black guys there stood waiting for us. Anyway, when we comes up to them, Mick introduces me to them. So this black guy gets out a nice velvet cover that he had with all these diamonds with big chunks and I mean big chunks. They were as big as bottle tops. And we stood there in that car park bartering with them. The rings were marked up at ten thousand dollars, some were five thousand and one ring was twenty thousand dollars. I said to Mick "Listen, these aren't real" But he says they are real, and he says look if you don't want to spend any money, lend me some. I ended up lending him a couple of hundred dollars. He had a few hundred himself, so he bought a couple of rings. I bought a couple as well spending about a thousand dollars in all. Well, I had to. Mick kept telling me that they were real.

'I finished up buying the bloody things because of Mick. I bought two rings. I spent about a thousand bucks. Mick had a bloody fistful of them. He had about three or four rings on his fingers. In fact, the rings looked that genuine that Mick was telling me how he was going to flog them when he got back to England for five or six thousand quid at a time, and buy a big BMW. I must have been soft as a brush. Anyway, we're all walking back to the Mirage, and we're all thinking that we've done a real good deal here. We kept looking at these rings, and they're shining in the sun. I mean they were really big carats these diamonds. Two or three hours pass, and I'd got these two gents rings on my fingers. So I decide that I'm going upstairs for a shower. So I takes this ring off, and it's green round my finger. So I gets on the phone to Mick, and I've got to admit this I didn't know how I was going to handle it with Mick. I didn't want him to come round and spark me out. I'd better handle him a bit careful. But I was so annoyed. I rang Mick's room. There was an answering machine. I said "Mick Mills. Phone Bernard, immediately at the Mirage." I got in the shower. The next minute I hear Mick shouting "Hello" as he does. He says "Your finger's green, mine is an' all."

I says to him "you better get down to that car park and see if them black bastards are still there, and you'd better knock them out. In fact, I want them knocked out and I want you to get my money back." We'd spent nearly two thousand bucks on bloody rings. The black guys were never seen again. Me and Mick, two street-wise kids from the roughest part of Rotherham had been ripped off in Las Vegas. I couldn't believe it. Mick tried for some compensation when he got home, by selling his ring. He sold his pair of rings to one of his mates for about three hundred quid. I gave him mine, and I told him I don't want to see the bloody rings ever again. I told him that if there's any money made on the sale, that he could keep it. I wanted nothing more to do with them. They just reminded me of the rip-off.'

In the course of this conversation Bernard had shifted somewhat from his usual laid back style into a state of some tension, as he relived the great rip-off in Las Vegas. 'Green bloody fingers', he was saying to himself. He had gone out there with one of the smartest most street-wise lads from Rotherham, and he had been the source of his humiliation. All this talk about green fingers directed my gaze towards those digits from which all trace of that green metallic colouring had been scrupulously erased. But something on one of his fingers held my gaze. It was the biggest, chunkiest diamond ring I have ever seen. Even in the half-light of this dark bar at noon, it sparkled. 'Surely not another Las Vegas special. Surely not another green genie?'

'Er Bernard . . . That's a beautiful ring there. Is that real?'

Bernard looked at me as if I had called his manhood into question. Here was a streetwise kid from Dalton who had become a millionaire, who had been to Las Vegas three times, who associated with boxers, who had taken this duffer for lunch only for this very same person to imply that despite having made one little mistake in his life in some dirty car park in Las Vegas he might be subject to other errors of judgement.

'Is this real? Of course, it's bloody real. That were five thousand quid. I had that made up in Las Vegas.'

I started to ask the next question, before I could even control it. 'Are you not worried about that not being genuine?'

Bernard nearly choked on his lump of steak. 'Not genuine. I got that in a proper shop. It was a jeweller's shop. It's a hell of a ring. I designed that. I told them what I wanted. It cost a lot less in the States than it would here, because the tax is a lot less over there. I haven't had it valued over here, but it cost me five grand to have it made.'

The diamond in this ring was the biggest I have ever seen. Large, thick chunky. Improbably large in fact, impossibly chunky. Sometimes one has to be extremely delicate in interviews.

'That's a hell of a big stone.' I laughed nervously for at least five seconds, as my comment terminated.

Bernard's affirmation came out low and deep, as if he was trying to work out what exactly I might be implying by this. Was it a compliment or a question, a statement or an interrogative, a shoulder pat or a kick down there in the nether regions from which the 'yeah' emanated.

'Did you buy that on the same trip as the one on which you were ripped off?'

'No. That were a different trip. I bought that in a shop where Mike Tyson was buying some jewellery. I can't remember the name of the shop but Tyson was there. If that shop was good enough for Mike Tyson, then it was good enough for me. You see, I've been okay on every other trip. The first time I take Mick "The Bomb" Mills out with me is the first time I get bloody robbed. I thought that I was taking Mick Mills out there for a bit of protection, that didn't happen, it was quite the reverse.

'On the trip with Millsie, my luck just wasn't in. I also had a thousand bucks on Buster Douglas to beat Evander Holyfield. He didn't, of course, so I came back well unhappy. I'm not a gambler, I just like a little flutter, but my luck wasn't running with me on that trip. I just thought that Buster Douglas would be too big for Evander Holyfield, but Holyfield floored him in the third round.

'The fight itself was very disappointing on two accounts. It didn't last long enough, and the undercard weren't very good. I think Buster Douglas just laid down in the third round. He got a clout on the chin, and he just laid down. He just took his money and run. I've learned that if you're going all that way – you might as well go to a Don King promotion, because that way you see all the top boxers right down the card. This one wasn't a Don King promotion. I'd brought these lads all the way from Rotherham with me, and it were all a bit disappointing.

'But I'd still rather travel to Las Vegas than London to watch boxing, because you've got freedom of movement over there. You can move around without having burly bouncers telling you what to do. You can have a drink in your seat. You can have a cigarette. I can walk around shaking hands with Jack Nicolson, as I have done at the Razor Ruddock–Mike Tyson fight. Tyson brings all the stars in. I've shaken hands with Mr T. I've even got a photograph of me and Mr T. I've shaken hands with Clint Eastwood. I've shaken hands with all these guys because they're all ringside, and I always sit ringside. It's about eight hundred pounds for a ringside ticket, but it's worth it. Eight hundred dollars, I mean, I get dollars and pounds mixed up. It was a bit of a nobble having Mick along with me, because Mick can do the business, if there's any trouble. There's no two ways about that. Mick would just knock them out and that's it. People like Jack Nicolson would have bodyguards with him, but the funny thing is that we didn't see them. Arnold Schwarzenegger were there. He probably had bodyguards as well. I shook hands with him as well, but his bodyguards didn't stop me. They kept out of sight as well. I arrived at the fight with Mick and Gary. Superstar. The secret in shaking hands with the stars is the approach. You have to let them know that you're going to approach them, rather than just rushing up to them. If you just rushed up to them, then that's when the bodyguards do close in. You're far better off shouting "Hi Jack! Can I shake hands?" I think that if you just rushed up and put your hand there, then they might think that you were going to shoot them or something. When Tyson fought Razor Ruddock the first time around, I was ringside but maybe six rows back. I went down to see Tyson when he got into the ring and I was standing just a foot away from him. I could have touched him. The supervisors asked me to move back. This guy from CBS heard my accent and started talking to me. He gave me a pass which enabled me to stand touching the ringside. It were a controversial decision in that fight because the referee stopped it in the sixth round. Anybody who was anybody got into the ring. This guy from CBS suggested that I should move away from the ring because he told me that "there will be more pieces in that ring than in the average Western." When he said "pieces", he meant "guns". He told me that there was going to be some fireworks. It frightened me to death. I thought to myself "Aye, aye, somebody's going to get shot here. I moved away from the ring, because everybody were throwing punches. The boxers, the promoters, the minders. That's not why I took Mick on my next trip, because I don't think that Mick Mills could do much with somebody with a gun anyway. It's just very nice to have somebody who's handy to the side of you. The funny thing is that they hadn't really heard of Mick "the Bomb" Mills over there. But the chap in London, who organised the flight had heard of him. He knew Mick were an ex-boxer. But nobody else knew him out there. But that didn't bother me that much.'

'You see Millsie and me have a lot in common with these boxers, and promoters, from the Bronx or wherever. People like Iron Mike and Don King have had it rough, but the fight game let them come through in the end. That's what I love about it. But my trips to the States have taught me something else about life over there. It's tough out there. I thought that I knew the score, coming from Dalton, but over there they're even meaner. But the next time Millsie and me go to the States, we'll be ready for them. If I've learned anything coming from Dalton, it's that you only get burnt once. Just the once.'

July 1993

Distractions

The worker comes home tired and exhausted from his labours. He finds that his comfortless and unattractive dwelling is both damp and dirty. He urgently needs some stimulant; he must have something to recompense him for his labours during the day and enable him to face the prospect of the next day's dreary toil. He is out of sorts; his nerves are on edge and he feels thoroughly depressed . . . Moreover, his need for company can be satisfied only in the public house, for there is nowhere else where he can meet his friends.

In these circumstances the worker is obviously subject to the strongest temptation to drink to excess, and it is hardly surprising that he often succumbs. Given these conditions, it is in fact inevitable that a large number of workers should have neither the moral nor the physical stamina to resist the temptation. (Friedrich Engels, *The Condition of the Working Class in England*, 1845)

The club trip

It was half past seven on a Sunday morning in the middle of a British summer. The British weather was living up to its reputation, and being rather unpredictable, to say the least. There may have been a drought, even days earlier, but now the rain was lashing the pavements. A queue on the pavement stretched all the way from outside the Working Mens' Club right down to the roundabout at the bottom of the road. It was three deep. Most of the women wore thin anoraks, and had brightly coloured umbrellas with spokes broken by the wind. Some of the men wore nylon ski jackets, usually in grey, many of the others just wore tee shirts, yellow for some reason, and which were wet through already. The long day of pleasure still stretching out ahead of them. The children were dressed in track suits for the most part in this year's colours – crimson, mauve, shocking pink. These were the cheap imitations of the High Street brands. Thin material – soaked already. And the wind was tearing through them.

A member of the committee supervised the goings-on. 'The coaches will be here in a moment, lads. Don't worry. Then we'll be off to Skegness.' He tickled some little girl under the chin. 'Cheer up, Lisa. You'll be in Skeggie in a few hours' time.' Little Lisa scanned the wet bleak streets and the cold, iron grey skies, in order to imagine what it would be like when she finally reached that Eldorado of the East Coast. 'And don't worry', continued the committee man – 'it'll be lovely there. The sun will be shining. It's just raining in Sheffield today. Take my word for it. It can't be like this in Skeggie . . .'

He turned away. 'This trip has been planned for a whole year. It's the only holiday some of these kids will be getting. Trust the weather to change today. We collect all year for this trip. All the kids today get £7 in their hand spending money, donated by the club. They travel free. Adults pay four quid for the trip. Not bad for a flipping day out to Skegness.' Only one of the coaches had so far arrived. The Queens Road Social Club sat next door to a used-car lot selling a whole load of exclusive and customised cars. The committee man's gaze had left the iron, grey skies and fixed instead on a Porsche. 'Marvellous that. Absolutely marvellous.' There was no envy in his voice, or not much. 'But my mate drove into a Merc on his way home last night from the club. You should have seen the damage. That's the problem with cars like that. You'd be frightened to go out in them. Too much to lose.'

We turned away from these millstones to looking for the coaches. A female in her mid-twenties in a tight black dress with a thin cotton jacket over the top, tottered past in high white stilettos. She was accompanied by a much smaller man, who was balding and looking very depressed. 'She doesn't wear any knickers, you know', the committee man whispered. 'Or a bra', he added thoughtfully. 'They say in the club that she's got three kids from three different fathers. I don't know about that, but I do agree that she's one of the best lookers who go down club.'

It was now five minutes to eight, and the remainder of the seven coaches pulled slowly up. The committee man explained that he would not be going on the trip. 'Don't forget to mention the lads who have to stay behind while

Queen's Road Working Men's Club trip to Skegness, 1991

you lot are away having a great time, to mind the fort', he said. 'It's alright for some', he shouted as he hurried back to the comparative comfort of the club. The rest of us shuffled wet and dripping onto the coaches.

All of the seats on all seven coaches were taken. A smell of damp clothing pervaded the bus. There were no smoking signs prominent on every window. An old man wearing a Tam o' Shanter and a hearing aid was the last onto the bus. 'Hurry up, or we'll miss the show', somebody shouted from the back. I didn't think that the man in the Tam o' Shanter heard anything. I didn't know what show they were talking about. I wondered if the man in the Tam o' Shanter did. The buses pulled away. The committee men waved from the windows of the club.

Ladies' loo, club trip to Skegness, 1991

Immediately in front of me sat Dave, a telephone engineer and Ann, a cleaner at the Queens Road Club. She normally starts work at half seven on a Sunday, but that morning she had to be in at half six. She looked worn out. Ann was thirty-six and a grandmother. Her daughter who was 'seventeen and a bit' sat with her baby, who was one and a half, and her husband on the back seat. Ann was immediately concerned about the no smoking sign. 'If you want a fag, you have to go to the back of the bus', she said helpfully. 'There's no stickers down there. It's like being back at school.' Her daughter, meanwhile, had already lit up on the back seat. Audrey, one of the commitee, responsible for orgainising the trip was called down. She looked worn out as well. 'I didn't sleep a wink last night, worrying that everything would go well today. It's a big responsibility to organise the club trip.' She was delegated to go and speak to the driver. The negotiations were successful. 'He says he doesn't mind if you smoke even at the front', said Audrey – 'Well a day like that what could he say?' Ann immediately lit up. The sound system of the bus played 'Hi, ho, silver lining', as the coaches snaked their way out of Sheffield. The whole bus now seemed to be smoking. Ann was already coughing.

The coach was now creeping up some hill or other, heading towards Lincoln. Crisps and a cheap Cola drink were distributed free to all the children on the coach. It was ten minutes to nine. Several of the youngsters were wearing peaked caps, made out of paper, stating that 'Pepsi' was 'The choice for a new generation', but it was only a Cola-like drink that was being given to them.

The first stop for the toilet was soon after that. Two huge queues – one for the toilet, and one for the tea, snaked out of the little roadside cafe. Some braved the elements, stood for a few minutes in the pelting rain, and then

Girl and baby, Skegness, 1991

hurried back, having failed either to relieve themselves or get any tea. Some had the sense to stay where they were. On the seat behind sat William, a self-employed electrician, and his wife, with their two children – Natalie and Jemma. William's father-in-law and mother-in-law sat opposite. The mother-law was eating a cheese and tomato sandwich. It was now half past nine. William explained that he couldn't afford a holiday this year, because he and his wife had been involved in a hit-and-run accident, and he had been off work for six weeks. His foot had been broken. Last year they'd had a week in Bridlington, but this was beyond them this year. They'd managed to get half of the number of the Sierra that had hit them. His daughter Jemma had her arm bandaged as well, but this was not connected with the accident. She had got her arm trapped in a door. Luck was not running for the family this particular year. 'The kids have been looking forward to the trip for months', said William. 'They've been asking when are we going on our holidays to Skegness, dad? It's only a day trip really, but it's a holiday to them.'

It was now 10.00 am. A woman of indeterminate age in white cotton pants and a white cotton top moved carefully from seat to seat with a card with numbers on it. You had to guess the number where the prize was located. 'We call it spot the ball', she explained – 'it's twenty pence for one square, and the winner gets four pounds.' Puddles of condensation were forming at the base of the windows. As the bus jolted this way and that, tiny rivulets started forming and making their way onto the seats.

We pulled into the coach park Skegness at 10.55. Some child at the back of the coach was immediately sick. It could have been the excitement of finally arriving in Skegness after three hours on the road, or it could have been all that cheap Cola and crisps. The boy showed a sense of responsibility and ended up carrying the bag to the front of the coach, having first sprayed the bag and its contents with air freshener. Someone at the back of the bus, perhaps a veteran of club trips, had a canister of air freshener handy in her bag.

The bus finally ground to a halt, this sudden final movement causing a grey ski jacket from the overhead locker to fall onto Dave's head. There was a muffled moan, as Dave tried to dislodge it by shaking his head. After what seemed like an eternity his head finally emerged into the fugue of the bus. His wife, Ann, the cleaner, was much amused. 'I bet you thought that you'd just had a blackout', said Ann. Dave looked slightly shaken by the experi- ence, as if that might be exactly what he had thought. The ski jackets were buttoned up for imminent disembarcation. One child already sucking a large · bright blue teat, had some matching blue sunglasses placed on him. 'He looks a picture', said his mother – 'a right picture', as she carried him down the steps onto the tarmac of the coach park in the torrential rain. Only little Lisa spoke – 'I thought that it was always sunny in Skeg, mum.' Her mum didn't answer, as she had already stepped into a large black oily puddle.

June 1991

All dressed up and nowhere to go

'I'm really sort of bored with nightclubs in Sheffield basically,' said Dom, sitting in his office in the centre of Sheffield, where he works as a self- employed graphic designer. A rather well-thumbed copy of the *Modern Amer- ican Poster* sat prominently on the desk in this little box of an office. The room was heated by an electric fire with just one bar on. The small room was very cold. Dom was dressed in a sort of distinctive tan colour, right from his cap down. He stood out from the crowd alright. His speech was also quite distinctive, he liked to drawl on the last syllables of words – 'really' and 'basically' seemed to go on forever. Some 'House' music went on intermin- ably in the background. 'Sheffield doesn't provide an exciting enough night scene, so we travel to Nottingham or Manchester for a night out. House music is the current big thing, it's the most exciting thing to happen, since punk. The only thing to happen in my opinion. My partner Chris and I organ- ise 'The Beat Route' – the ultimate trip, we like to say. We take a group to a club in a different town – there and back by coach for about a fiver, includ- ing the admission to the club. It's one long party, in the coach we have intransit sounds from Graeme Park and Winston and Parrot.' 'Yes, *the* Graeme Park and *the* Winston and Parrot,' said one of Dom's friends.

I was none the wiser.

'We go to the clubs with the DJs, we'll follow them around to hear the best sounds. This is the scene today with House music, you know – the cult of the DJ. My partner and I make about eighty quid if we manage to fill the coach. Tomorrow night we're going to the Hacienda in Manchester, it's really

Heavy metal night, Rebels Nightclub, Sheffield, 1994

hot. One girl is coming up from Covent Garden to go on the trip. She'll be back in Sheffield for about half three in the morning, then she'll catch the first train to London and be at work for 10 am. This is serious business – really exciting. The bus leaves at 8.30, so don't be late.'

There followed a night of nervous planning about dress. 'It's going to be Acid House music,' said a friend, 'so wear a fluorescent shirt or a Smiley tee shirt.' But what kind of fluorescent shirt, or what kind of Smiley tee shirt? I had already learned that Dom regularly forks out £15 for a pair of socks, and Chris £20 for a toothbrush ('well, it's a Paul Smith toothbrush, well worth it and instantly recognisable, if you're in the know'). This level of expenditure on socks and toothbrushes shocked me a little, especially when I learned that Chris, the better off of the two, earns about nine grand a year as the manager of a cinema in Sheffield. Chris's underpants cost more than his weekly rent. Here were men with an eye for detail, and some not insignificant dedication to what they currently thought was fashionable. So what kind of buttons should there be on the shirt that I would wear? And how many rips should there be in the tee shirt, or my jeans? I went off to sleep pondering such important issues.

The following night was late-night shopping in Sheffield, and the town was positively heaving, but despite this I could still spot Dom's crowd congregated in front of the City Hall from some considerable distance. It might have been the hats and caps, it might even have been Dom's satin shirt with the wing collar and his leatherette jacket. 'Seventies retro,' whispered one devotee – 'very cool, very cool indeed. Old Dom does it again, always ahead of

Disco dance sisters, Sheffield, 1982

the crowd. And just look at that hat – brown corduroy, it takes real style to wear a hat like that. Wow, *brown* corduroy.' I nearly told her that I'd just got some brown corduroy trousers from Next, and that I was thinking of lending them to Dom to go with the hat, but I decided to keep my mouth shut. It was as if she could read my thoughts. 'We're the opposite of townies, you know. We're into style, fashion, X-cess, with a capital "X". We're individualists – the opposite of Townies, who all buy the same old boring blazer from Next.' I nodded in agreement before hurriedly boarding the coach.

Now, Acid House has got a lot of publicity from the tabloids because of the apparently heavy reliance on drugs in this particular cult. So like any self-respecting scoop, I was keeping an eagle eye out for any little tablets chang-ing hands or any little pellets being surreptitiously popped into the mouth. But the only thing that I could see being popped into the mouth were rather large bottles of Lambrusco, and some rather smaller bottles of Bell's whisky and Gordon's gin. I called Dom over and asked where all the Ecstasy tabs were. 'Oh, we don't bother with that stuff here. The whole drug thing's been really exaggerated. I wouldn't even know where to get hold of any. A friend of mine tried to score some Ecstasy in a club a few weeks ago, but all they got for their twenty quid was a Valium. I know why people believe it – when you see some of the dancers in the Hacienda, you'll wonder what they're on as well. But they're not so different, Chris always says that they look as if they're just squeezing an orange box. So, if you want to dance and fit in, just pretend you're squeezing an orange box, and you'll be okay.'

Our conversation was rather suddenly disrupted by the first song of the specially commissioned tape of House music. 'Boolie hoolie, boolie hoolie, boolie hoolie, it went. The volume was intense. I was being deafened and we hadn't even made it past Sheffield Wednesday's ground in Hillsborough yet. The atmosphere was building up, people kept changing seats. I was joined by Thomas. 'I'm not into all this seventies retro stuff, I'm into any clothes that go with my hair, basically.' His hair was in a pony tail, which was set off with an expensive black leather jacket and ripped jeans. His knee, clearly visible through one of the large rips, was bleeding profusely. I wondered for a moment whether the cut was functioning as a fashion accessory. I asked him whether, like Dom, he would consider paying £15 for a pair of socks. He looked at me as if I was personally responsible for the hole in his knee. 'Look,' he said, grabbing my attention by biting the top off a bottle of lager, 'I'm only a snob about two things – women, food and wine.' Thomas continued, 'When I go to clubs, I always eat in restaurants. That way the management knows you're a good punter. I eat in the Millionaire's club in Manchester and Mr Craig's in Leeds. There the food is out of this world, but when I was there last week, I was too pissed to eat.' Now the problem here was that none of this sounded terribly *nouveau*, quite the opposite in fact. I was wondering why Thomas needed to travel all that way to the Hacienda, when his concerns were so, well, basic. He seemed to anticipate my question. 'I'm barred from Josephine's, by the way, the top club in Sheffield, because of my appearance.'

My musings were disturbed again by Thomas. 'Time for wee wee,' he suddenly cried. Now, I'm not that familiar with Acid House slang. I asked Thomas about this mantra. 'Let me show you,' he said as he and three friends got off the bus and proceeded to urinate on its wheels. 'It's only the men who ever do this,' said one female devotee in 1940s' gear, 'it's all that lager. We're hardly even out of Sheffield yet, they'll need to stop again before they get to the club.'

'That's better,' said Thomas, when he got back to his seat. 'Now what do you want to know about Acid House? About where it came from? It's like this, when I was a DJ, I was playing Acid House music three years ago. It's basically funky music, and boring funky music at that. The truth is I can't stand the bloody music. If some other producer worked on these records they'd be able to do a lot more with them. But that's just my opinion.' I wanted to point out that almost everyone I spoke to had claimed that they, and they alone, were the first to play Acid House music in Britain, but bottle after bottle was being passed from the back of the bus for Thomas to take the top off with his teeth, and this ritual was somehow inhibiting any provocative questions that I might have liked to ask.

Instead, I stuck to more innocuous questions, like asking Thomas what he did for a living. 'I own a small engineering company,' came the immediate reply. 'What kind of engineering company, exactly?' I asked. 'Well, um, a domestic appliances company – I fix broken vacuum cleaners. I call my firm – the Sheffield Vac Hospital, not bad eh? Our motto is that your vac can be broken, even without you realising it. I supply free safety and efficiency checks – there's usually something wrong with them in the end. But I really want to get in to selling credit, then you can sell anything – cars, holidays, the lot. All my mates are entrepreneurs – see that guy over there, he's a top entrepreneur. Did you see *The Clothes Show* when it had these sun glasses on with the flashing lights – £4.95 they were. He's selling them for four quid. He's got the brains, you see.'

A different tune was now playing. This one had more elaborate lyrics – 'You want this party started right.' I asked Thomas about Ecstasy. He said, 'Look, put it like this, you can get an awful lot of lager for twenty-five quid. I was approached a couple of weeks ago in a club, and this guy asked me if I wanted to buy some 'Windowpane'. I told him that I'd never heard of it – Windowlene yes, but Windowpane? Acid House isn't about drugs, it's about staying ahead of the pack. I organise coachtrips to clubs as well, you know, but more up-market clubs. I don't make a fortune, but it's a start.' And on that note Thomas disappeared to the back of the bus because there was a queue of bottles waiting to be opened.

Chris, the co-organiser, made his way over, and started telling me about a friend who had just paid £750 for a suit and £195 for a shirt. The friend in question was a hairdresser. 'He had a real Northern accent, and they laughed at him in this trendy shop, until he produced his wad of notes. Just imagine their faces.' I could see that there was real power for Chris in this – something to keep inside your coat more deadly than any concealed weapon. 'The assistants just froze, you should have seen their faces, he killed them stone dead.'

The group on the bus kept drinking and chatting and changing seats – all one long party, and we weren't even there yet. Josie sat beside me. 'Do you want to know why I come on these trips?' she drawled in that awfully trendy way, before inserting the usual inordinately long pause . . . 'It makes me forget.' There was another significant and very meaningful pause. 'Do you know what it makes me forget?' I shook my head. 'The way everyone is so oriented towards money today in Thatcher's Britain. You just can't get away from it no matter how far out you go.'

And we both would have laughed at this double entendre, if it hadn't been quite so uncool.

January 1989

'Yippee yi, yippee yo – the goalie in the green polo'

It was the middle of an English winter, and the weather was causing problems yet again. Jean Thomasson, who was fifty eight, listened to her radio for any information about the match. 'The snow's not that bad, surely. If they work at it through the night, they could clear it. I'd go down and help myself, if they'd let me.' Jean Thomasson was a dedicated football fan, a lifelong supporter of Bolton Wanderers. 'More than a fan', she said – 'it's in my blood. To be a fan, you have to start young. You can't become a fan overnight. I remember when I was a little girl, my father's nose blood red from the cold from watching the Trotters play on a freezing afternoon. Mother

Girls' night out, Sheffield, 1994

always had the tea ready for him when he got back from the match. Every Saturday, he'd say "never again". I used to go with my father to the game. I had a brother, who was nine years older than me, but he wasn't that interested in going to the match. I always think that he didn't really like standing about in all weathers watching football. I, on the other hand, have always loved the winter. I love going down to see a match at night. There's a tar works near the ground, and if the wind is going in the right direction, it blows the smoke right across the ground. There's this lovely smell of tar. It's great down there on a winter's night.'

'My week revolves around football. You start the build-up to the match on a Wednesday, it's then that you start thinking about the team for the following Saturday. Friday night's paper has the team selection, then there's the local TV programme to follow. Then on Saturday, you have the match itself. We always have the traditional meat and potato pie before the match. When you come back, you look at the match from all angles. On Sunday, you have the Sunday papers to analyse the match all over again. On Mondays you have the evening paper, and another chance to read about the game. And if you're very lucky, there's a match on Tuesday, which just keeps you going until you start all over again. If I have to miss a match for whatever reason on a Saturday, I carry this little transistor around with me all the time. I also have the radio on in the kitchen and a radio on in the lounge, and the teletext on the television. If all those fail, there's always the club call on the telephone – you get the match commentary on that. Football occupies quite a lot of my life. When you get to the end of the season, you get withdrawal symptoms just like from a drug. In the summer I like to watch Lancashire playing cricket, but it's not the same. There's no substitute. I've got some other interests apart from football, mainly Third World issues, and I'm a member of Amnesty International, and an organiser for Christian Aid. But, I've been known to go to these serious meetings with a little radio, hidden on me, to hear the latest match scores if Bolton have been playing away from home that night.'

'I'm a teacher at West Houghton High on the outskirts of Bolton. There are some Man United and Liverpool fans there, and they give me a bit of stick for supporting Bolton. But it's like water off a duck's back. That by the way is a saying often used by Bolton's manager. I'm a dedicated fan, and the kids at school know that. I've been in a few scrapes through football. When we played Sheffield United, before they had proper segregation, I walked up the steps and the whole section where I was to sit was occupied by Sheffield United fans. The friend I was with wanted us to go and sit somewhere else, but I said that I wanted my seat. So I went along the row and just said to this big bloke "Excuse me, but you're sitting in my seat." He said "Oh, sorry about that. You can sit down here, luv. Don't worry, you'll be alright – unless you score, that is." He sounded really quite threatening. But eventually my friend persuaded me to move, which is just as well, because the Trotters did score. I've also been searched going into grounds on loads of occasions, and I've even been told off for carrying a flask in with me, because it's considered to be a missile. Can you imagine me throwing a flask at the ref? I've been told to shut up by stewards for shouting at matches. Well, you don't realise what you're shouting sometimes, do you? I shout things like "Get off you black bugger", referring to the referee of course, not black players. I do take exception to racist chants. I've only been in trouble the once though. Where we sit at Burnden Park, our home ground, there's a fence just by us, and down below that there's the standing section. One Saturday, there were these people climbing up out of the standing section to get in to our spot. We, of course, were pushing them back. I recognised one of those who were climbing up. He was one of our sixth formers and I can tell you he had a right bloody nose. He'd obviously been scrapping, and he didn't look very pleased to see me. I pushed him back, but I was told off by the police for that. The police didn't thank me for my assistance. Somebody else had seen this boy as well, and he was reported to the headmaster on the Monday. So he wasn't very pleased either, but I can tell you that he was a bit surprised to see his teacher right in the middle of things.'

'But there's always been trouble of one sort or another at football matches. I was at the Burnden disaster in 1946, when thirty three people were killed. That was the first of the big football disasters. Bolton Wanderers were play-ing Stoke City in a cup tie. They'd won 2–0 at Stoke, this was the second leg, in front of 65,000 people. Or at least in front of 65,000 paying fans. Others climbed in from the back – over the railway line, and pushed forward. The barriers collapsed at the corner of the ground. The fans were just crushed. I remember my mum waiting for my dad and me at the gate, because we were late back. She didn't stop either of us going to the match though.'

'I started going with a friend from school when I was twelve. We used to go to all the home games, and the away games that were near enough to reach. I used to collect all the pictures of the players in a colourful plastic wallet. My father had worked in a plastics factory during the war, you see. After every Saturday's match the order of the players in my wallet got shifted about. My favourite was the goalkeeper – Stan Hanson. I used to fiddle the order of the players in my wallet so that he was always at the top. Me and my friend used to stand behind the goals. My friend, Margaret, thought that Stan was fat. I used to say that he wasn't fat, he was just well built. We used to live nearby and plague the lives out of these players. Stan used to go down to the ground on the bus in the morning. We used to sit close to him, so that we could hear what he was whistling – to see what kind of music he liked. I made up a little poem about him:

> Know a man in a green polo
> Down at Burnden Park
> Now he lives in Springfield Road
> Grand place in the dark.
>
> Do I love him? Do I love him?
> Yes on your life
> Can I have him? Can I have him?
> No, he's got a wife.
>
> Living round at Harper Green,
> Not far from his home
> At the end of every day
> Round his place I roam.
>
> Who makes my heart sing,
> Yippee Yi, Yippee Yo
> The goalie
> In the green polo,

That was in the forties, that culminated in 1953 when we went down to London to watch the FA Cup Final against Blackpool. We were winning for a large part of the match, and then we had a couple of very bad injuries – there were no subs in those days. In the end it was obvious that we were going to lose. The final score was 4–3. We wept on the way home.

'After that I moved away to Manchester University. I talked about football a lot, but I didn't go to that many matches. But then comes what I can only describe as an 'aberration'. I met the man who is now my ex-husband, who was a Manchester United supporter. Now if you mention Manchester United to a Bolton Wanderers' fan, you get an immediate reaction. Manchester United is the team that Trotters fans hate the most in the whole world. At matches Bolton fans will chant "We only hate Man United", when there's not much happening on the field. My husband started taking me to Man United matches. We were both teachers. I have to admit that the atmosphere was fantastic. I remember watching one game where Busby's Babes beat Anderlecht 10–0. The crowds were huge. You'd be carried out at the end in a sea of people, your feet would never touch the ground – quite literally. You'd be carried on

a huge wave right into the street. I remember waving an umbrella at somebody once, because I thought that I was going to be trampled under their
feet. But it was really good, I mean I really enjoyed it. I even watched Bolton
play Man United at the cinema in 1958, and I remember that I was torn in
terms of loyalty. I thought at the time that my husband had managed to turn
my loyalty away from Bolton. That would have been some feat.

'Then we moved away from the area for several years. If you're away for
any length of time from a football team, then the players change. You don't
recognise the team anymore. While I was away I used to keep an eye out for
Bolton's scores on a Saturday, but that was about it. They'd moved down to
Division 3 by that time. Then one particular night in 1971 I was going to see
my mother on the top of this bus, and it went past the ground. Manchester
City were playing Bolton in a cup tie. It was like looking at that Lowry picture
called "Going to the match", which is actually a painting of Burnden Park. I
felt that I was in the wrong place – I shouldn't be on this bus. That was my
home in there. I persuaded my next door neighbour to go with me to the
next match. I didn't know the players, because I'd been away a long time,
and the team lost 6–0 to Chelsea, but it didn't matter. It was like going
somewhere I'd already been – it was like going home. My husband wouldn't
go to watch Bolton, he despaired of me – going back to Bolton after all
those years. But I felt that I'd never been away.'

Anna, her daughter, a twenty nine year old student has a different memory
of the family and football. 'I remember all the arguments. My dad used to
say things like "At least Man United are in the First Division. It's a set of
amateurs that you've got there in Bolton Wanderers." He used to criticise my
mum's judgement about football all the time – "Are you sure you know
which way that they're supposed to play?" My father was a headmaster and
less open at school about his interest in football. Everyone at school knew
that my mother was fanatical about the game. She used to take me every
week with my hat and scarf embroidered with all the players' names. I would
wear the same jeans and the same jumper for every match as a kind of good-
luck charm. Mother would be listening out for weather forecasts all week. It
wouldn't have been the same if the weather forecast was good. You needed
the uncertainty, just as you needed the rain itself on the big day. It wouldn't
be the same either if you weren't wet through whilst you were watching
the match. My favourite Bolton player was Gary Jones. I liked him because
he was the underdog. He was a striker that rarely scored any goals. The lads
would shout things at him like "It's raining, Gary will be dashing inside to
blow dry his hair." Or the lads would just whistle at him. I just thought that
he was lovely. Mum was more objective about the football than I was. She
was also more objective about Gary Jones than I was. My mother always
says that to be a proper fan you have to start young, and I certainly did.
My mother used to go to matches with her father, but it was she who took
me. My father was content with watching Man United on the box, but me
and my mum would be at Burnden Park come hell or high water. I followed
the team week in, week out until I was eighteen then I moved away from
Bolton to do nursing. Now it's a bit difficult to get to the match because
I'm a full-time student at Sheffield University. I don't get a grant, so I have

to work nights in a hospital at weekends to pay my way. That makes going to the match really difficult. But mum and me still discuss the game all the time.

'I've always been drawn to the energy of football, but sometimes that energy works the wrong way. I was in my flat in Sheffield on the afternoon of the Hillsborough disaster. I saw the news flash on the TV. I rang the hospital where I worked and they told me to come up immediately. I remember that it was really difficult to get there because so many roads were closed off. I got there at about 4 o'clock, and it was just chaos. I worked in the angiography department which is attached to the main X-ray department. In angiography, you inject drugs into the patient to see which arteries are ruptured. But nobody needed that sort of investigation that day, they'd all been asphyxiated. Also an amazing number of medical staff had turned up, so there wasn't a lot for some of us to do. So I had a wander round to see who needed help.

'It was a scene that anyone who was there will always remember. Every stretcher that the hospital owned was in service that day. Some stretchers had been brought out of storage, some had been brought out of the knacker's yard. I don't remember any noise, but what I do remember were all these football scarves and football programmes all over the floor. It was a bit of a shock to see the injured and the dying completely surrounded by all these little things – scarves, bobble hats, programmes, that usually mean so much. These were the things of my childhood, and my mother's childhood, the innocence of singing about the "goalie in the green polo". But it didn't seem so innocent any more. I honestly don't think that I could bring myself to wear a Bolton football scarf today, even though Bolton's colours are blue and white, and not a bit like Liverpool's which are red and white. Funny that.'

November 1991

Dominoes

'Hey, man! Is that the best you can play? Give me a break. Why did I team up with you? You're useless, you're crap!'

The shouting took me by surprise, and I took a step back away from the table, quite instinctively. The other games seemed to pause for a moment, as heads turned towards the epicentre of this sudden explosion. A man in a black sweat shirt was visibly shaking with anger in his seat. The eyes only stayed on him for a moment. This was obviously nothing out of the ordinary.

'Crap!' the man in the black sweat shirt shouted for emphasis. 'This is total crap. It's bullsheeeeeeeet.'

I noticed that he was so angry that spit flew out of his mouth as he shouted. It landed on the chin of the man sitting opposite him. He was the object of the first man's abuse. He was also on the same side as the man in the black sweat shirt. With friends like that . . .

Suddenly the man in the black sweat shirt started banging the table with his fist. The argument, you could say, was getting quite heated.

Sheffield United Dominoes Club, 1993

'Relax', said Lloyd to me, out of the corner of his mouth. 'He'll calm down in a minute. He's just overreacting a little.'

Something told me that Lloyd might not be right here.

'You did it all wrong, man. You couldn't keep up with me, man. I thought that you were supposed to be able to play. You can't play. My mother can play better than that, and she's nearly blind.'

The recipient of all this abuse made a languid sort of gesture with his eyes, as if to say 'Who gives a fuck? Shout all you like asshole. You don't bother me. I'm an ace player and if you don't see that, then it's you who must be blind.'

The irate player was incensed. 'That's right. You just sit there. Who's worrying anyway?'

The man in the black sweat shirt pushed his chair back from the table, knocking over one of the fire buckets packed with sand, which stood on the ground functioning as ash trays. When he stood up, you could see that he had massive shoulders. He looked as though he would pack some punch.

'He is a bit angry', said Lloyd, who I could see was the master of the understatement. 'He is a ferocious player though, a bit like the Mike Tyson of the dominoes' world.'

Iron Mike then turned to the wall, and started punching it repeatedly. He may not have punched holes in the wall, but there were certainly dents. Meanwhile his two opponents just sat there smiling. I feared for their safety.

'Come, on, sit down man. Relax. Take it easy', said one older grey-haired black man. His advice was falling on stony ground.

This was just another practice night at the Sheffield United Domino Club held upstairs at SADAC – the Sheffield and District Afro-Caribbean Association in Sheffield. 'The problem was that his partner misread some of the signs that he had sent', explained Lloyd. 'The whole skill in dominoes is based on the ability to read certain codes of secret communication between the players on the one team. You have to be able to signal to your partner what hand you've got, and you have to be able to do this without talking. We use a whole series of very fast signs. You have to be able to do this so fast that your opponent can't see them. We have a club code and also a private code between different sets of partners. Every player in the club must know the club code, in case their particular partner doesn't turn up. In the club code, if somebody pulls their ear lobe then that means that they've got a "deuce", if they cross their fingers that means a "double-two". If they point down then that means a "three". You can't print that, by the way, because it's top secret. Other clubs are still trying to work out our secret club code. There are opposition clubs who would pay to discover our secrets.'

I put my pencil away, for a second.

Lloyd said that he trusted me. 'I know that it sounds basic, but the idea is that you do all of these things so quickly that your opponents can't see what you're doing. As well as the club code, individual sets of players have their own secret code. Ricky Bennett, our club secretary, for example touches his beard for a "six", wipes his mouth for a "five" and points up for a "one". These are his personal signals.'

'Only good for men with beards', I added helpfully.

'If you partner Ricky', continued Lloyd, 'then you have to learn the secret signals that he uses. Ricky is fast, as fast in dominoes as some of the West Indian fast bowlers are in cricket. Ours is one of the best domino clubs in the world. In fact, Sheffield United Domino Club is as famous in dominoes as Sheffield United Football Club is in soccer. Probably more so. We consider ourselves the world champions. We won the British Airways and Appleton Special Competition last year. This is the toughest domino competition in Britain. The final was held in Brixton Town Hall, and we had 400 people down there watching and shouting and clapping. Even Lord Scarman came to watch. He had a great time. We also had the Mayor of Brixton in the audience and one Open University lecturer. We won twelve tickets to Jamaica. There they take their dominoes really serious. The Jamaican domino team is as good as the West Indies cricket team. They have professional players out there. We went out there and played the best, and we won five matches and lost two. That's why we consider ourselves number one in the world. The tops. Apart from the British Airways and Appleton Special Competition, we've won the Moonshot Big 12 League three years running. This is like a premier league, but we're too good for it.'

Lloyd Edwards is the team captain. By day he is a machine operator in Sheffield. By night he is one of the world's greatest domino players and captain of the squad. 'It's a very serious game. Clubs are run just like football clubs. We take players on a one year trial and there's a strict code of conduct. We check their attitudes and behaviour during that year. We have a playing strip – a black blazer, white shirt and tie, with handkerchiefs emblazoned with a domino in the top pocket. We are a very professional side, and we

Dominoes, Sheffield, 1993

have scouts coming from other clubs trying to poach our best players. But you don't get the recognition in this country', he said. 'We get ignored by the media here. In Jamaica, on the other hand, we were treated like royalty. Everybody knew who we were. The TV and newspapers there all carried our matches. We had groupies following us around from match to match. Well groupies always go for the best teams. In Jamaica it is part and parcel of life there. For most of us it was our first time back in our home country and we had the time of our lives. We were superstars. It was great to return there in that style.'

'It disappoints me that dominoes isn't rated as more important in England. But they always say that the three most important things to a West Indian are sex, cricket and dominoes in that order. But as you get older the order shifts a bit. We get some of the men coming up here to practice and their wives want them for sex, but they won't leave for that. No way! The women know how important dominoes is. They wouldn't try to interfere. They go home on their own.'

Sheffield United Domino Club has 36 playing members. Twelve players are fielded at any one time in a match. The match lasts for four hours, so Lloyd explained it is a game that requires a lot of stamina. Lloyd was described as a very cunning captain by his players. 'You have to take firm control', said Lloyd. 'The captain can win or lose the match. He is the only person allowed in the "ring" – the playing area – when the match is in progress. The captain selects the pairs and watches their progress. He also makes sure that his players don't get too heated. It is his job to keep his men cool, calm and collected.'

'There's an awful lot of skill in this game. A good domino player can tell you what their opponent has got in their hand 80 per cent of the time. Our top men are Don Parker, Delroy Malcolm, Neville White and Cecil Simpson. Don Parker is the Mohammed Ali of dominoes. He is the greatest, Delroy thinks he's the greatest. There's a lot of rivalry in this sport and a lot of passion, and it's funny because it can be just as competitive when you're practising, as you've seen tonight.'

I looked around at the tables. There were no white players, no very young players, and no female players. I commented on this. 'Well teenagers have other things on their mind, and as for white people they tend either not to be that interested or that good. Leeds Domino Club though has a white lady as secretary who plays, but there aren't very many good white players around. Some women do play in the leagues, and we have played against women, but on the day, you don't care what sex they are as long as you win.'

I remarked on the 'disagreement', which had been in progress, when I arrived at SADAC. 'You get disputes in any competitive sport', said Lloyd. 'Things can get a little heated sometimes, but there's never any violence. As captain I make sure of that.'

By now, the noise level in the room meant that Lloyd had to shout into my ear. Players banged the table to pass, and everywhere I looked there were middle-aged black men stroking their ear lobes, touching their chin, and wiping their beards (if they had one). Some were shouting simultaneously, sometimes in Jamaican Patois. It might have been my imagination, but there seemed to be quite a few disputes in progress.

'It's all part of the game', said Lloyd. 'Sometimes, players will pretend to have a dispute with their partners to throw the opposition off. You see, the game really involves sitting there for four hours watching every little twitch, hand movement and grimace of the opposition to try to work out what hand they've got. You have to be able to do all that and not be put off by all the noise and all the arguments. My players are very successful at doing that. That's why we're number 1.'

'The Liverpool of dominoes', I added helpfully.

'Riiiiiight', said Lloyd.

'Bullsheeeeet!' The racket from table 1 had started up once more, and I noticed that Iron Mike was banging the table again.

'Gamesmanship?' I suggested.

'Now, you're learning', said Lloyd. 'Now watch him take his opponents to pieces. This is a very cunning sport alright.'

April 1993

Koi carp capers

I was sitting in a large garden just outside Barnsley with Norman. 'But you can't give the address', pleaded Norman – 'just say somewhere in Yorkshire.' The security light came on suddenly, Norman jumped. 'You have to be vigilant at all times. They came about 11 o'clock last time. They took only one

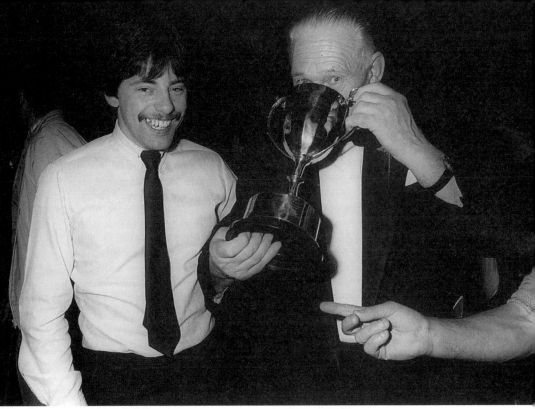

Retirement party, Dial House Working Men's Club, Sheffield, 1983

fish, my very best Koi carp. It wasn't my biggest, but it was my best. It was a beautiful Yamabuki. It was a right big beauty, probably worth about two thousand pounds. They knew what they were looking for alright. My security wasn't tight enough. I didn't let on that I had got Koi carp in my garden, I told everybody down in the pub that it was just an old fish pond, but somebody obviously came for a closer look. My wife says that it's like leaving your jewellery out on your front lawn. I got the security lights installed. But that wasn't enough. They came back exactly one week later and took my second best Koi. It was a beautiful Aigoromo. Again they only went for one fish. Those boys knew what they were after. Since then I've had this grill put over the pond. It's ornamental, and I think it doesn't spoil the view of the fish. But what can you do? The grill has got twelve locks, so now there's no chance of the thieves putting a net in and trawling for the fish.'

Norman sat forlornly gazing at his fish through the metal grill. He pointed out the beautiful markings on a Taisho Sanke, but all I could see were the markings on the metal grill. 'I can't bear the thought of any of my other carp being taken. I have photographs of all of them and I circulated the photographs of the stolen fish to all the enthusiasts in the area. I thought that if anybody tried to peddle my fish then other enthusiasts would inform on them. But so far I've heard nothing. I've rung a number of the Koi carp importers and breeders, but they tell me that they never buy Koi off the public to prevent this sort of thing, which is becoming more common. My Koi are probably in some pond in Leeds or Manchester, missing their old home in Barnsley. They were as tame as anything. They would rise to the surface and take food from my hand, they would even let you stroke them.'

Koi carp are the status pet of the nineties. But they are more than a pet, they are an investment. Norman, a small businessman, careful with his money had watched his Koi appreciate over the years, from a few hundred pounds to several thousand. You can pick up a four-inch Israeli Koi for ninety pence, but a good Japanese Koi can set you back four thousand pounds. Then the prices really start to rise. The most expensive Koi ever sold went for £330,000, and that was in Japan some fourteen years ago. In Great Britain the prices are more modest. One was sold for £28,500 three years ago. Some press reports of the prices that Koi in this country have fetched, have apparently been greatly exaggerated, but nevertheless nearly thirty grand for a fish is still rather a lot of money. But the profits in Koi carp have made the thieves move in. The thieves and the cheats. The value of a Koi depends partly on its overall size and volume, but mostly on its colour and the uniqueness of its patterning. If a Koi is nearly perfect, but not quite, it can have cosmetic surgery to improve its pattern and increase its value. I talked to Peter Waddington of Infiltration in Warrington, the biggest importer of Koi carp in this country. 'Say you have something like a Kohaku with a deep-red colouring on a white background, and say it's got champion potential with nice crisp divisions between the colours, with a definite edge. But say this Koi has a little black freckle. This can ruin the fish's potential, but it can be removed with cosmetic surgery. The fish has to be anaesthetised, but it is a fairly straightforward operation. You can add thousands of pounds to its value in this way. Cosmetic surgery is not something that I approve of, but some breeders in Japan do use it.'

Fish, of course, cannot be guaranteed. These carp may live for thirty five years, but then again they may not. The irony is, of course, that you may end up with a Koi with a unique pattern, but one partially achieved through artificial means. You could end up putting your money into a fish traumatised by cosmetic surgery, only to find the value of your investment sinking like a stone along with the fish's lifeless body, which has failed to recover from even the most skilful cosmetic surgery.

Unfortunately, for Koi enthusiasts everywhere, the opposite of cosmetic surgery also occurs. Norman attended a Koi carp show recently where the champion Koi, as tame as anything was being stroked by members of the public. 'This Koi was worth literally thousands of pounds. It had a beautiful red pattern. I saw this woman stroking it and the next minute one of its scales came off. It looked like nothing without that scale. Its value must have dropped by about ten thousand pounds in that one second. The stock market was never as precarious this. But as my wife says to me if it's an investment you're after, you're better off putting your money into a building society rather than into Koi. But then again, if your money's in a building society, you don't have all this beauty to appreciate.'

I left Norman staring down through a metal grille somewhere in Yorkshire.

July 1990

'Game to the last'

The setting was a barn just outside Scunthorpe. The venue had been kept secret, known only to the select few, until the very last minute. And even then you had to be in the know to get sensible directions to this barn in the middle of nowhere. The entrance fee was a fiver. It was 1.00 am, and it was very wet and miserable, but they didn't seem to feel it. There were about fifty of them all gathered around the twenty-foot-square 'ring'. This was the one that they had all been looking forward to. The big one. This was Sledge, the local hero, and his big chance against a champion called Peace. You could tell that Peace was a champion just by looking at him – he had one eye and one ear. Most American pit bull champions are missing some important part of their anatomy. Peace's missing parts were plain to see. The stitches looked very crude indeed. 'Well, you can hardly take them to a vet,' explained one of the ringside buffs.

The two American pit bull terriers were being displayed – not so much like race horses, more like boxers. Or gladiators. This was going to be a real display of guts, in every sense, and the crowd knew it, and loved it. Peace was being carefully scrutinised. 'Awesome', said one regular. 'Awesome,' said another. It was already obvious that the specialised vocabulary of the American pit bull ferrior fraternity was somewhat limited. Their world, I couldn't help think, must be just as limited, limited and very, very mean.

Peace was led our way. 'Peace has been through the wars, you know,' said one of the regulars pointing at the awesome creature in front of us. A dog with the most incongruous name imaginable, as well as the most incongruous teeth. The teeth, which were really fangs, dwarfed its stocky little head. 'Peace isn't technically a champion, which would mean that it's a three-time winner,' said my informant seeking to clarify things. 'Peace is what you call a "two-time winner", but that's still pretty good.'

I could see already that if three victories made a dog a 'champion' then the fighting life of these dogs was really rather short.

My new acquaintance continued. 'But old Peace has got a lot of fight left in him yet. He may be half blind, but he's still as game as hell. That dog likes fighting more than fucking. All good pit bulls do, you know. I owned one pit bull who was up this bitch, and just after it had finished the business it was trying to bite the bitch's head off. But that's pit bulls for you. They're great dogs, and great companions, they're all very game. See Rottweilers, they're useless. As soon as you injure them, that's it – they're off with their tails between their legs, if they could get them between their legs that is. It's exactly the same with Alsatians and Dobermanns. They're good guard dogs, don't get me wrong, they're good at biting people, but they can't fight. My pit bull killed an Alsatian in the street a few weeks ago, and the Alsatian was a right big brute as well. I kept my pit bull in a pen at the bottom of the garden, and it got out somehow. A friend of mine saw it run across the road after this Alsatian. But the Alsatian had no chance against my dog. My dog topped it in a few minutes. My dog's a big 'un, mind you. It stands 23 inches and weighs 60 pounds. It has a 21-inch neck as well. It's right solid, really awesome. It'd tackle anything.'

My informant leaned back, relishing every minute of the tale, basking in the pride that emanated from this great breed. 'Pit bulls never give up, they're one of the few breeds that'll fight to the death. They're dead game and I've heard that old Peace is especially game. They're bred for gameness. But even some pit bulls quit after they've given everything that they've got. But I've heard that Peace never quits. It just keeps going and going. I've got great respect for that dog, and I've spent all my life with dogs so I should know. Pit bull fighting does come in for some criticism, but the way that I look at it is that the dogs love it. These dogs have been bred for it. And when you watch them fighting, the first thing that you'll notice is that their little tails are going all the time. They love it.'

This ringside *aficionado* was getting into his stride. He was drinking neat vodka out of a bottle. He continued, 'Pit bull fighting is just like boxing really. It's like two trained, fit men fighting. It's all run in a very professional way with a referee, a time keeper and judges. There are some idiots who own pit bulls, but there are idiots in all walks of life. I know of one guy who had a pair of dogs and he set them at each other when he came in from the pub one night. He had them fighting right in his front room. They wrecked the place, the ornaments were all over the place. There was such a hell of a commotion with all the breaking glass and yelping that his neighbours actually rang the police. He panicked when they told him. He couldn't get the pit bulls separated so he ended up having to drag the dogs outside and stab one of the dogs, to get them apart. Idiots like that shouldn't be allowed to own any dogs, let alone pit bulls. They're also the guys who get away with fighting pit bulls. Those that organise proper fights get prosecuted. You see the way I look at it is that it's like the difference between a scrap in the street and a professional boxing match. There's rules here. The main rule is that when one dog turns away from its opponent it's taken to its own corner. The other dog is held in its corner. The dog that has turned is then given ten seconds to go after the other dog and cross that line there, or it's lost. It's a way of seeing that the dog is still game, that it wants to get stuck in there one more time. Of course, if the owner of the dog touches it during a contest, then that dog has lost. That's really like throwing in the towel, you see.'

At this point in the proceedings, I noticed that the dogs were being scrubbed. My informant noticed my perplexed expression. 'That's to make sure that their owners haven't put any stuff on the dogs to stop the other dog biting it. Before big contests, the owners always swap dogs and wash them to make sure that they haven't been coated in anything. Just look at the shape that Peace is in – it's awesome. Greyhounds are bred for running, pit bulls like Peace are bred for fighting. Just look at the neck on Peace. It's a bit like Mike Tyson. Of course, like boxers, pit bulls fight in different weight divisions. This particular pair of dogs have been matched at fifty-five pounds. Peace has come in overweight tonight so its owner has had to pay a £200 forfeit. It's not his night, let's just hope that it will be Peace's.'

It was time for the fight to begin. 'Face your dogs,' shouted the referee. 'How long is a round?' I asked. 'There's no rounds, they just fight to the end,' said my new acquaintance. But the end was a long time coming. One hour forty-five minutes, to be exact. At that point Peace was picked up by his owner. Not before time – his bottom jaw was hanging right off. But the contest was not stopped on humanitarian grounds or whatever the equivalent is for canines, as my informant pointed out. 'He's gone,' he explained. 'With a jaw like that he can't bite properly. There's no point in letting the fight go on, he's useless now.' Sledge's owner picked up the £600 prize money.

But the entertainment wasn't over for the evening. The consensus around the ring was that Peace was still dead game, so it was decided to give him a courtesy scratch. His owner held it in the ring to see if he was still game to fight. He stood there motionless half blind and half deaf, with his lip hanging off like some freshly cut liver on a butcher's slab, and with his lower jaw resting at a very odd angle. He stood there trembling with anger and determination. And presumably pain. There were all these people hanging over the ring egging him on. His owner's eyes seemed momentarily to fill with tears – of pride rather than sorrow. Peace bolted forward – blindly, obediently, instinctively – beyond sensation, indeed beyond sense. Sledge, still held firmly by his owner, seemed to brace himself for round two. The seconds should have been out, as Peace tried to bare his heroic fangs which could not grip or bite or even meet any longer. Sledge rolled his muscular shoulders bracing himself for the impact – that never came. Peace was dragged up and out of the ring. 'Game to the last, what a dog. What a scrapper. They'll be talking about this fight for years. Your dog is a hero, mate.'

The hero, which couldn't even eat after going the distance that night, was kept for one week after the event, and then shot. I remembered what I had been told about not being able to take such dogs in that condition to the vets. 'It was good for nowt,' said his owner afterwards – 'perhaps I should have dragged it out of the ring sooner, but there was Peace's pride to consider.'

That was a wet windy night outside Scunthorpe, now it was a bright winter's afternoon in Dalton, outside Rotherham. I'm sitting in the front room of Mick 'The Bomb' Mills, an ex-professional boxer and a dog lover. His lurcher sat on his knee, licking Mick's face affectionately. Drawings of his favourite pit bull, Eli, occupied pride of place in his living room. Mick saw me looking at the drawings. 'I had to get rid of it, because of all the bad publicity that pit bulls were getting. If you've got a pit bull everyone expects you to fight it. I got fed up with all the hassle. A lot of people were asking me when they were going to see it in action. It would make a change, they said, from watching all the druggies around here topping themselves.'

Despite all the hassle that he'd had, Mick had agreed to try to explain to me not so much the thrill of pit-bull fighting – because he considered me too soft – as the inevitability of the sport. 'Pit bulls need to fight. It's like some people. They're bred for it. It's best to put them in against something that can fight back. It's just like professional boxing, and like boxing, the sport is well regulated.' I felt I had heard all this before, but from a boxer it sounded different – not necessarily more convincing, just different. Mick continued, 'In America, it's an even bigger sport, but the Yanks always do everything in a big way. I went up to Newcastle a while ago to see one of the all-time greats from America. This pit bull was valued at ten grand, the stud fee alone for that dog was a grand. The dog was truly incredible. It had the biggest teeth I've ever seen on a pit bull, they were $2\frac{1}{2}$-inches long. This dog was a real champion – a three-times winner. In its first two fights it had killed both its opponents in half an hour each. In its third fight it was put up against another champion. Now that, believe me, is a real test of the character of a dog. But this particular animal managed to break the other dog's pelvis in forty-two minutes.'

I flinched. I didn't like to think about broken pelvises, I didn't even like to hear about them. I mentioned Peace's broken jaw from my night in Scunthorpe. Mick knew all about this classic fight. He reached for the video-recorder in the corner of the room. I assumed that he was going to re-run the fight in Scunthorpe from a pirated video – all one hour forty-five minutes of it, in all its glory, but no, this ring was different. This ring was out of doors, and I could make out Mick's stocky form laying punch after punch into another boxer called John Ridgman. Mick was tearing at him, wearing him down, snarling around the heels of the taller boxer. In the second round Mick floored him. Whilst the viewers watched the re-run of Mick's bomb landing, Mick explained that something happened at that point in the fight. 'That's when he broke my jaw,' explained Mick. 'He broke my jaw and dislocated it and split it right down the middle.' And sure enough when the camera eventually returned to the action, you could see that Mick's jaw was now resting at that improbable angle. I had only seen a jaw at that angle once before, and that was on a dog.

'I had to retire at that point in the fight,' explained Mick, 'in front of my home crowd at Bramall Lane, but I'm not finished yet – I've had two fights since. They say that I've made more comebacks than Frank Sinatra. And don't worry, I've broken a few jaws myself – six to be exact, and only one of them in the ring. I broke my first jaw when I was sixteen in the car-park of the pub at the bottom of the hill, and that's the only one that I've ever been prosecuted for. I'm thirty-two now, but I still keep on training. Did you know that the referee Harry Gibbs described me as having the hardest punch since Randolph Turpin. When you've got a punch like mine, there's always a place for you in boxing. Perhaps one day I'll be back. I'm still very game, you know – very game indeed.'

'As game as old Peace,' I added, 'and used probably just as much.' But my half-hearted comment was drowned out by noise of the video-recorder and the crowd at Bramall Lane baying for blood. It was almost funny.

April 1990

Driven to distraction

Aldo is an Italian barber, in his forties, with two shops. Not a wealthy man by any means. There is just something rather odd about his shop. On that space just outside reserved for his car, I realised that the car kept changing. I was admiring his red BMW 520i one day, the next it had gone replaced by a Renault 21 Turbo Quadra. Weeks later the space was filled by an aqua blue G reg Porsche 944. A few weeks later it too had gone, replaced by a Ford Fiesta RS Turbo. But Aldo is not a car dealer, not even a part-time car dealer. In fact, he tells me that on every deal he loses some money. He just enjoys changing his car, frequently. In fact, very frequently. Usually every few weeks. And this is no stairway to heaven, the cars do not necessarily get progressively flashier and more expensive. Indeed, there seems to be little progression of any sort. Down from a BMW to a Renault then up to a Porsche then down to a Ford Fiesta. Always one car at a time, not a collector with dozens of cars, just an average car owner, but a far from average consumer. As he talks about his car exchanges, you can't help wondering what is going on.

This is not a man in pursuit of some record or other. He doesn't off hand know how many cars he has had. He stands with his clippers in one hand trying to count them. He works through the BMWs, Porsches and Alfa Romeos on up though the Capris in their various shapes and forms. The 1300 Capri, the 1600 Capri, the 2-litre laser Capri, the 2.8 injection Capri, all lovingly described, their best features identified, their worst features painfully elucidated. Then it's the turn of the Mazda RX7s – he has owned both the non-turbo and turbo versions. He has had numerous Volkswagen Beetles, all subtly different he says. He reads motoring magazines avidly – *Autocar*, *Car* and *Autoexpress*. He is the ultimate consumer, the ultimate target for all those glossy car adverts. 'I like reading all the details about new cars. I just like cars', he says by way of understatement. It is only others who think that his car-buying behaviour is worthy of some explanation or other. I ask him to reflect on his motivation. He ponders the question for a few minutes. Eventually he comes up with an explanation. 'Envy', he says. 'I see other people in cars, and I think that's a nice car that. I would like to drive that. Then I get the car, and to be honest sometimes I'm a little disappointed. The most disappointing car that I've ever had was the Porsche 944. The engine was too lean for my liking. I could go for a fortnight on a full tank of petrol, instead of a week. I had a chip put in to enhance the performance of the car. It pepped it up a bit, but not enough. The BMW 520i wasn't any good on the hills around here. I was having smaller cars passing me. That was no good at all for somebody who likes a little bit of performance. When a Fiat Panda passed me I knew that the car had to go. I've had two Fiat Pandas in the past, and they pull pretty well. But I'm happy with the Fiesta Turbo. It's an excellent car.'

Then you see that look in his eyes. You can almost guess what's coming next. 'The funny thing is that I've seen a rather nice Toyota Supra today. The Fiesta is fun to drive, but in a week's time I might want a bit of luxury, so I might trade her in for the Supra.'

The objective in this constant quest is not to make money. 'I've never made a cent on the deals. In fact, I've lost on every deal that I've ever done. On the deal of the Porsche against the Fiesta Turbo, I did pretty well. I got the money back what I paid for it. More-or-less. I might have lost a few bob on it. The Porsche cost me around twelve and a half. I got around ten and a half for it. So it's not a few bob really. You're talking about a couple of grand I suppose. But these deals are always on paper anyway. I always have finance on the cars, I've never been in a position to pay cash. I've had some expensive cars this way. I had a Mazda RX7 Turbo, which cost me around twenty three grand, but it only cost around £570 per month on a lease purchase. This might seem expensive, but I could just about afford it. Aldo also does not enjoy the actual buying process. "I don't even haggle", he says apologetically.

So what deep psychological reasons could underpin this minor obsession. 'I think that there is always something better out there. It's not something which has sprung up in middle-age, it started when I was seventeen. I've always been into changing my car. My first wife said to me – I'm surprised that you're still with me after all the times that you've changed your car. But what she said was prophetic in a way, because eventually I traded her in as well.'

But surely even he can see that his list of virtually random swaps has no pattern to it, it does not represent any sort of logical progression towards an ultimate goal. 'The funny thing is that I know what my dream car is. It would be a new Toyota Supra. It cost thirty seven grand, which is too expensive for me. Forget your Ferraris, I'm not too keen on Ferraris. They've got the performance, I'll give them that. But I like a little bit of luxury. That's why I dream about the new Toyota Supra. I don't even want to go and see one to tell you the truth, because although I couldn't afford it, I would still want to find out how much it would be on a lease purchase. I suppose that I'm avoiding my dream car. I just want something better.'

But 'better' here is irrational, worse than irrational, it sets one off on a quest that is bound to fail. Cars are too different to be just better or worse. Aldo ponders this. 'It would probably make sense if I had three cars at the same time – one for sportiness, one for luxury, and one four-wheel drive for the snow, but I can't afford that. So when I've got my sporty coupé, I start missing a bit of luxury. When I've got my bit of luxury, I miss the acceleration, and the whole thing starts again. Even when I've got most things in the same car, I see somebody else out there with something better. The problem is that there aren't enough car manufacturers to satisfy my needs, so a lot of the cars that I've owned have been duplicated. But they're always right at the time.'

November 1993

Voices from beyond the grave

'Mr Smith' from the Stretford end of Manchester is reputed to be one of the best mediums in Britain today. Mr Smith is not his real name, but it could be. He seems very ordinary. He is very well known in spiritualist circles, but he didn't want to be exposed to the great British public. At least not yet. So Mr Smith he remains. I went to visit him with as open a mind as possible, which was difficult given what I had heard about him. Mr Smith greeted me at the door with a firm handshake. It was a wet and bitterly cold day. 'Not a great day to be out and about,' I said. 'Not a great day for the spirit people either,' said Mr Smith. 'You mean that the weather can affect them?' I asked. 'Of course it does. The spirit people have told me so themselves.'

Mr Smith had been recommended to me by someone who had spent the best part of forty years investigating the claims of mediums, and exposing the charlatans in their midst. However, according to this one expert, 'interesting' things were said to happen in Mr Smith's seances. 'Like what?' I had asked. 'Oh the usual – talking ectoplasm, ectoplasmic voice boxes – that sort of thing. Just the normal stuff really, but the materialisation of spirits still isn't at a very advanced stage yet.' I was already starting to wonder how I would cope when faced with an ectoplasmic voice box. I was also starting to wonder how I would cope when confronted by any skeletons from my past. You see I had also recently talked to a lorry driver who had been to one of Mr Smith's seances, and had one old and particularly nasty skeleton dragged out of its cupboard. It seems that the experience wasn't very pleasant. The lorry driver in question had attended one of Mr Smith's seances, in his own words, 'for a bit of a laugh and to give me something to talk to my mates about down the pub.' He gained access to the group because his mother was a regular member. But the joke backfired. 'During the seance, this child's voice said "Hello, Dad" right to me. I thought to myself that they hadn't done their homework very well. You see I had a daughter, but no son. But anyway, this child's voice started telling me all sorts of things about my daughter, about watching her in her playground at school and it all started to feel a little eerie. Eventually, I asked the voice how old it was and what was its name. It said. "I'm thirteen, and my name is Terry." I was dumbstruck. You see, what nobody at that seance knew, was that thirteen years previously, my wife had had an abortion. Before we decided on the abortion we'd decided that we were going to call the baby "Terry". Nobody at that seance could have known anything about this. I locked myself in the toilet after the seance for three hours and wouldn't come out. When I eventually came out my mother and I had a row about the abortion. But now I know there's nothing to be afraid of, and I regularly talk to Terry.'

I was trying to prepare myself for a few surprises as I was led into Mr Smith's drawing room. I noticed the thick velvet curtains, and the smell of a pet dog. Mr Smith eyed me suspiciously. 'You know some people come here rather sceptically. Some so-called intellectuals think that there's no such things as spirits and that contact with the spirit world is all in the mind. I think that some of these people should see a psychiatrist,' he said. It had been decided that I would not yet be allowed to attend an actual seance, instead I was to be allowed to hear some tape-recordings of spirits talking. I settled myself back in the chair for my first experience of the spirit world. Then the little pet dog of the house, wandered in. I reached out my hand to stroke it. 'Don't touch it,' yelled Mr Smith, 'it bites.' I had already jumped into the air and we hadn't even started yet. The little dog wandered out again. 'The evidence of the spirit world is plain for all to see,' said Mr Smith. 'Now you're going to hear some of that evidence. You'd have to be a fool not to believe it.' He continued to look straight at me. He pressed the play button. An eerie sound emanated from the machine. I nodded knowingly. 'That's not the spirit people. That's just us singing "Let me call you sweetheart",' explained Mr Smith – 'we always start with some good old-fashioned songs.' Then the singing slowly died away. Suddenly a child's voice spoke, 'I enjoy the singing, you

know.' Mr Smith stared at me – 'there was no child present at the seance.'
'Just listen,' said Mr Smith.

Woman's voice: 'Is it Terry?' [the lorry driver's aborted foetus apparently thriving in the spirit world].

'Hello Auntie Rose.'

'Hello my love. Where's my kiss?'

This was followed by a kissing noise. After Terry came a whole series of spirits recorded from different sessions. The first thing that struck me about them was how well spoken they were. Indeed, Mr Smith had pointed out that some of these spirits were 'better spoken than the Queen.' But, as I listened to the tapes, I discovered that the spirits that frequent Stretford are not just well spoken, they're fairly outspoken as well. Stretford spirits do not mince their words. Referring to practising Christians, one spirit, a Mr Powell, referred to them as 'misguided'. He continued, 'They are ignorant peasants. They are compensating, so do not worry.' Mr Powell had apparently delivered this message in a darkened room through an ectoplasmic voice box, although he was hoping to deliver this and similar messages in person later, as he himself explained. 'We were hoping that we could have shown ourselves before now, but at least you can hear us speaking to you for the time being.'

I was relieved to discover that day that spirits retain their sense of humour. One spirit was holding a conversation with a scientist called Ronald. The spirit began by insulting him. 'Your theories are not quite right. You're only scratching the surface. You think you're an egghead and clever, but you wait until you learn about our world.' The spirit then told him his name. Ronald, the scientist, misheard it – 'Crook?' The spirit corrected him – 'Cooke! Just think of your dinner,' he said. It wasn't much of a wisecrack, but at least it was something.

Mr Smith just nodded – 'marvellous these spirits. There's nothing they don't know.' He then played me a section of tape where he discussed my impending visit with one of his spirit guides.

Mr Smith: 'God Bless you – Just a second, Mr Powell, we've got a Gerald Beattie coming to talk to me tomorrow.'

Spirit: 'Oh yes, you have many people coming here, he'll be one of many who will come – he will go away with his own ideas.'

Mr Smith: 'Yes.'

Spirit: 'But I think you will give him a lot to think about.'

Mr Smith: 'That is good.'

Spirit: 'A *lot* to think about – you could open a whole new world to this gentleman.'

Mr Smith: 'Yes.'

Spirit: 'If he cares to learn, but he has to learn the truth and to be well-read on the subject. You carry on, my friend, telling him to read – because there are books we value very much.'

I wanted to point out that there were clearly some things that these spirits did not know. My name was Geoffrey for a start, or as these spirits would probably put it – 'Geoffrey! As in just think of that sheepish Deputy Prime Minister.' But I left it. I asked instead when did Mr Smith first realise that he had psychic powers? He said that it first dawned on him when he was about four. His father had gone to the races and left him and his mother alone on their farm in Cheshire. 'This particular night mother said that the two of us would sleep in the guest room of the farm. I woke up in the middle of the night and mother was shouting at something to go away and stop it. I said, "What is it mother?" She replied, "I think it's Alice Healey." Alice Healey had been dead for some years. I could see these unseen hands pulling at the bottom of the bed, so I dived under the bed clothes. Mother told everybody that the spare room was haunted and that I had psychic powers. All the neighbours heard about my psychic gifts after this.

'One other incident convinced me of my psychic powers. During the war, I was stationed in India. In 1944 I had to take a special message to divisional headquarters. I passed this signal operator in a trench. He asked me to take over for a few moments, while he relieved himself. A message came through for one particular soldier to report to Bombay for repatriation to the UK on special leave. That soldier was me! There were about 150,000 troops in that area, and just by chance I received the radio message. When we were two days out of Bombay, we heard that a 30,000-strong Japanese army invaded the area that I'd just left. Most of my friends were wiped out. The Japs even bayonetted the patients in the field hospitals. I realised there and then that there must be something I had to do in my life – that I'd been chosen for something.

'When I got back home to the farm in Cheshire, my father hardly recognised me. He hadn't seem me for six years, and he was shocked by my appearance. I'd gone down from fourteen stone to nine stone. He said, "By God, they've taken their toll on you alright." When I was demobbed in 1946, the vicar came round to say that he hoped to see me in church on Sunday. I told him that church was the furthest thing from my mind after what I'd seen in the war – ministers blessing guns for killing people with. And I didn't believe in the stories either – Noah's Ark and all that tripe. If it were true just tell me how the Kangaroo came to be in Australia, eh? I was more interested in gambling than church to tell the truth. Whilst I'd been away mother, who had 2,000 poultry on the farm, had been saving the egg money for me. There was a bank book with £140 in it, waiting for me when I got home. I said to her, "Mother, what a delightful person you are." We used to go to these steeplechase meetings, and one day I backed horses in eight races and had eight winners. I must have been psychic, or so mother said. About that time mother became a spiritualist. It was about the only thing we ever argued about. I said. "Don't bother me with that tripe." In 1952 I decided to give it a try. We sat in what's called a development circle with a red light above the circle. It was so dark that you couldn't recognise the person sitting opposite you. I saw this light on the wall of the church, but I was sitting there real arrogant. I was thinking to myself that I bet there's a hole in the curtain and all these mugs are taken in by this. Suddenly something happened to me. I could feel my eyes pulling out, and my face being contorted. I thought to myself, what the hells's this? There's some bugger here sitting with me – their legs in mine, their face in mine. Then this man from across the room shouted at me, "Young man let that spirit doctor come through." I was panicking. That was my first experience. Later I found myself talking like a Scotch man in that church. The Scotch man's name was Jock McCullough. Jock McCullough entered my body. Shortly after this experience I became a spiritualist.'

Shortly after this, Mr Smith's mother encouraged him to go to a very well-known medium where materialisation was common. 'We all had to pray at the start of the seance, but because I wasn't used to going to church anymore, I wasn't sure what to say. So I just said, "Dear God, I've come here by invitation." You have to pray, by the way, so that you don't contact lower evolutionary forms of life, such as the lower ape man. We've had cases of dogs materialising, and little dogs sitting on people's knees. So we always pray. After the prayer, as we were singing, this bright light, the size of a sixpence but brilliant like a diamond, went round the room and stopped in front of me. Suddenly there was this huge noise like a 'whoooosh' and it materialised as an angel. She walked up to me and said, "God bless you in the name of Jesus." She told me her name was Sister Helen. She was the most gorgeous figure I'd ever seen and had this beautiful face. She told me that we had been brought there for a special reason. "Do not believe the priests," she said. "You do not lie in the grave until some far off day of judge-ment, when the great trumpets sound. I am proof of that."

'One man at this particular seance had a wife who was dying of cancer. Sister Helen told him that if he did what she told him, that she would get up off her sickbed in three weeks' time. Sister Helen told him to go to the chemists and buy these Dutch drops – capsules with cod liver oil in them. She told him to give her two in the morning and two at night. She also told him to take her to hospital in three weeks to have her inspected. Up until then she had this huge cancer as big as a coconut – doctors could feel her cancer by poking about up through her rectum. But now it had gone. The doctors were baffled. Sister Helen was lovely. She told my mother that she would be there to meet her when it was her turn to pass into the next world. She had a lovely voice – very soothing, and far more educated sounding than you or I. In fact she also spoke in a way superior to the queen.'

At that point, I nearly put my foot in it. It had already been explained to me that your spirit body can transform after death. Terry was after all now thirteen, and not a foetus any longer. Were voices also transformed? Did you lose your accent in the afterlife? Would my mother be pleased that I had lost my Belfast accent after all? Unfortunately, I blurted this question out. Mr Smith looked at me as if I had just spewed up some ectoplasm onto his lap. 'Of course not. Sister Helen was educated in this life, Mr Beattie, unlike some people.'

Mr Smith's mother passed away three years ago. She was ninety-two. In a seance shortly afterwards she explained that Sister Helen was there to meet her on the other side, along with her sister Winnie. Mr Smith continued his account. 'Nobody except me at that seance knew about Sister Helen's prom-ise thirty-five years previously. My mother stayed in the astral plane for fourteen days before being led to the spirit world. For fourteen days you could smell her perfume all over the house and then it was gone. It was the same with Jesus – that's why his disciples reported seeing him. Jesus was a great medium. He never said he was God. It's the same with all religions. All the great religious leaders were mediums. The problem is that ordinary people want to turn these great mediums into gods. The astral plane is a world of our own mental making, the spirit world is a world of anti-matter. When some people die, they think they're in a nightmare. Others are brainwashed into thinking that they will sleep until the trumpet sounds. So they do sleep because they've been hypnotised. But a belief in the spirit world would change the way that people live. How could one person kill another knowing that they would have to come face-to-face with him again one day?'

'Or indeed abort your unborn foetus,' I added, thinking again of the poor lorry driver, as I made my way out on to the cold streets of Stretford. It may indeed have been my imagination but the temperature seemed to have dropped sharply in Manchester that day.

May 1990

Aliens over Gleadless

'The first time I saw aliens was in 1979 in Gleadless in Sheffield, when I was on my way up to the chip shop. I was going up for two fish suppers at about nine o'clock at night and I bumped into a neighbour of mine, Ken, and we just stood chatting for a bit. Then I just happened to look up into the sky and there it was. Ken saw it as well, but he backed out. He had learning difficulties and he thought people would just laugh at him. He was frightened as well by the UFO, more frightened than me. The space craft was a saucer shape, like they are. But it had a dome on top, the same colour as the space craft. It had a plum-coloured light down beneath it, but it looked like it was turned down low. It was just stood there.'

Jean's eyes opened wider in an almost involuntary manner. Her pupils seemed to dilate, as her excitement rose. 'There were two people inside – beautiful looking people. Both had blond hair and very pale complexions. I couldn't tell whether they were men or women, but they had an all-in-one ice-blue suit on. They had hair a bit like Cleopatra with the fringe and that, only they were very blond. One was stood looking down at us – just watching me, the other was just standing to attention, like a soldier.'

I looked around at Jean's very ordinary kitchen in Hyde Park flats overlooking Sheffield. I could see into the bedroom where Jean's husband, Tom, a hospital porter had his binoculars poised and focused on the horizon waiting for the next visit by alien spacecraft.

Jean continued her story 'I could see right into the spaceship, it had neon lights just like my kitchen. When I saw the UFO everything went quiet. There were no cars anymore, whereas before that there were. I had a word with my friend Jenny, and she says it's what they call the "Oz" factor – when everything goes dead, and all you can see is the spacecraft. I think the aliens are keeping an eye on us, just watching how we're developing. They go all over the world, mainly America. But that night they were in Sheffield,

Jean and Tom watch the sky and wait, Sheffield, 1995

probably flying over the Pennines and they saw the lights in Sheffield, and they just decided to go in for a closer look. After a couple of seconds the UFO just vanished. When I went back home the first thing I had to do was draw it. That's what everybody does when they see a UFO. You think that people aren't going to believe you, unless you draw it. My husband Tom didn't believe me. He said that it was probably the Russians, just over to spy on Gleadless in a secret spy craft that could just fly anywhere, stop anywhere, go anywhere. But when he saw my drawings he changed his mind.'

Tom sat nodding in the corner. 'I got worried when I saw the drawings', he added. 'No Russians would be driving around in a machine like that.'

'But that wasn't the only time, I saw aliens', said Jean interrupting. 'In 1990, I learned I had cancer and I was just about to go into hospital for a mastectomy. I was a bit nervous and scared about going into hospital. I fell asleep in front of the telly. Something woke me up, and I could sense somebody at the back of me. I couldn't move. I felt this hand go onto the top of my head, and I felt these vibrations. I still couldn't move. I went back to sleep again, and when I woke up I felt great. The aliens had cured my fear of cancer. When I went into hospital, I had no fear. The doctors couldn't believe how well I was coping with it. But they didn't know what I had experienced. It changed my life. I look up driving. I passed my test and bought a car. It wasn't the cancer which made the change, it was the visit. There's more to life than what you see around you.'

This all sounded like a faintly religious type of experience. I suggested this to her. 'I don't believe in God, but I do believe in aliens. I think that it's aliens that watch over us. After all, I've seen them with my own eyes.'

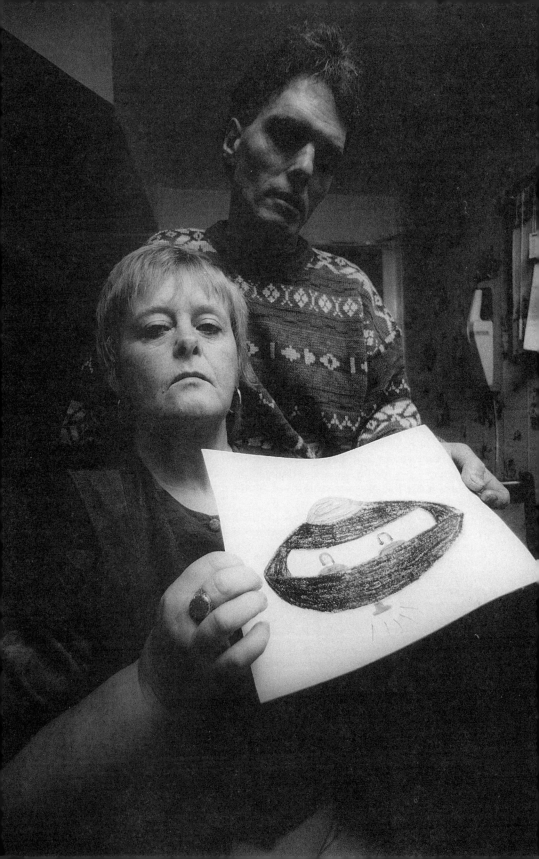

But couldn't she have been mistaken? If aliens are so common in Sheffield, why didn't others report a sighting as well? Jean had a ready-made answer to that. 'A lot more people than you think have seen aliens, but they don't want to talk about it. Take Ken, because he had learning difficulties he thought that people would just laugh at him, so he kept quiet.'

Tom got up to adjust the focus on this binoculars. Dusk was drawing in. 'There are different types of aliens, of course', continued Jean. 'The blond ones don't mean us no harm. They're quite like us. They're called Norviks. They've got their own planet, at least that's what I've heard. The others – the ones with the long arms and the big eyes kidnap human beings, and do all sorts of horrible tests on them. They're called the 'Greys'. I haven't seen any of them, but I think they're a grey colour. The Greys seem to be more common in America, for some reason. I've read that the Greys have no digestive system, and they don't eat meat. But I wouldn't fancy meeting a Grey on a dark night, I can tell you that.'

For fourteen years, Tom had felt a little left out of all of this. Jean had by then had two experiences of aliens, but the closest he had come to a UFO were a few bright lights in the sky over Sheffield that turned out on closer inspection to be planes. Until a trip to Skegness in 1993 that is. Jean leaned closer. 'Tom and I both saw this UFO at Clumber Park. It came down in some trees just before this big roundabout. It was right close. Tom wanted me to stop the car. But no way would I stop. I was scared that time. I don't know why. Tom begged me to stop, he even swore at me. But I just wouldn't. He's never let me live it down. We still have arguments about it to this day.'

Tom sat staring out of the flat in Hyde Park flats with his binoculars beside him. 'I remember that night well. Manchester United were playing Sheffield United at Bramall Lane, but we were going to Skegness. I was listening to the game on the radio, and then I saw it. At first I thought it was the Russians at it again, then I realised that it was too quick even for them. I couldn't believe Jean wouldn't stop. The spacecraft was only fifty feet away. I saw the lot. It was black and shiny, just as if it had come out of a car wash. It looked like a boomerang. I don't know what they were doing here, but I wanted to find out. I think they were resting. They weren't going to a cafe, because aliens don't go to cafes. There's a lot of people say that the aliens are killing cows and all that sort of carry on, but there were no cows in this field. If Jean had stopped, I would have gone over that fence to find out what they were doing behind those trees.'

Tom looked wistful. Jean had been touched by an alien, he had only managed to glimpse them through some trees. 'It was an opportunity of a lifetime that I missed there. I hope they'll come back. I'd go with them. Some of my friends have said that they might want to do experiments on me and stick things up me, but I think that's a load of rubbish. I think that they'd look after you. Anyway, they might have things that keep you alive forever.'

'After all', he added 'what's there to lose in the end?'

February 1995

The machine itself, 1995

Epilogue

From social observer to hanger-on

'Hey!'

'Hey!' It was louder the second time. The sounds had come straight out of the darkness, and I stood there quite still, like an animal caught in the headlights of a car. A rabbit transfixed momentarily, as if I was trying to decide which way to run. I always react in the same way at times like that. Just in case the sounds aren't intended for me. You see, I have that kind of natural embarrassment which prevents me from going in search of the kinds of people who shout across the floors of crowded night-clubs. Besides, I had been there enough times to know how to behave – how to really behave when you belong in a place like this, like the famous footballers, the ex-famous footballers and the assorted selected hangers-on who have been there enough times to know the score. You don't just jump, when somebody calls. If you can help it.

I suppose that I've always been a hanger-on. At least since I started this project – writing about people and places, observing, trying to know the score. If you don't fit into any neat category you have to be. I don't mind. They get a bad press though. Whenever a great celeb falls, the media always blame the hangers-on. They're the scapegoat. I suppose that it's easier than blaming an ethos, or a lifestyle, or a way of interpreting or seeing the whole wide world. Just blame the men in the shadows, the men like me. There are different types of hangers-on, of course. I'm one sort. We all want something for nothing. I want people to talk to me. On the record if possible.

'Hey!' somebody shouted again. I just stood there in the dark, trying to feel comfortable. If you feel comfortable, then you look comfortable. That's what somebody had told me once. 'Just use your body language to project who you are', he said. Others use props to tell everyone else who they are. I had met VIPs who were all front and all mouth, who would talk about ordering butterfly cocktails just to show who they were. One hundred guineas each and two bottles of champagne in each one. Two bottles of champagne in each one! They'd arrived up North in the eighties, the cocktails that is. For years they'd been knocking them back in the South in Stringfellows, in the Hippodrome, in all those clubs where all the flash Southerners hung out, with some bimbette to impress. Now they'd made it back to Pete Stringfellow's home town. And didn't they just love them up here. As Bob from Rotherham liked to say – 'You'd think that they'd been invented for the North.' But it wasn't an original line. I knew that.

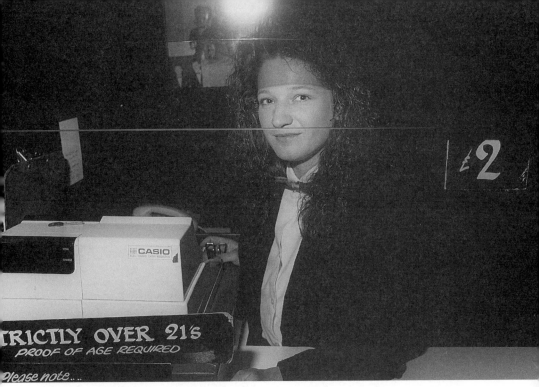

Cashier, Josephine's nightclub, Sheffield, 1992

I should say that I have never actually seen a butterfly cocktail. I have heard about them, but I haven't actually witnessed one being drunk, or being assembled. Cockney was one of my interviewees, he could *talk* about these cocktails for hours. He liked to talk about anything expensive, anything beyond my means. I suppose that it was a sort of verbal prop, a prop of the imagination. 'One of my mates ordered eight butterfly cocktails last week', he told me. 'Eight! Do you know that one of them's meant for eight people.' I didn't know that. My look told him that I didn't know that. Cockney liked that. He liked me not knowing. That was my role. Out there, permanently surprised.

He continued his tale. 'The barmaid queried his order. "Excuse me, sir, are you sure you haven't made a mistake here?" My mate just looked at her. He took his time. He didn't get all flustered, like you would when some snotty bitch tries to put you down by querying your order like that, and then he came right out with it. "You're quite right, luv – I have made a mistake – I forgot you – make it nine." And we all fell about laughing.'

I was in on the joke. I had to laugh with him. That was part of what he wanted. They wanted to surprise me, to shock me, to give me a glimpse of a world close to mine that I really didn't know.

'But that's what you call style', said Cockney. 'Nine hundred guineas for a round of drinks. Mind you, he got barred a week later for running up and down the bar with his trousers down round his fucking ankles. He was a scrap dealer by the way, and he looked a bit ridiculous when he dropped his bags. You can be a big spender and still end up being barred. It's not enough just to splash your money about, you have to have class as well as style. And I've got both.'

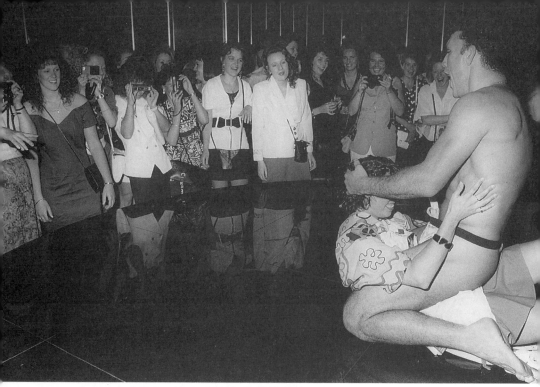

Ladies-only night, Josephine's nightclub, Sheffield, 1994

I always liked to think of Cockney at times like this, because despite his obvious faults Cockney got by. Or he did once. The last letter I got from him was from a prison somewhere. He wanted me to send him a copy of the article that I'd written about him. He had told somebody inside about the fact that there had been a full-page article about him in the *Guardian*, and they obviously hadn't believed a word of it. He needed proof. He needed to show off his story in cold print. He needed another prop.

But Cockney had been a survivor, and when he was out and about, he got even more free drinks than me. And that was saying something. That's an important part of being a hanger-on of course – not paying for anything. It's not the lack of funds, although that can come into it. It's just that the famous don't pay, so why should anybody else? Anybody with style, with class, with a little savvy. I had to have some savvy, whether I liked it or not. I had to learn the rules and then follow them. I had to become one of them – a survivor living in the North during its period of negative de-industrialisation, getting by with limited resources.

Perhaps 'survivor' is too strong a word here, but perhaps not. They were times of confrontation. The Conservatives took on the steelworkers and then the miners, and at times it looked as if the government intended to go the whole hog, and close the whole place down. We were told time and time again that the recession was to blame. 'What recession?' said one of the few steel magnates who was doing rather nicely through these times. 'Which recession?' said Cockney, who was sensitive to rhetoric, and who had heard everything at least once before.

The impression I got sometimes was that there would only be a few survivors left, running around the industrial ruins scavenging for what they could, begging or borrowing props to play the few roles which were left open for them.

'Hey!' I heard the shout again. Cockney wouldn't have been rooted to the spot by embarrassment by someone calling in his direction from the neon glow of the wine bar, Cockney would have known exactly what to do. He was a friend of all the stars who ever made it to Steel City, although to be honest it was hard to remember why his friends were once famous. They were all ex-this and ex-that. But you still had to be polite when you met them, and develop a sort of generic deferential greeting. It's not acting. It's just politeness, and everyone who has been an ex-this or an ex-that expects the deference. I was getting very good at deference.

Suddenly, there was a tap on my shoulder. 'Don't you remember me then?' I turned to face a middle-aged man with slightly receding black hair brushed into a nineteen fifties Teddy boy style. 'Of course, I remember you. You're Mad Pete . . . er . . . Pete . . . Pete isn't it?'

It's at times like this that you wonder, perhaps for the very first time, about the potential ambiguity of nicknames – irrational mad, mad beyond logic or reason, or just devil-may-care mad – mad, spontaneous and full-of-pleasure. Sometimes such distinctions can be important when you're stuck alone in the headlights like this.

'That's right, Pete', said the man with the old-fashioned haircut. 'So you do remember me. I thought that you were ignoring me for a second there, but then I thought 'No, not Gerry. He's not like the poseurs you find in places like this, with more front than Blackpool and even less behind it. He's alright. He's a decent sort of guy – normal. Right normal. Right fucking normal.'

Mad Pete was still staring at me, at a distance that most would find uncomfortable. He had been drinking brandy. It was a warn type of smell. There was a glow to it. I wanted to point out that he had got my name wrong again. He told everybody that he was my great pal, but he always got my name wrong. This annoyed me, but I didn't say anything. I hated being called 'Gerry'. A lot of people called me it. It must be the way that I say 'Geoffrey'. I swallow some of the sounds.

'Now how's the writing going?' he asked. 'Still writing for that paper? What's it called?'

'The *Guardian*', I said.

'That's it. That's the one. That's the fucking ticket. I always mix it up with that other one. It's a big one as well. What's it called?'

I just shook my head.

'Um, the *Observer*?' I suggested.

Pete looked as if he hadn't heard. 'Lots of words. Lots of fucking pages to fill with writing.'

I nodded. 'It's a big paper alright.'

'It's a fucking big paper', said Pete. 'I bet nobody's ever read it all. I mean I bet nobody's ever read the whole fucking lot from start to finish. I mean every fucking word of it. Every single fucking word.'

Pete had this look. I wasn't sure whether he was asking a question, or challenging me in some way.

'I've read it all', I said.

He looked almost hurt when I said it, as if I was trying to undermine him, so I softened my claim.

'Well, not every word. You wouldn't read every word after all', I said.

'No, you wouldn't, would you?' he said. 'Not every fucking word. Unless you didn't have a life yourself.' He reached out and took hold of my lapel and pulled me a little closer, as if he was going to confide in me.

'Are you looking for any stories at the moment?' he said, 'because I may have one that's right up your street.'

There was a silence starting to form, filled only by the Human League in the background. On Thursdays they liked to play the classics in this night-club, the classics from fifteen years ago to make all the young mums out with some friend from work on her hen night feel young again. 'Don't you want me b . . . a . . . b . . . y . . . .'

I could feel my cheeks starting to glow. I didn't like this situation. Why couldn't I just tell Mad Pete that I didn't really want any story out of him. I had tried to get the one good story from Mad Pete, the one-time bouncer with the baseball bat, the bouncer who liked to nut people when they were least expecting it, but I had failed. I had tried to coax that story out of him. It had been a long, painful experience because Pete liked crowded, noisy night-clubs as, if the truth be known, did I; like a lot of hangers-on. But he always said that he didn't want to go into details. 'No details', he made me write it down. 'No details', he said slowly again. But there was no story without details, so I had finished with him.

I had finished with others too. I felt guilty about this sometimes. I knew that I was in the business of reducing lives to a few thousand words after all. But it was still better than reducing them to statistics, that's what I liked to tell myself. I reduced them and then the Northern editor from the *Guardian* labelled them – 'the burglar's tale', 'the pimp's tale'. I always felt a little guilty because they weren't burglars or pimps, this was just part of what they did, part of their survival strategy. They were right to ask for more. I knew all this and yet my heart was sinking fast.

I always got a little nervous when Mad Pete, or Big Paddy or even Cockney came up with the idea for a piece, especially because money was then usually mentioned fairly early on. I never mentioned money – at least not to any of my informants. This was my one golden rule – try to avoid mentioning money in the course of the interview. I had picked up this rule from John Course, The Northern features editor of the *Guardian* which I worked for on a casual basis. The newspaper wanted stories about everyday life in the North, but they also wanted to distance that great paper from the tabloids. 'The *Guardian* never pay for stories, remember that', John had once warned me in an imperious sort of way, an unusual tone for him. And what stuck in my mind most about this pronouncement was the way that John had said *stories*, as if they were things that the man-in-the-street, exactly the kind of person that I liked to write about, would generate *stories* as soon as money was hinted at. Stories as opposed to the truth which we reduced as appropriate.

But the *Guardian*'s great moral standpoint on cheque book, or even back pocket, journalism could lead to all sorts of problems, especially when you are dealing with the likes of Cockney. Now I had to agree that there was a story in Cockney. Cockney wasn't his real name of course. Cockney was not from the North. He was from London, but quite unlike the rest of the country, he had moved North in search of work, which in his line of business made some sense. Cockney was a 'plastic surgeon', heavily into credit card fraud. His real name was Richard, but to everyone else in Sheffield, and Armley jail, and Hull prison, he was Cockney, because Richard, who was full of useful aphorisms, liked to tell everyone who was prepared to listen, and quite a few who weren't, that you couldn't have a decent night out, or a right good drink, past Watford. London was the place, the only place to be. So Cockney, it was. He was also a hanger-on and a good one.

Now, Cockney had once given me an interview in the comfort of his council flat surrounded by teddy bears and David Cassidy posters, because his wife was crazy about teddy bears and David Cassidy. 'I saw David when I was fifteen, and I never got over it', she used to say. Now nobody ever mentioned David Cassidy, except Richard's wife. She wanted a nose job but Richard wouldn't pay for it. But Richard had a ready answer to this, as he had to everything else. 'Well I had the bags under my eyes done by one of the top cosmetic surgeons in England, but I never paid. Did I?' he told me. 'They weren't quite right, you see. I've got very high standards, so why should I pay for a job only half-done?'

I would nod back at him, as if I too wouldn't pay for a job half done, as if I wasn't the kind of mug who would pay up front.

'You can have anything for free in this country, if you're prepared to ask', he said. 'If you're not too lazy to ask, that is.' He told me that he was Margaret Thatcher's biggest fan.

I would talk to Richard about credit card fraud or butterfly cocktails, and he would sit in his flat having a chip at his wife.

Richard asked for all that he could, and a good deal more besides. Richard also had an answer for everything, and if my interview with Richard wasn't exactly pleasurable, it was very easy, because Richard was an extremely good talker. The only problem was that after it was over he demanded money for it. No, this is wrong. He didn't demand money. He just made it clear to me that we had now reached the point in our professional relationship where I was to put my hand in my back pocket, and pull out the appropriate wad.

I didn't. Instead, I told him what my editor had told me. I tried to imitate his tone as well. I watched his look change, until I couldn't bear it. With a sharp staccato movement I pulled my gaze away from him and fixed it instead on David Cassidy on the wall, with his pink healthy skin. I could feel Cockney's skin reddening. 'What do you mean the *Guardian* don't pay', he said. 'They'll fucking well pay me.'

'Oh, no they won't', I said. 'That's their editorial policy.' I even thought that I sounded sanctimonious saying this.

Cockney was not convinced, and that is putting it mildly. 'Editorial policy my bollocks. I'll tell you what if you don't want to pay me in money, you can pay me in silk suits. Two silk suits would be fine. I'll even get you a discount on them, five hundred quid for the pair of them. Now what could be fairer than that. You owe me money, and I'm prepared to save you money. How much fairer could I be?'

I tried to explain that the *Guardian* wouldn't pay in pounds, lire, silk suits or whatever other currency Cockney had in mind, but to no avail. It wasn't my personal decision not to pay, I explained. Why if it was up to me, Cockney would have been paid immediately in hard cash with a few silk suits thrown in for good measure. But it wasn't up to me. But Cockney just ignored all this pathetic pleading.

Cockney knew that he had certain things going for him. He may have been a stranger to the North of England, but he could recognise that Sheffield was a very small place – 'the largest village in England' they said. So in that small place wherever Cockney saw me he would shout out the reminder that I still owed him money. 'You'd better pay up soon. You and that paper telling people's stories. You got paid for the article, why shouldn't I? Just pay me half of what you got for writing it – just half. I'm not a greedy man. You owe me money.'

I could take this constant barrage for days, weeks even, but no longer. Not months, not six months. The barrage greeted me everywhere – in restaurants, in shops, even in toilets. 'There's the man who's cheating me out of my money', he would say to anyone who would listen in the toilets of clubs, as we stood side-by-side at the urinal. He always said 'my money', as if I was just holding it for him, which I suppose I was.

There was an important lesson here. Writing stories is one thing, but living with the characters, the individuals concerned, brings its own problems. It all looks so clean sometimes – stories from the North, but there was all this personal stuff to get through for years afterwards. Obligation, debt, that sort of thing. Relationships. Money that doesn't belong to you, burning a hole in your pocket. I didn't want to succumb to Cockney's pressure, but I did in the end. He knew I would. I thought that I wouldn't. That's how much I knew. But I had a plan. I was learning you see. 'You always need a plan', said Cockney. So I ended up taking the payment slip from the *Guardian*, tippexing out the amount paid for the article, substituting a new figure approximately half the original, and paying Cockney half of that new amount instead. I was very pleased with my initiative. I was becoming street-smart, in an extremely limited sort of way.

Cockney, on the other hand, was horrified to see the evidence of the *Guardian*'s stinginess. 'Jesus, is that all that paper pay you for articles? It's a bloody disgrace. Give me the name of the editor, and I'll ring him up for you and give him a right bollocking.' I never gave him the number. He was bad enough without having a phone as an offensive weapon.

But despite all his protestations, Cockney was happy. I had quite unconsciously provided Cockney with a new opening line. 'Pleased to meet you. Did you know that I am the only man the *Guardian* has ever paid for a story? The first man ever. But even papers like that, who know nothing about the common man, can recognise class. I'm pleased to do business with you.'

I never wanted a repeat of this episode. I wanted to find the stories within

people. I wanted to draw them out. I wanted to be the instigator, the origi-
nator. I didn't want anything on a plate, because it was clear that people
only offered things on plates if they wanted something in return, and like
many other writers I tried to avoid too much reciprocation in this writing
game. Mind you, I still wrote applications to the probation service on behalf
of someone else. I composed advertisements for a debt collection agency. I
gave personal references. I gave advice. But more often I took advice. I went
to their homes. Very occasionally, they came to mine, sometimes without an
invitation. 'You didn't think that you could hide from me', said Big Paddy
one Sunday afternoon. 'It wasn't very hard to find where you lived.' I had
sometimes been a bit vague about my personal history. I was miserly with the
truth about myself. I wanted to remain anonymous somehow – a fly-on-the-
wall. The shadow. Paddy wanted me to know that this was not possible, so
he sat in my front room one Sunday afternoon as my children played in front
of him. He was grinning away, as he sipped his tea. 'It's handy knowing
where you live. I might pop round again if I ever need to see you in a hurry –
if you ever get up my nose.'

Pete was still standing in front of me waiting for a response. 'So what kind
of idea for a story, did you have Pete?' I asked 'Were you thinking of a
profile of Sheffield's oldest surviving bouncer – something along those lines.'

Pete shook his large, pendulous head.

'No, my friend, something altogether different. You should be writing big
stories, not little stories, and I have one big story for you. What about the
secrets of the Hungarian revolution? I was there at the beginning. I saw it all
with my own two eyes.'

Mad Pete's eyes started to stare into space, they were quite moist. I felt a
momentary sense of shame and embarrassment. For years I thought that Pete
spoke the way that he did because he had a speech problem. I had never
realised that Mad Pete was Hungarian. That, I suddenly realised, explained
rather a lot about him.

Mad Pete was still staring. 'I killed my first man there. He was a right evil
bastard – secret police I think. I shot the knobhead – bang, bang. Goodnight
Josephine. Goodnight dickhead. I have the secrets in my head. I want to tell
them to my children. My son is nineteen and a bouncer just like me – great
big shoulders just like me. I try to tell him my stories and he says 'Fuck, off.
Baseball bats are more your fucking line. You wouldn't know what to do
with guns.' My son thinks that I'm old fashioned! Me, who saw the Hungarian revolution first hand. I predicted the fall of the Berlin wall. I saw it all. I
started it back there in my little village. Without me none of this would have
happened. We would still have Cold War. My son says that he's not interested, that he couldn't give a fuck. He won't listen to my stories, to my
adventures. I want to tell him that I was using guns when he wasn't even a
glimmer in his mother's eye. God rest her soul. That's why I want to talk to
you – you write it all down, then he might believe me.'

Mad Pete adopted a pleading expression. He wanted his son to know what
he had seen, if indeed he had seen anything. I was to be the conduit for the
family history, real or imagined. Without me there would be no notes, no
piece, nothing for his son to read and believe. Or not. I sipped my lager,

slowly, considering my responsibilities. I was always cautious with these types of offers. For genuine reasons, and for more selfish reasons. Every time that I had interviewed someone, they would themselves spontaneously and without any encouragement come up with some sequel. I had written an article about an entrepreneur in Rotherham, whose entrepreneurial inspiration was to base an Ibizan night-spot right next door to the Jobcentre in Rotherham. 'Style city right in the centre of Rotherham – more *Miami Vice* than *Saturday Night Fever*.' Their self-declared managerial policy was 'not to wallow with the poseurs.' But this article was only the start, the entrepreneur assumed. 'Next on the agenda is my days as a randy DJ in all the best clubs. Just to give you a taster, I was approached by one girl who, I think, worked in the town hall who said to me, "I don't know whether you're a tit man or not, but I've got the biggest nipples in Barnsley."'

Sequels were often bad news. I tried to avoid them. I glanced back at Mad Pete, who had frozen his pleading, little boy lost look.

'We can do a whole book on my life. Me and Hungary. It would be like that film with that bird with the sexy mouth – *Doctor Zhivago*. All history happening and me in the middle shooting that knobhead secret policeman.' And Mad Pete cocked his hand in the shape of a gun. 'Bang, bang fucking dickhead', he shouted into space.

'Steady on, Pete, you don't want to injure yourself playing silly games, now, do you?'

Pete was embarrassed at having been caught out like that. Don had slipped up to him unawares, right up behind him, and Pete hadn't known a thing about it. 'You must be getting old Pete', said Don. 'I could have been anybody. Perhaps one of the punters that you've escorted off the premises over the years.' And Don trapped Pete's head in a vice-like grip and pulled him backwards so that he was slightly off balance. Even though he was being choked, Pete still tried to talk. Worse, he tried to talk humorously.

'Escorted off, that's good, boss. I always carried them out asleep. That was my style, boss.' Pete was now choking.

'Well, Don't you start falling asleep, now. You always have to watch your back, don't you.'

Pete tried to nod his head.

Don laughed. He was the owner of the club, and he moved with a certain stealth through it, watching the punters, learning a few of their secrets. Don was in his fifties, with grey receding hair, and starched cuffs which he constantly played with. Pete seemed flustered.

'I was just telling Gerry here about the good old days in Hungary', said Pete, 'and what we used to get up to.'

'Boyhood pranks, Pete, boyhood pranks. You want to forget about such things. We all do things when we're young that we may feel a little ashamed of later in life. It's best to draw a veil on such things.'

Don turned away from Pete and towards me.

'And how's the writer today? Made up any good stories lately? I don't know why you bother talking to people, you make it all up anyway. All writers do. They write what they want.'

Don's tone became even more confrontational. 'So what are you working on tonight? Is this a social visit or something else?' I told him that I was working on a book about the lives of people in the North. It was a big story, not a little story – about the work and the days when the work had gone. Their hopes, their fears. Their vices. The threats. This seemed to amuse Don. 'Well, hang about. You never know your luck. Perhaps Pete and myself could arrange for something to happen right in front of you, so that you don't miss any of it. Now, how would that suit you?'

Pete suggested that I should volunteer for the head vice. 'Show him how it works, boss. Get him to pass out. Just for a second.'

I couldn't help thinking that Mad Pete had added 'just for a second' as a bit of an afterthought. Then Don said that he had some business in the restaurant. I went back to studying the scene. Thursday night was hen night up in Sheffield. The various clubs invariably filled with gangs of women – the hen parties, gangs of men – the stag parties, plus the old faithful – the punters that go to night-clubs every night regardless of the weather or the economic conditions in the country. The punters that never have to rise that early. The punters who have plenty of money but never seem to work. The hangers-on. The survivors.

And there they stood, talking business, or trying to. It was after all that time of the night. The floor show was on – somewhere in the background, but those on stage were amateurs, and it showed. All brides-to-be prepared to go on stage on their hen-night, all prepared to slide along a greasy pole for a bottle of champagne, or rather for a bottle of sparkling wine pretending to be champagne. There was a lot of pretending.

None of the amateurs could make it more than a few inches along the pole. 'Go on love, show us your knickers', bawled the DJ – 'Oh, she's not wearing any! That woke you up, didn't it. It doesn't pay to sleep when I'm on, you know.'

One rather large bride-to-be mounted the pole rather noisily and very unsteadily. She was dressed in a funny milkmaid's outfit, festooned with inflated Durex and decorated with pictures of men's sex organs, with captions cut out of newspapers pinned just below – 'What a whopper!' and 'A right Charlie!' That sort of thing. It must have taken her friends weeks to find the right captions in the headlines of their various newspapers. Her friends had to help her onto the pole. The DJ held a microphone close to her. 'I'm pissed', she screamed into it. Suddenly, and without any warning, she gave a great heave along the greasy pole. This one heave took her all the way along the pole and then off the other side. There was a loud bang as her head hit the ground. 'Jesus, she's probably concussed', said the DJ, his microphone picking up every word. 'Doorman to large bride-to-be on stage. Doorman to large bride-to-be on stage.'

The bouncers looked confused. 'What the fuck does he want us to do?' said the one nearest me.

Meanwhile, the large bride-to-be was stirring. 'Eh up, I'm alright. It's only because I'm a bit tipsy.' The DJ presented her with her bottle of champagne and, with some relief, led her off the stage. She looked as if she would have trouble remembering anything about her once-in-a-lifetime hen-night in this top night-spot the morning after.

'Don't sue us, remember that', said the DJ. 'Unless your name's Sue.'

It was now time for the climax of the show. The DJ asked if there were any stag parties in the club that evening. One group in the corner raised their hand.

'Then get the lucky man on stage, let's see what he's got', bawled the DJ.

One very thin young man, in his early twenties, bolted for the exit, but he was dragged back and lifted onto the stage. He stood surrounded by the girls in their funny brides-to-be costumes with the inflated Durex billowing out behind them.

'That's right girls, crowd in on him. Don't let him escape', ordered the DJ. The girls didn't need to be told twice. 'Now, when I give the word, and not before, wait for it! – take all his clothes off. Go for it', screamed the DJ.

Three pairs of hands grabbed at his shirt, five pairs grabbed at his trousers. The bloke didn't really resist, there wasn't much point, he just ducked and dived as best he could to prevent the audience seeing everything. Hands were being thrust inside underpants – 'He's got bloody holes in his Y-fronts', screeched the DJ. 'Is that going to be your wedding night surprise? I think we've seen enough of that. Now get the curtains closed quickly. Quickly!' There was real panic in the DJ's voice. And the thick velvety brown curtains closed swiftly around the scene. But you could still see bumps in the curtains, with the bumps moving rapidly one way then another. The bridegroom-to-be was obviously continuing to bob and weave and duck and dive for his modesty's sake, even with the curtains shut.

Meanwhile up in the VIP bar, a different kind of bobbing and weaving and ducking and diving was going on. The VIPs ignored the brides-to-be show. 'It never changes, does it?' said one man in his late forties with white slip-ons. 'Seen one of these hen shows, seen 'em all. Where do they get these awful looking birds from? Now let's get back to talking about that Corniche', he said turning to his companion. To his right, stood a man in his early thirties chatting to one of the bouncers. Suddenly, he seemed to recognise a face in the crowd, and he started to weave his way unsteadily towards him. 'You were the fella looking at that black Merc I'm selling, isn't that right?' he slurred. 'Have you got fixed up yet? I've still got the car. It's not that I've had trouble selling it, it's just that . . . well I like it so much I can't bear to part with it. Honest to God. I don't like talking business on a Friday, when the pair of us have had far too much to drink, but why waste the opportunity? Answer me that one.'

His friend had to nudge him to remind him that it was Thursday night, not Friday night. 'Oh', he said. 'Well, I'll be pissed again tomorrow night, so what's the odds.'

Other deals were being struck, and other bright ideas tested. George, who had aspirations to be a club owner, was swapping stories about money-making schemes to some other men in the corner. 'I had a friend who put an advert in the local paper', he said, 'advertising a guaranteed safe and one hundred per cent foolproof method for killing rodents and other vermin. Only £9.95, the advert said. You know what – for a tenner he sent the punters two bricks and a set of instructions saying "place the rat midway between the two bricks and bring the bricks rapidly together on the rat's

Men watching stripagram in pub, Sheffield, 1995

head". Nothing dishonest about that, now is there? Hundreds of mugs replied as well. Just shows you what a rat-infested hole we live in.'

His friends all laughed. George could be very funny. He had a hair transplant done recently, but it hadn't worked properly. His head looked like a tea towel with thread knitted into it. He said that he hadn't paid for the transplant because it wasn't a proper job, but the rumour was that he had. Up front, on the button, like a mug. Cockney just shook his head when he heard this. 'Well I never', he said. 'I can't believe that old George fell for it.'

George was still telling his tales. Tales about pulling the wool. 'But that one's only if you're desperate. I'm into leather jackets now. There's a sign at the front of my store that says "genuine leather jackets", then there's jackets at the back of my store for forty five quid. How can they be leather at that price? When it says "genuine leather" at the front of the shop, it doesn't mean that all of the jackets in the store are leather, now does it? But some punters have tried taking the forty five quid jackets back because they're not leather. The nerve of some people. That's what it's all about, you know – ducking and diving, keeping one step ahead of the ordinary punter.'

Meanwhile the large lady from the brides-to-be show had made it as far as the steps of the VIP bar, clutching the remains of her sparkling champagne. But all the fizz had long since gone. She clambered wearily up the steps. But, when eventually she made it to the final step, the bouncer standing there to keep the ordinary punter and the VIP apart, stepped in and turned her away. The bouncer hadn't forgiven her for all the excitement earlier. The man in the white slip-ons and his cronies had, however, started to attend to the spectacle, designed to make them feel special. It seemed to work.

'Let her up Gary, we need a few fat birds up here for a bit of a laugh.'

'That's going to be my next little scheme', said George – 'mass-produced brides-to-be costumes complete with pictures and captions.'

And his entourage guffawed with laughter, as the large bride-to-be sat herself wearily down on the bottom step leading to the VIP bar, and started to cry, ever so gently. She cried for a few minutes and then went off to look for her friends. Before anyone had time to notice, it was the time for the slow dances at the end of the night, the erection section. And then time to go home. For the ordinary punter.

The VIPs stayed behind. Don fetched the drinks. 'Put your money away, it's after hours.' Requests were put in to Don. 'Play "Come on big 'un".' It was a video recording from the security video, without sound. One lone punter in a white shirt stood outside the front door. He had blond permed hair. The film was a few years old, it was a classic. Don provided the narration. He spoke the words that he claimed were actually said by those featured in the film.

'Go on big 'un, let us in.'

'No, you're barred.'

'Go on big 'un.'

'Look I've told you once. Clear off.'

'Go on.'

'Clear off.'

It went on and on. Don was very practised at this skill of over laying the soundtrack. 'It's authentic', he would claim. It was a boring enough film I was thinking to myself, until 'boom', the big 'un landed a left hook right around the door of the club on the chin of the punter. Down the punter went, like a sack of spuds. The big 'un sat astride him and you might have missed the second one. But the doormen didn't. One of them nudged me – 'boom'. The big 'un landed another one, as the punter's head bounced off the flag stones. You couldn't see the head. It was just out of camera, but you could see the arm action.

Everybody laughed. Then the friend of the man with the perm came to drag him away. A lifeless body pulled slowly away. 'They always leave the club one way or another', said Mad Pete who had joined us again.

The second film was even better, I was assured. This one had sound. An Asian guy was having an argument with his wife in the doorway of the club. She was screaming in his face. The camera captured it all. 'You kicked my sister in the fucking fanny, you son of a bitch. Look at her! Look at her!' She kicked him and kneed him, and head-butted him, knowing that he wouldn't retaliate in the presence of the doormen. She was trying to get him to hit her, so that everyone would see what kind of a man he really was. I found the film embarrassing, but the rest of the audience were creased up with laughter. There, also captured on the video, was the audience witnessing the original scene, huddled in the doorway of the club. They were clearly enjoying the spectacle of raw passion unfolding in front of them. This film went on forever. The violence was episodic. Every now and then one or other of the protagonists would disappear down the steps away from the club, and the other would sidle up to the door and attempt to persuade the bouncers that they were not at fault. They would try to do this as calmly and as rationally as possible. Neither wanted to be the one that was barred from the club. In the middle of all that violence and screaming and blood and pain, that's what they were most concerned with. But they were both barred in the end.

So there we were – the selected hangers-on in a Northern city enjoying a big night out. This was the kind of VIP evening just waiting for those who eventually made it. Those who wanted to show this select *demi-monde* of a Northern city that they had indeed arrived. But there were stories, some more exotic and more improbable than you might imagine behind every one of those faces lit up by the TV screen in the corner, where the big 'un went through his paces again and again on request. We were there until dawn.

The *Guardian* got many of the stories, then *The Independent*, and occasionally the *Sunday Telegraph*, *New Society*, *New Statesman and Society*, or the *Observer*. But John Course was right. You don't have to pay for stories. You just have to listen and try not to miss a trick, and be wary of sequels that go too far beyond the mundane, which turn out, of course, to be anything but. Then, of course, you have to learn to keep a few secrets back, to develop a little savvy just to show that you know the ropes and that you can be trusted. And you have to be prepared to stay in the club until the death. That's what they call it anyway – 'the death' – kicking-out time, because if you don't, you might miss it all. And then again, if you're not invited to stay to the death, you're nobody in the first place, at least nobody worth talking to.

I started writing about the North soon after Thatcher came to power. I was a young university lecturer who had recently moved to Sheffield. I started writing because my wife fell below a train at Sheffield station, and lost her arm. I wrote my first piece out of anger and frustration about what it was like for her to get a false arm. When Paul Barker stepped down many years later as editor of *New Society* he wrote to me saying that this piece had always stuck in his mind. I moved on from there. Many of the pieces look quite dated now. Life was changing. The very fabric of life in the North was in a state of flux, as the traditional industries went, and unemployment rose. Whole communities were destroyed and new cultures started to emerge. I lived in Netherfield Road in Crookes in Sheffield in those early years, and this is the first piece I reproduce here. I called it 'Brick Street' in my first compilation of pieces. I don't know why. Netherfield Road sounded quite posh. It didn't sound quite right for the street. Then again, I didn't want to hurt anybody's feelings.

John Course used to ask me how I found some of these people. 'Nearby' was the answer. I lived two doors away from an unemployed steelworker. It was very handy. If the truth be known, all of the pieces were opportunistic in this way – just whatever came up. There was no grand plan, no abstract scheme. I was summoned as often as I did the summoning. It wasn't just Mad Pete who had the odd story for me. There were, of course, many stories which I could have told, but didn't. This is just one set in a way – one version of life in the North under the Conservatives.

When Friedrich Engels wrote the preface to the original German edition of *The Condition of the Working Class in England* in 1845 he wrote 'Working Men! To you I dedicate a work, in which I have tried to lay before my . . . countrymen a faithful picture of your condition, of your sufferings and struggles, of your hopes and prospects. I have lived long enough amidst you to know something about your circumstances.' I would have loved to have been able to preface my book with these words. But life was constantly changing for the working class in the north of England during the successive Conservative governments from 1979 to 1997. There was no fixed picture of the condition of the working class to be lain before anyone. There was just a series of fleeting images of lives captured from different angles and a succession of vignettes and descriptions of people living sometimes in quite desperate circumstances. Then there was the multitude of self-constructions, self-justifications and emergent self-identities which went along with all this, as we all changed. Forever.

This, I suppose, is what this book is all about.

DATE DUE

GAYLORD			PRINTED IN U.S.A.